PHILANTHROPY AND ECONOMIC DEVELOPMENT

PHILANTHROPY AND ECONOMIC DEVELOPMENT

edited by
Richard F. America

Contributions in Economics and
Economic History, Number 162

GREENWOOD PRESS
Westport, Connecticut • London

Library of Congress Cataloging-in-Publication Data

Philanthropy and economic development / edited by Richard F. America.
    p.   cm.—(Contributions in economics and economic history,
  ISSN 0084-9235 ; no. 162)
    Includes index.
    ISBN 0-313-28809-7 (alk. paper)
    1. Corporations—Charitable contributions—United States.
  2. Community development—United States.   I. America, Richard F.
  II. Series.
  HG4028.C6P45   1995
  361.7'65'0973—dc20   94-30933

British Library Cataloguing in Publication Data is available.

Library of Congress Catalog Card Number: 94-30933
ISBN: 0-313-28809-7
ISSN: 0084-9235

First published in 1995

Greenwood Press, 88 Post Road West, Westport, CT 06881
An imprint of Greenwood Publishing Group, Inc.

Printed in the United States of America

The paper used in this book complies with the
Permanent Paper Standard issued by the National
Information Standards Organization (Z39.48-1984).

10 9 8 7 6 5 4 3 2 1

To Dino

Contents

Figures

Tables

Preface

Private and corporate decision makers can target grants, investments, and other assistance to accelerate the growth of jobs, small businesses, and incomes in distressed areas and restore them to full health. But there are experience gaps that block opportunities for creative public–private financing of training, technology transfer, small business, large business retention, applied research, and housing innovation. This book was developed to stimulate corporate and private foundations and their clients and associates to take more creative action in this field.

There is chronic economic distress in too many communities. And in many other areas, once stable thriving local economies have declined because of complex factors that undermine the economic base and discourage investors and potential entrepreneurs.

These conditions are not inevitable and do not have to be tolerated long term. Successful intervention is possible and can raise incomes and generate jobs. But small business and economic development in too many communities is chronically underassisted and undercapitalized.

This volume reviews these situations and offers innovative remedies that can increase the flow of the right kind of capital and assistance, in the right quantities in the right ways.

Philanthropic grants and portfolio investments do help revitalize distressed economies and generate businesses, new products, jobs, and income. But available capital from all sources, public and private, conventional and unconventional, is inadequate. In this book, remedies are examined that will allow private and corporate philanthropic decision makers to work with local public and private leaders to intervene. They can leverage resources to accelerate development.

Self help is part of the solution. So are traditional investment and entrepreneurship. And strategic philanthropy can assist both processes. Housing, job training, commercial and industrial site development, and small business assistance and development are key activities needing philanthropic help. So too is behavior and attitude change. Crime prevention, shifts in values, and the "work ethic" can be helped along by imaginative philanthropy. And without these changes, economic development cannot occur in some areas.

The chapters especially concentrate on innovations in public–private partnerships to make possible greater leverage in financing to support small business and job creation. They examine how loans, guarantees, and grants can be best structured. And they are forthright in seeing that capital grants to for-profit businesses and to locally controlled banks, savings and loans, and credit unions are appropriate and essential to promoting competitive strength, especially in minority businesses.

Statewide and regional strategies also come in for attention. One notion is that in every state and major metropolitan area, at least one umbrella organization in the form of a public trust nonprofit corporation be formed to act as a holding company for a series of for profit subsidiaries, whose profits could in turn finance economic development related social projects, especially in training and human capital investment.

The chapters discuss direct grants, loans, and guarantees and also indirect approaches through various intermediaries. The papers are critical, and make careful distinctions, recognizing the value and strengths that make some approaches more suitable than others for selected situations. These aspects of philanthropic strategy are thoroughly analyzed. Similarly, the use of philanthropy to create and sustain secondary markets for the kinds of investments being channeled into small businesses is discussed.

In general, the chapters specify and define an important problem or opportunity facing philanthropic executives and review and summarize a key strategic issue. Then they offer case evidence of philanthropic success or failure. This is followed by innovative recommendations on how philanthropy can do better. Special attention is given to how corporate philanthropy can work successfully in areas where the company has no plants or employees. The restrictive policy, all too common, of limiting efforts to locations in which there is a physical presence is called into question and alternative policies are offered.

The chapters also suggest, in some cases, analytical techniques, so that projects might be subjected to greater scrutiny and hard analysis to insure that feasibility is adequately determined and expected value established. Several chapters also examine how philanthropy can escape the straightjacket of limiting support to projects only. They discuss the policy of providing general operating grants to improve the management and organization of local economic development organizations, to build capacity and upgrade management. Likewise, strategies that include support for important functions like legal services, economic analysis, and other specialized consulting are addressed.

In all, the volume will aid philanthropic managers in working with many other players to tap the latent entrepreneurial talents in the distressed or underdeveloped communities. Taken as a whole, the volume offers an extraordinarily useful guide to moving philanthropy beyond conventional thinking and to curing the myopia that prevents many corporate philanthropists from engaging community development problems creatively.

Acknowledgments

This book evolved out of years of experience in consulting, teaching, writing, and working with government and corporations seeking to find better ways to accelerate development in chronically distressed areas. Colleagues and students at the Stanford Research Institute, The University of California at Berkeley, and at Stanford Business School provided the early spark. Thanks to Ed Epstein and Richard Holton at Berkeley, and to George Bach and Jim Van Horne at Stanford.

Thanks also to Eddie Williams at the Joint Center for Political and Economic Studies in Washington, to the late Jack Gloster of Opportunity Funding Corporation, to Parren Mitchell, and to Alice Rivlin for various consulting and staff opportunities to develop aspects of some of the ideas that are represented here.

Thanks to colleagues in the National Economic Association. They continue to provide a unique forum in which all aspects of the development of the African American economy can be examined.

Thanks to my wife, Dino, and my daughter Amy for being good sports.

And thanks to Cynthia Harris, Jim Ice, Ann Smith, Elise Oranges and Marcy Weiner at Greenwood Press for sponsoring this project and helping it through to completion.

Introduction

This book evaluates the progress, performance, and emerging opportunities for foundations in domestic economic development. It examines the level and quality of philanthropic attention to community-based development. And it pushes the boundaries of conventional thinking by also looking at how trade associations and labor unions can participate in community renewal. Few have seen this work as suitable. But they have much to offer and should be more fully engaged.

Foundations have been created by a few unions and trade associations. For example, the health insurance industry has invested directly in social development. That approach has wider applicability.

Finally, the book examines how most Fortune 1000 firms, that have not been active in economic development, and those that are active but only minimally, can target resources directly or through national, state, and local intermediaries, to accelerate new business and job generation and revitalization in chronically distressed communities, rural and urban.

The book will interest economists and planners. And it will interest CEOs, vice presidents, and directors of public corporate, government, and community affairs, and board members of companies that have:

- no foundation
- no or low contributions
- a habit of reactively giving only small amounts and responding to many requests, rather than proactively giving larger amounts to fewer organizations
- a habit of giving only to United Way and selected universities, arts and cultural groups, hospitals, and other traditional recipients.

LEVELS OF CORPORATE PHILANTHROPY

Corporations fall into three categories: Type 1 includes firms that, so far, provide most of the funding for serious sustained economic and community development. They have decided this priority is important and have been early supporters of innovative development. Examples include Levi Strauss, Arco, Equitable Life, Bank of America, Hewlett Packard, Amoco, and British Petroleum.

Type 2 includes firms that have active philanthropic, contributions, and community relations programs but have concentrated on health, higher education, the arts, or scientific research, and the United Way.

Type 3 firms, unions and most trade associations, give little or no support to any programs. When they do give, their contributions lack a clear strategic focus of any kind. This group includes most firms in the Fortune 1000.

Some leading trade associations have logical business reasons to do much more and to join Type 1 corporate leaders. Some groups that might be prime candidates to provide creative participation include:

Securities Industries Association

Chemical Manufacturers Association

Pharmaceutical Manufacturers Association

Edison Electric Institute

National Association of Manufacturers

Motion Picture Industries Association

Coal Industries Association

Associated General Contractors

Electronic Industries Association

American Gas Association

Iron and Steel Institute

Aerospace Industries Association

Computer Manufacturers Association
Semiconductor Industries Association
The Beer Institute
The Tobacco Institute

And trade unions that could establish proactive, professionally managed, economic development philanthropy include:

United Auto Workers
United Steel Workers
United Mine Workers
National Education Association
AFL-CIO
United Electrical Workers
United Chemical Workers
Brotherhood of Teamsters
American Federation of State, County, and Municipal Employees
Screen Actors Guild
Transport Workers Union

This volume is intended, in part, to help such organizations discover that this kind of philanthropy can pay social and business dividends.

SUMMARY

Part I examines broad philosophy, policy, and practice. Most of the papers conclude that contributions programs are effective, even if limited in scope and depth. But the first essay, by Richard Steinberg, counsels caution and restraint. It emphasizes corporate and political realities and the limits to what philanthropy can do and can be expected to accomplish.

Other papers test and stretch these limits. But Steinberg reminds, at the outset, of the traditional constraints on corporate participation.

Next, Wolch reviews the literature on corporate philanthropy. She analyzes issues facing executives in developing philanthropic social and community investment policy.

Several questions policy makers and managers should consider include:

Do corporations make grants constrained by a too narrow geographical focus? Do most companies concentrate their contributions too close to home? Why do so many companies give only where they have locations? Does this make sense, or is it based on an assumption and habit that needs review?

Why do firms give? Should they periodically review their fundamental rationales? How can companies measure the political goodwill and image payoffs of their philanthropy? Is it important that they do that? And how would they use the information?

How does corporate giving influence local government decision making and policy?

Should more firms explicitly adopt net income giving targets? Why? And should more firms create foundations as well as give through contributions programs? Would it make sense for firms in:

electric, gas, and sanitary services

agriculture

mining

contract construction

transportation

for example, to dramatically increase their philanthropy? Would firms in these industries make a major impact on economic revitalization by creative, proactive, targeted philanthropy?

How does size matter? And would it matter if more mid-sized and small firms adopted strong giving programs?

Next, Kenneth Bertsch also reviews the basic rationale for corporate philanthropy and sets the idea of proactive corporate contributions in historic context. He analyzes how contributions officers have justified economic development. Finally, he reviews three innovative approaches that show promise.

Ritchie P. Lowry puts proactive strategic philanthropy in the context of corporate ethics codes and standards of conduct. He concludes that corporations fail to recognize that lack of commitment to community development reflects an under developed sensitivity to general ethical concerns and is a symptom of a narrow view of corporate mission.

Lowry outlines how proactive programs can be pursued through nonprofit community development instruments using financial support and employee volunteerism. He finds positive direct connections between corporate philanthropy and profits. And he presents cases in which cause related marketing is tied to community development. This chapter also examines how foundations proactively work to stimulate local development through targeted, leveraged investment and grants and through partnerships.

Mescon, Tilson, and Desman elaborate further on how senior managers view philanthropy and how they might sharpen their approach. The chapter examines the professionalization of philanthropic management. It then discusses how contributions, philanthropy, and public relations and marketing are best coordinated so that appropriate acknowledgement, credit, and market benefit is assured.

The use of special events and tie-ins, as in cultural, sports, arts, and health, has been modified to work in community and economic development as well. And a creative tie between contributions, foundations, marketing, and even operations, has been successful for some corporations.

James Post and Sandra Waddock examine how active strategic philanthropy differs from more passive reactive approaches. They review the partnership approach to philanthropic management. And they analyze several corporate approaches and the benefits that have resulted.

The concept of strategy, as they use the term, refers to donors' overall competitive strategic interests. But other analysts and philanthropic managers, use the term to refer instead to focusing giving on defined long range outcomes. Partnership approaches have been important in many projects and the chapter examines the subtleties of partnership development and management.

Those first six chapters establish a sense of how corporate philanthropy is oriented, how well it is managed, and how it can be focused to produce desired results.

Part II examines in greater detail the central concern of the book, community-based economic development. These chapters evaluate an approach that has emerged in the past 25 years. With corporate and government partners, some CDCs and other similar organizations have learned to successfully address a wide range of development problems.

Hodgkinson summarizes CDC history, then focuses on how foundations' program related investments have been used in CDC development. She reviews several surveys conducted by the Council on Foundations and analyzes the findings on foundation social investments and financial innovation through intermediaries.

Clay critically examines CDC structure and performance. He finds serious limitations and takes issue with some more laudatory evaluations of their effectiveness. The chapter examines how CDCs have developed and how to evaluate their capacity to carry out projects. It also considers the context in which CDCs work and the local political realities of public–private partnerships.

Thelwell and Smith find that macro policy and macro trends can undo grassroots development efforts' results. Shifting income from poorer to richer, because of tax and budget policy, makes some attempts at development futile when weighed against countervailing public policies. Nevertheless, community-based development is worthwhile, in their view, if only to keep inequality from becoming even worse.

The chapter examines two formal evaluations of CDC impact. And it addresses how this information can influence foundation responses to

CDC proposals. It also examines how CDCs specialize and seek economies of scale.

Vidal and Howitt review a major intermediary, LISC, which has created a channel for philanthropic funding into community development. The chapter analyzes how foundations have used this and other intermediaries, and conceived and created new ones, to focus on particular regions or types of problems. It also examines how corporate philanthropy has underwritten general operating expenses, as well as project capital.

In the third and fourth sections, chapters consider how corporate philanthropy has focused on two priorities—African-American development, especially strengthening internal fund raising and philanthropy in black communities, and second, housing, employment training, and small business development.

Part III focuses on development in African-American communities. Over the past 30 years, this sector has been a focus of government attention, however mismanaged, under funded, or misguided at times. The two chapters emphasize development strategies under African-American sponsorship.

Buhl examines firms' support for community-based development. He reviews how corporations approach development through these organizations.

Carson analyzes how black philanthropy functions and how internal giving supports programs in health, education, training, housing, capital formation, and law enforcement and security. The chapter reviews how philanthropists have worked with this kind of broad based, grassroots, self-help giving.

Finally, America examines how philanthropy might build institutions that would strengthen communities and economic development through innovative proactive investment.

In Part Four, the chapters look at specialized targets for philanthropy. Waddock examines Private Industry Councils and finds them effective instruments for development. Many emphasize training. And corporate philanthropy enhances their work.

Kemp discusses how proactive philanthropy generated jobs, income, and wealth in distressed areas by investing in and subsidizing venture capital and by helping finance business acquisitions.

Lydenberg examines philanthropy's role in increasing housing availability through below market rate loans and grants and other social investments. These projects have been an entry point for some corporations. Housing investment has allowed them to participate at low initial risk. Then, with increasing experience, they have moved into business development and more complex program related investments.

Finally, Nelson discusses how philanthropy works with government at all levels to help emerging nontraditional entrepreneurs—public housing tenants, women on welfare, structurally dislocated workers, and others—to successfully launch and grow businesses.

The volume covers the field in depth. It will help readers evaluate the options available and think through and implement optimum strategies. Fads and fashions in philanthropy come and go. Government emphases change, and priorities shift among foundation and contributions executives. But chronic economic underperformance is a long term problem, and this volume is intended to have a long life and to be useful for many years. The specific techniques and programs will be altered to fit prevailing ideas about political reality. But philanthropists will basically use some variation on the techniques discussed here for the foreseeable future.

Part I
Philosophy, Policy, and Practice

1 Philanthropy and Economic Development

Richard Steinberg

The chapters suggest three themes for further research. First, whereas the chapters concentrate on "What can philanthropy *do* to help cure chronic economic distress?" there is a greater need to analyze "What can *philanthropy* do?" Although many charities and foundations sincerely care about broad issues of social welfare, it is wishful thinking to imagine that charities need only to be informed about recipient needs and then dramatic retargeting would occur.

Charity priorities primarily reflect the idiosyncratic wishes of donors. The institution of philanthropy is ill suited to address issues of social priority or to ensure that all ethnic, religious, professional, and regional interests receive equitable relief; these goals are the provenance of government. If charities are unduly pressured to serve one cause or another, there is the risk that the supply of new donations would dry up. How then should social responsibilities be delineated?

Charities should address socially acceptable individual impulses which cannot be accommodated through democratic political regimes because of a lack of consensus. Philanthropies may simply express heterogeneous preferences about social policy when diversity crosses geographic barriers (so that local governments are not a feasible alternative accommodation). Philanthropies may allow the expression of social policies which are constitutionally proscribed to government (such as the advancement of religion or of specified ethnic groups). Finally, philanthropies may fund new ideas through chancy demonstration projects which, if proven successful, develop the political support for continued public funding. By fostering these pluralistic values, charities are useful even if they do not address those social problems of highest priority to recipients.

Perhaps charities ought to pay more attention to chronic economic distress. Proponents of this view will have to persuade, not pressure, donors to reevaluate their priorities. To do so, one would probably need to go beyond the chapters in this volume and include an analysis of tradeoffs. Which previous donor priority causes should receive less aid, so that chronic economic distress can receive more aid?

Corporate donations may be more malleable, and corporations do have a direct interest in curing chronic economic distress. For example, following the urban riots of the middle and late 1960s, many corporations supported new training centers and community development organizations designed to stabilize the urban environment. However, corporate philanthropy is an unreliable and inadequate solution for three reasons. First, corporations will only invest in a community if they are strongly tied to that community (by the costs of moving, customer good will, etc.) and are major players in the community (a smaller firm would prefer to free-ride off the community investments of other corporations). Many urban communities will lack firms of this sort.

Second, although there is some overlap, there is no congruence between the interests of firms and the interests of the economically distressed. Corporations cannot stray too far from profit maximization without facing a takeover bid or bankruptcy. Indeed, most corporate donations are designed to enhance profits through improved public relations (hence sales) or an improved community environment (which cuts recruitment costs and boosts productivity). Community investments which reduce the local crime rate or otherwise make the locality more attractive for its work force can be profitable, but meeting the priority needs of the economically distressed will not generally assist sales or lower costs of production.

Third, corporations must steer clear of controversy. Donations to controversial community causes could alienate some potential customers, and most corporations avoid them. Thus, only 27 percent of corporate donations in 1987 went to health and human services. This percentage is clearly inadequate when one recalls that corporate donations constitute only about 5 percent of total donations and that aggregate donations constitute about 27 percent of the aggregate income of nonprofit organizations (Hodgkinson and Weitzman, 1989).

Democratic governments, at least in theory, serve both donor and recipient needs. Although political power is not evenly distributed in practice, reformers who anticipate an ability to assemble a reasonable consensus are better off lobbying government than philanthropies. Governmental institutions are better constituted to respond to pressures than are voluntary organizations. Further, unlike philanthropic institutions, governments can compel "contributions" through taxation, ensuring that some potential donors do not free-ride off the contributions of others. Finally, governments often implement their programs through targeted grants or contracts with nonprofit organizations, obtaining the best of both worlds. Thus, those wishing to "cure chronic economic distress" should focus their importunations on governments.

Granted that governments should play the primary role in addressing chronic economic distress, the second major theme for research asks, "What sorts of intermediaries should government employ?" Government can directly aid communities, contract out with private parties (for profit or nonprofit), or provide tax breaks and regulatory subsidies for private providers. It is true that, as one chapter observed, for-profit firms find low-income housing to be too risky to be worthwhile, but this is only because governments have not provided the proper tax breaks, contract offerings, or regulatory subsidies. Government needs to finance and direct a solution to chronic economic distress, but the actual implementation of these solutions can be delegated to private institutions. Should these institutions be nonprofit or for profit?

Conventional wisdom suggests that nonprofit organizations are less efficient but more trustworthy. Nonprofit organizations are defined by the "nondistribution constraint" (Hansmann, 1980), which allows them to make profits but not to distribute any profits to those in control of the firm. This constraint reduces financial incentives for productive and allocative efficiency, as no one within the organization can (legally) directly profit from reducing the costs of production or better meeting consumer needs. Further, there can be no financially motivated hostile takeover bids to ensure efficient performance.

On the other hand, the nondistribution constraint removes financial incentives to cheat the customer. Purchasers of complex products (such as housing services for the poor) must be wary of difficult-to-catch corner cutting. Housing suppliers can construct units with hidden defects that cause them to wear out prematurely, economize on maintenance, fail to ensure adequate security for residents, or fail to ensure that only eligible recipients reside in their units. It is difficult to contractually obligate every aspect of performance and to verify compliance with such a contract, so the degree to which the contractee can be trusted is critical.

For-profit firms may profit financially from shortchanging government contractors in ways that are difficult to catch and hence leave their reputations intact. Nonprofit firms lack this financial incentive to take advantage of patrons (Hansmann, 1980). Therefore, nonprofit firms constitute the superior intermediary when it is less costly to police the nondistribution constraint than to write and enforce a complex performance contract (Weisbrod, 1988).

Recent U.S. housing policies emphasize a greatly expanded role for nonprofits in the provision of low-income housing. The recently enacted Cranston–Gonzalez National Affordable Housing Act provides incentives for current for-profit owners to sell federally assisted housing projects to nonprofit housing corporations. In addition, the Act sets aside money for the development of new low-income housing units by nonprofits. It is unclear whether this is good policy. True, nonprofit housing organizations have been relatively trustworthy in the past, but this may be because they have been such small players. If government funding and tax breaks for nonprofit housing corporations become far more lucrative, it would become correspondingly harder to enforce the nondistribution constraint and keep nominal nonprofits from acting like for-profits in disguise.

The experience of other countries is instructive here. For example, using a somewhat broader definition which includes labor unions and housing cooperatives, nonprofit investors completed 55.1 percent of dwellings in Sweden, 6.7 percent of dwellings in Great Britain, and 35.7 percent of dwellings in the Netherlands in 1985 (U.N. Economic Commission for Europe, 1987). In Germany, the nonprofit share has fallen dramatically, and recent public policy has turned hostile to nonprofit housing associations. Hills et al. (p. 149) attribute this to "inefficient expansion, immobile management, and a large scale corruption scandal within the largest company followed by a financial collapse." Cross-national institutional comparisons of this sort can fruitfully advance research on the topic.

The third question suggested by the chapters is, "What can community development organizations (CDOs) themselves do to enhance their abilities to fight chronic economic distress?" I suggest three concrete steps. First, CDOs can work towards enhancing their professional competencies by integrating more closely with the broader nonprofit management training opportunities. Managers and other staff can obtain training through certificate programs such as the Fund Raising School in Indianapolis or can obtain college degrees such as the Master of Nonprofit Management degree offered at Case Western Reserve University in Cleveland. Boards of directors can become more effective if they seek the training resources of the new National Center for Nonprofit Boards

in Washington, D.C. Skills can be refined and advanced through professional participation in the various practitioner and research conferences
(such as the Association for Research on Nonprofit Organizations and
Voluntary Action, Association of Volunteer Administrators, Nonprofit
Management Association, and Independent Sector).

Second, CDOs can form (or join) state and national umbrella groups
specializing in housing and community development issues. In many
states, each small CDO must rediscover the wheel. There is no convenient mechanism for keeping track of state and national legislation af-
fecting daily business (let alone for lobbying the legislature). There is no
buying consortium allowing CDOs to obtain scale economies in purchase
orders. There is no convenient way for one organization to learn from
the experiences of another. State and national level community development consortia would address these needs.

Third, CDO members should cautiously endeavor to change the power
structures in "pass-through" nonprofits. They should lobby community
foundations for more aid and seek membership on the board of directors
of local United Ways. Caution is in order, because united fund raising
organizations like United Way must avoid controversy to function well.

Can philanthropy solve chronic economic distress? Of course not.
Does philanthropy have a major role to play? Decidedly. These papers
help us to better understand the current and potential role of philanthropists and nonprofit organizations.

REFERENCES

Hansmann, Henry. "The Role of Nonprofit Enterprise." *Yale Law Journal 89,*
    1980, pp. 835–901.
Hills, John, Franz Hubert, Horst Tomann, and Christine Whitehead. "Shifting
    Subsidy from Bricks and Mortar to People: Experiences in Britain and
    West Germany." *Housing Studies 5,* 1989, pp. 147–167.
Hodgkinson, Virginia Anne, and Murray Weitzman. *Dimensions of the Indepen-
    dent Sector: A Statistical Profile (third edition).* Washington, D.C.: Inde-
    pendent Sector, 1989.
Steinberg, Richard. "Nonprofits and the Market." In Walter W. Powell, ed., *The
    Nonprofit Sector: A Research Handbook.* New Haven: Yale University
    Press, 1986, pp. 118–140.
United Nations Commission for Europe. *Annual Bulletin of Housing and Build-
    ing Statistics for Europe 1986.* New York: UN, 1987.
Weisbrod, Burton. *The Nonprofit Economy.* Cambridge, MA: Harvard Univer-
    sity Press, 1988.

2 Corporate Philanthropy, Urban Research, and Public Policy

Jennifer R. Wolch

Corporate philanthropy has become increasingly important. It is vital to organizations providing voluntary services and to understanding community and economic development. This is particularly true in light of reductions in government funding. This chapter reviews the literature on corporate philanthropy. It argues that research on the rationales and patterns of corporate giving has focused on national observations and analysis. It has left many unanswered questions about geographic variations and about the role of corporate giving in local politics and policy making. An agenda for additional research is outlined. It focuses on questions that need to be addressed if governmental decentralization and expenditure cuts are to be adequately evaluated on equity and efficiency grounds.

INTRODUCTION

The importance of the voluntary sector has come into sharp focus since the advent of tax limitation movements and federal reductions in social expenditures. Increasingly, both government and private sector have turned to voluntary organizations to fill gaps created by revenue shortfalls and service cutbacks. This has put pressure on service providing organizations to raise more nongovernmental funds from donors already contributing to charitable and philanthropic causes. Although aggregate individual charitable contributions exceed the level of corporate giving, contributions by businesses are a significant source of philanthropy.

To illustrate, corporate gifts represent 10 percent of total private contributions to nonreligious voluntary organizations (Maddox, 1981, p. 5). This probably understates the importance of corporate gifts. Many companies report gifts under operational categories such as advertising. And they provide in-kind donations of labor and products. The value of these donations is not typically reported as corporate philanthropy per se.

Moreover, corporate cash giving has risen considerably over the past 40 years. It increased at three times the rate of the gross national product between 1940 and 1970. In the late 1970s and through the 1980s, the rate of giving lingered around 1 percent of pretax net income. But there are indications that corporations realize the necessity of giving and will continue to respond. In fact, in 1980, Tuthill pointed out that in the previous three years, corporate giving rose an average of 16 percent annually. This was "faster than giving by any other sector of society" (Tuthill, 1980, p. 67).

Unfortunately, research on motivations and patterns of corporate contributions is still limited. Most studies have been biased toward the largest corporations. But smaller enterprises may exercise greater influence on local communities. Further, past research focused at the national scale, instead of at the metropolitan level, where corporate funds have their most direct impact and are most essential for meeting collective service requirements. This lack of information and analysis at various scales presents several problems. First, voluntarism has become a cornerstone of the federal program of governmental decentralization and spending cutbacks (Kirschten, 1981). So, it will ultimately need to be evaluated with respect to efficiency and equity. This requires an assessment of the geographic variation in corporate giving. For instance, does local corporate giving mirror national trends? And do regional variations in industrial structure affect the relative ability of a region's voluntary sector to operate effectively or to provide services?

Second, the literature on urban political geography, and local politics, is silent on corporate giving and its impacts on government decision making and policy. Are business gifts strategically targeted to local purposes? Or do corporations give to nonlocal causes and organizations? Are contributions made in order to create employee satisfaction, community goodwill, and a local political climate favorable to business? Or do other aspects of corporate presence in the community, such as jobs and multiplier effects, provide businesses with enough influence in local political life?

Answers to these questions are vital to a more complete understanding of public–private interactions and their role in urban political and geographic processes. Acknowledging these gaps in our knowledge, I critically review the literature on corporate philanthropy, providing an agenda for future research.

PATTERNS OF CORPORATE GIVING

Tax deductibility for corporate contributions was started in 1935. The Internal Revenue Code was amended to permit deduction of charitable contributions by corporations up to a maximum of 5 percent of pretax net income.

There has been a steady increase in business giving since the end of World War II, when giving first exceeded 1 percent of net profits. This rate stabilized through 1970 (Baumol, 1970, p. 5; Vasquez, 1977, p. 1839). In 1968, corporate giving went over $1 billion and equalled 1.17 percent of total pretax net income. Since then, however, giving fell below 1 percent in 1974, 1976, 1977, and 1979, although it hit 1 percent again in 1975 and in 1978, when contributions were 5.3 percent of total charitable contributions of $39.6 billion (Tuthill, 1980).

Overall, aggregate corporate gifts have increased markedly since 1970. In 1982, corporations provided $3.1 billion, or 5.2 percent of all private contributions to voluntary organizations (religious and nonreligious), up from $1.2 billion, or 4.3 percent, in 1974. From 1960 to 1970, corporate giving grew by 38 percent. This was slower than other donor categories. But from 1970 to 1980, corporate gifts increased 60 percent, outstripping growth in giving by foundations and from bequests. And it equaled the rise in individual contributions (IS, 1984, p. 23).

In addition to corporations with giving programs, many large companies have their own foundations. Although the rate of establishment of company foundations has slowed since the 1969 Tax Reform Act, which offered disincentives for foundations, the trend toward business giving via foundations is important. The foundation mechanism allows corporations to sustain their contributions when profits decline. For example, according to the American Association of Fund Raising Council (AAFRC), corporate donations to company foundations fell significantly during the 1974–1975 recession. Nevertheless, foundations were able to draw on accumulated assets, not only to sustain past levels, but to increase total gifts (AAFRC, 1980, p. 17).

There is no reliable estimate of the total number of corporate foundations or their holdings. But the Foundation Center reports on corporate foundations with $1 million in assets or more or which gave $100,000 or more in grants. In 1977, there were 545 such corporate foundations. Together, they held $1.6 billion in assets, received $0.4 billion in gifts, and gave $0.3 billion in grants. By 1981, there were 701 foundations, a 29 percent increase. They held $2.5 billion in assets, received $0.5 billion in gifts, and contributed $0.7 billion (IS, 1984, p. 32).

Not all charitable contributions are actually reported to the Internal Revenue Service (IRS) as such. Therefore, most figures on corporate philanthropy understate the corporate role. Recently, the Conference Board and the Council for Financial Aid to Education (CFAE) surveyed 286 corporations about their nonreported assistance (IS, 1984, p. 33). In 1982, these firms provided cash and in-kind assistance of $258 million. Of this, $74.8 million was in cash, $22.9 million was in loaned personnel, and $86 million was in property and products. $31.9 million was in low interest loans, $4 million was in the facilities and services, and $38.8 million was for administrative costs for these contributions. The median was $92,500 (IS, 1984, p. 33).

I now turn to variations in reported contributions by size and industry and examine the distribution of gifts to various purposes including: health, education, arts, welfare, community and economic development, and geographic variations in levels and patterns of philanthropy.

Variation in Giving

Giving levels vary widely. Most firms give very little in cash. Only one quarter of firms with net income reported charitable deductions in 1977, for example. They gave an average of $3,400 (IS, 1984, p. 33). Primary variations in giving, identified in past studies at the national level, relate to corporate size. Typically, size is measured by assets and is related to primary activity, such as manufacturing, services, or agriculture. Surveys in metropolitan areas generally mirror national patterns. But there are too few surveys to make definitive conclusions about local trends.

Corporate Size

The biggest contributors are a handful of the largest firms (Vasquez, 1977, p. 1843). For example, in his analysis of size distribution of corporate givers, Vasquez found that over 50 percent of total contributions, in 1970, were by the largest firms over $100 million. They were a mere 0.05 percent of all corporations reporting taxable income.

This dominance suggests that if large and generous companies give disproportionately to local causes, cities in which they are located would enjoy higher levels of largesse than other cities. Although voluntary services funded by corporations do not necessarily substitute for public programs, these cities may experience fewer difficulties providing services. Moreover, if corporations favor their local areas, large and generous firms may wield greater local political influence than less generous ones of the same size. Thus, for planning the delivery of services, for planning development projects, and for political analysis, it is useful to understand how corporate contributions vary by firm size and how this affects public policy.

Large corporations have played a dominant role in charitable giving as far back as 1940. Then, firms with assets of $100 million or more, and in control of over 48 percent of total assets, gave over 20 percent of total contributions (Vasquez, 1977, p. 1839).

By 1970, 36.5 percent of firms with net income made charitable contributions, and these firms controlled 83.4 percent of total U.S. assets (Vasquez, 1977, p. 1848). In the same year, nearly 29 percent of total gifts came from companies with assets over $1 billion (Harriss, 1977, p. 1813). By 1977, this situation was even more pronounced. Corporations in the $100 million and above asset class represented only 2 percent of all corporations. But they gave 62 percent of all gifts. And they held 73.9 percent of total corporate assets (IS, 1984, p. 32).

However, other studies indicate that companies with fewer employees, and fewer assets, gave a higher percentage of income to charity than did larger companies (Baker and Shillingburg, 1977, p. 1858). In fact, these studies indicate that the rate of giving by asset size class follows an inverted V-shape pattern. Giving ratios in 1970, for example, declined from 1.2 percent to 0.8 percent of pretax net income as assets increased from $5 million to the highest asset classes. But contribution ratios also decreased from the $5 million asset class to the smallest ($0) asset class. This pattern has been documented from the mid-1940s through the late 1970s. (IS, 1984; Johnson, 1966; Nelson, 1970; Whitehead, 1976). In 1977, firms in the largest asset class ($100 million or more) gave 0.7 percent of pretax net income, those in the $1 million to $4.5 million class gave 1.19 percent, and firms in the $100,000–$250,000 class gave 0.74 percent.

Interestingly, the very smallest firms in that year (with assets under $100,000) gave 1.74 percent of pretax net income (IS, 1984, p. 32). In 1979, firms in the largest asset categories gave an average of 0.76 percent of pretax net income. But the average for all firms was 1.04 percent (Troy, 1982, p. 5).

Industrial Sector

In addition to variations by firm size, there are also marked differences according to industry group. Manufacturing is, and has historically been, the most generous to all sectors. In 1966, the IRS showed manufacturing, with 55 percent of total net income, gave 58 percent of all contributions at a rate of 1.06 percent.

Textile mill products, rubber and plastic products, printing and publishing, stone, clay, and glass products, and producers of transportation equipment made gifts at over 1.75 percent (Fremont-Smith, 1972, p. 44). In 1970, 48.1 percent of manufacturing firms with positive net incomes, although accounting for only 19 percent of total assets and 12 percent of all firms, made contributions of 50 percent of all contributions.

In 1977, manufacturing concerns accounted for an even smaller percentage of all firms (11%). But again, they contributed more than 50 percent of all gifts. In comparison, retail trade had 19.2 percent of firms but gave only 8.8 percent. Finance, insurance, and real estate, with 19 percent of firms, gave 15 percent. Wholesale trade, with 12 percent of total companies, gave 7 percent. And services, with 22 percent of all firms, gave a mere 4.3 percent (IS, 1984 p. 33).

Despite a declining number of firms, manufacturers continue to give more generously than others. They made 62.3 percent of all contributions in 1978 (AAFRC, 1980, p. 19). And they gave 0.72 percent of pretax net income. But nonmanufacturers gave only 0.58 percent in 1979 (Troy, 1982, p. 18).

Other industry groups have been catching up. For example, by 1970, the percentage of net income contributed by agricultural concerns had increased seven times over its 0.5 percent level of 1940. And mining, communications, wholesale trade, retail trade, and the services doubled from 1940 to 1970 (Vasquez, 1977). And, although the proportion of total contributions made by retailers dropped between 1940 and 1970, from 13.3 percent to 9.3 percent, the rate of giving increased and actually exceeded that of manufacturing. Retail trade in 1970 made gifts of 1.43 percent of pretax net income while manufacturing gave 1.19 percent, an exception to the rule that manufacturing is more beneficent than nonmanufacturing (Vasquez, 1977, p. 1842).

These variations, by industrial group, can have significant implications. Regional economies, with strong manufacturing sectors, may receive more corporate dollars than service oriented areas if companies target gifts close to home. For example, one study indicated that, although the average proportion of employment in manufacturing in the 50 largest Standard Metropolitan Statistical Areas (SMSAs) was 24 percent in 1977, it ranged from 17.4 percent in southern SMSAs to 30 percent in the north central region (Noyelle, 1983). Thus, regional economic structure may strongly determine what to expect from corporate philanthropy.

Distribution of Contributions to Recipients

Individuals give largely to religious organizations. But corporations contribute to health, welfare, and higher education (Baker and Shillingburg, 1977, p. 1853). Conference Board surveys in 1959, 1962, 1965, 1968, and 1970 indicate that the relative attractiveness of these three areas to corporate givers has shifted. Contributions to education increased between 1965 and 1968. But grants to health and welfare dropped (Fremont-Smith, 1972, p. 48).

In two specific years, the 1968 Conference Board survey of 401 corporations indicated that 39 percent of gifts went to education. But 37 percent went to health and welfare organizations (Watson, 1972, pp. 12–13). By contrast, health and welfare had received 50.7 percent, and education 31.3 percent from the 180 companies surveyed in 1955. The two surveys are not strictly comparable because of differences in sample size. But they are nonetheless indicative of the shift in corporate priorities.

The Conference Board surveys indicate another trend that emerged during the 1960s. Beginning in 1965, corporations showed increasing interest in civic causes and urban affairs. It is reasonable to conclude that this was a response to the growing urban crises. In 1967–1968, Cohn surveyed 247 Fortune 500 companies. He found that "175 of these companies have revised their annual donations list since 1967 to include grants to national and local groups associated with urban affairs and that of these, 45 had actually cut back on donations to traditional charities" (Fremont-Smith, 1972, p. 55).

Watson's 1968 survey also led him to comment that "4 out of 5 of the companies reporting contributed funds to help meet the crises in the cities. Almost 50 percent of the companies allocated up to 5 percent of their annual contributions for this purpose. Another 20 percent gave larger amounts, in some instances up to 10 percent of their contributions" (Watson, 1972, pp. 12–13).

An examination of giving in the 1970s indicates a continued and growing emphasis on civic affairs and on the arts. Whether or not this trend was accompanied by an increase in corporate attention to their own communities is not clear. At any rate, the 1972 Conference Board survey indicated that 42 percent of contributions went to health and welfare and 33.6 percent to higher education. Civic improvements received 9.14 percent (Baker and Shillingburg, 1972, p. 1858). By 1978, 35 percent of total contributions went to education and health care, and 11 percent was allocated for civic projects (Tuthill, 1980). Similar results were reported by the CFAE. Between 1975 and 1980, giving to the arts more than doubled. And from 1967 to 1978, contributions to the arts rose from $22 million to $250 million (Tuthill, 1980, p. 70). In 1978, culture and art received 10.1 percent of contributions, up 2 percent in two years (AAFRC, 1980, p. 18). Thus, a reallocation of contributions occurred during the 1960s and 1970s. It reflected a growing emphasis on education and labor force training and increasing attention to civic problems, social needs, and cultural enrichment.

Although the clamor of urban social movements of the 1960s has subsided, urban crises have intensified in many respects. And corporations have continued to respond by channeling resources to projects and organizations that have the potential to alleviate social distress or into highly visible projects in the arts that can improve businesses' images.

Current federal policies of social spending reductions have intensified these socially directed efforts. But, the shift in giving toward education, and away from health and welfare, implies that although the most severe cuts in public social expenditures have been in health and welfare, voluntary health and welfare agencies should not expect an increasing share of corporate donations. Similarly, cities with high "misery" indices, and most in need of health and human services, may not be bailed out by rising business gifts.

The distribution of corporate philanthropy raises questions for research and policy. We need to know if the distribution among purposes mirrors the distribution preferred by citizens and, in some instances, required on the basis of human needs. For instance, does the pattern of giving reflect social choices about the types and levels of health, welfare, arts, or education services that ought to be provided, no matter who is responsible for funding? Or do differences between private and social allocations leave preferences unsatisfied and needs unmet?

Since corporate donations are subsidized by public tax expenditures, knowledge and analysis of the differences between public and private allocations have always been necessary as a justification for tax favoritism. But the needed analyses have not been forthcoming. Now, with government reductions in social expenditures and increasing calls for corporations and other donors to bridge the widening service gap, greater knowledge is essential.

Geographic Variations in Giving Levels and Targeting Patterns

There have been only six studies of corporate giving at the metropolitan scale (Galaskiewicz, 1982; Maddox, 1981; Wolpert and Reiner, 1980; see Fremont-Smith, 1972, for a review of three earlier studies). Some simply repeat what has been done in national surveys for a local area. And they report total contributions, contributions per employee, contributions as a percentage of pretax net income, industrial group differences in giving, and proportion of gifts to functional subareas of voluntary activity. Their findings are difficult to compare. In each case, survey designs, sampling techniques, and time periods are different.

Some of these studies also address issues related to geographic targeting. For example, a 1952 study of Cleveland corporations revealed that companies with headquarters there gave more per local employee than nonheadquarters (e.g., branch plant) firms. And it found that more monies were targeted to local charities than to all other causes (HBSCC, 1953). Galaskiewicz (1982) surveyed giving of 150 corporations in Minneapolis–St. Paul and found that smaller companies tended to give all their contributions to local causes, whereas large firms gave on average only 63 percent of total gifts to local activities. And Maddox (1981) surveyed 142 corporations in ten cities and although there were too few in any one city to provide intermetropolitan comparisons, she found that headquarters firms gave more per headquarters city employee than per branch community employee.

Wolpert and Reiner (1980) collected 1973 and 1978 data from 60 Philadelphia corporations and corporate foundations to discover differences in giving by industry, employment level, and headquarters or branch status, as well as to document the allocation of contributions, local and nonlocal. They found that in this sample, skewed toward the largest businesses, 66 percent of Philadelphia headquartered corporate and corporate foundation contributions, 93 percent of non-Philadelphia-based corporation gifts, and 20 percent of gifts from non-Philadelphia-based corporate foundations with regional or division offices in Philadelphia stayed in the area in 1978. With respect to industry specific giving, in 1978, the 34 manufacturing concerns surveyed provided 34 percent of contributions, 16 service firms 12 percent, and 21 financial firms 48 percent. Services and finance targeted most gifts locally (73 percent and 84 percent, respectively), in contrast to manufacturing (29 percent). But the small sample size and its nonrepresentative nature seriously compromise generalizations concerning industry patterns or employment giving relationships.

This lack of comparative metropolitan surveys, or analyses of the impact of local factors, leaves gaps in our understanding. It also hampers both the estimation of the revenues needed to meet local public collective goods requirements, and the evaluation of public policy alternatives. Although national levels and patterns of corporate philanthropy have been documented, in rough terms, for more than 25 years and shifts in targeting patterns have been identified, there is little definitive information on local levels or patterns of corporate giving.

First, how do levels of giving vary across metropolitan areas? Are there significant differences between snowbelt and sunbelt cities; declining and growing cities; factory towns and service centers; cities with reform administrations and cities dominated by political machines? Second, what share of corporate funds stay at their origin? And how do local/nonlocal allocation decisions vary by industry, corporate size, and other factors? And third, when companies target locally, do they allocate the same proportion to specific purposes as their national pattern of giving would suggest? Conversely, what kind of targeting pattern arises when companies give to areas in which they have no facilities?

Any useful evaluation of the current program of the past decade's "new federalism" and "privatization" policies, which shifted human service responsibilities onto lower tier governments and voluntary sector organizations, suggests the importance of answering these questions.

Reasons for Giving

What compels corporations to donate? Many explanations have been offered. But these rationales can be categorized into three main motives: (1) corporate social responsibility, (2) through-the-firm consumption of managers or owner-managers, and (3) profit maximization.

Corporate Social Responsibility

Turner (1968) suggests that corporations have historically responded to five internal pressures: (1) from stockholders for dividends; (2) from employees (and unions) for cash compensation and other benefits, (3) from governments for taxes, (4) from customers for quality goods and services, and (5) from suppliers for purchase of their materials and equipment. Today, according to Turner, there is a sixth pressure: (6) from the community, to redistribute some of the corporation's community derived benefits back to the public and to conduct business in a manner consistent with the public's health and safety.

Such redistributive behavior is commonly referred to as the exercise of corporate social responsibility. Efforts to be socially responsible include initiatives to enhance product safety, environmental protection, consumer education, consumer services, and cash and in-kind contributions to charitable activities, including community and economic development. According to the theory of social responsibility, firms direct efforts and dollars to these areas because of their duty to employees, and the communities in which employees reside, and in which negative environmental impacts of company activities are likely to result in external costs (Maddox, 1981). The corporation should be a "good citizen", as corporate leaders asserted. It has a responsibility to the community and therefore should support local philanthropic causes and help meet public service needs (Baker and Shillingburg, 1977, p. 1853; Levy and Shatto, 1978, p. 20).

This "social responsibility" motive is popular among corporate leaders. It implies that support of philanthropic agencies in a community is given without ulterior motives of enhancing manager or owner satisfaction or profits. This contention is debatable, however. Maddox (1981) argues that "without any connection to some kind of benefit accruing to the firm . . . this motive lacks logical substance for explaining corporate contributions" (p. 30). Similarly, Moskowitz (1977) contends that corporate philanthropy is not the route to social responsibility but is actually a strategy to dodge social responsibility.

After interviewing corporate executives from some of the largest corporations, Moskowitz found that corporate leaders saw their contributions as providing support for the problem solving efforts of others (Moskowitz, 1977, p. 1828). "Their philanthropic expenditures were largely applied to the symptoms of social problems, but had little impact on causes; furthermore it was generally not in the interest of business to develop significant programs that addressed causes." He concludes that the only reason companies make contributions is because they believe it is in their selfish interest. They use resources to help communities in which they operate only because the corporation will not otherwise thrive (Moskowitz, 1977, p. 1829).

Owner-Manager Philanthropy

A second motive suggests that owners and managers are displaying their own personal philanthropic motives when they give through the firm (Johnson, 1966).

Following Nelson, Maddox (1981) points out that they also garner more financial benefits by channeling gifts though the firm. These benefits accrue as a result of Internal Revenue Code provisions that tax the corporation for income distributed as dividends, but allows gifts to be deducted from taxable net income. Owners, or managers who are stockholders, save by replacing some dividend payments with tax deductible giving through the firm. Otherwise, owners or managers would be forced to make contributions out of already taxed dividends and other income.

Profit Maximization

Instead of adhering either to the social responsibility rationale or the through-the-firm giving hypothesis, many analysts contend that corporate giving is actually a device to enhance or maximize profits. Two variants of the profit maximization approach are worth noting.

First, a "political" theory of corporate nonprofit activity (Nelson, 1970) suggests that giving helps firms meet the following corporate objectives: (1) protection of investments, (2) earning the goodwill of the community, and (3) achieving better relations with labor, customers, and other interest groups. These objectives seem consistent with the motive of corporate social responsibility (Neal, 1968). But the underlying reason for support, in order to assure the goodwill of groups and interests, is that their cooperation and assistance are absolutely essential to the existence and growth of the company (Baker and Shillingburg, 1977).

A second variant of the profit maximization hypothesis, but one which also puts business in a most favorable light, is Eells' prudential investment theory (1956). Benefits to the company result from the successful pursuit of objectives like the protection of investment, better employee health and education, community and labor goodwill, a neighborhood attractive to executives, and, of particular importance to Eells, preservation of pluralism against encroachment by the state (1968). All of these benefits become "part of the intangible assets of the company" (Baker and Shillingburg, 1977, p. 1867).

Decisions about corporate contributions are made on the same level as those about corporate investments. Gifts are motivated by the expectation of an increased monetary return. These returns may not be immediate, as simple profit maximization strategies would strive for, but in the long run, gifts may serve as indirect inputs to enhance the public image of a corporation and advantageously shift the demand curve for the corporation's product (Schwartz, 1968, p. 480; Maddox, 1981, p. 29). At the same time, beneficial and prudent corporate giving, such as in innovative community and economic development, helps society too. It becomes a creative force for solving social problems.

Baumol (1970) has fused the ideas of corporate social responsibility and profit maximization in his concept of "enlightened self-interest" as the stimulus for corporate philanthropy. He points to a mutually dependent relationship that exists between private and public enterprises. "Gifts by private firms are justified not merely as a matter of their indebtedness to the nonprofit institutions for their past accomplishments, but also as a matter of self-interest, inasmuch as the deterioration of institutions such as universities and hospitals would no doubt have serious consequences for private enterprise" (1970, p. 3). Voluntary organizations rely on corporate contributions for their subsistence. But, at the same time, many corporations depend both on the voluntary and on the public sectors to carry out those functions that will ensure the well-being of their employees. This implies that corporations will most likely provide funds to causes that best serve the firm's interest. That can be narrowly defined in terms of profits or more broadly construed as a healthy business environment.

In summary, corporate giving levels have risen over the past quarter of a century, along with philanthropic contributions from other sources. Giving levels vary with corporate size and industry group. The largest corporations give the biggest dollar share, while not necessarily giving the greatest proportion of pretax net income. Manufacturing concerns

have historically been more generous than other businesses and they are
the source of most corporate gifts. Voluntary agencies in health and welfare and education services have attracted most corporate contributions.
But since the 1960s, civic affairs and the arts have both become more
popular targets. Only a minimal information about corporative giving is
available for urban regions, and there are no comparative metropolitan
studies of corporate philanthropy.

The most common explanations for corporate philanthropy center on
the short term and long term benefits that contributions make to the
firm. Although owners and managers may receive tax benefits by giving
through the firm, instead of making gifts from their personal income,
most analysts conclude that corporate gifts are made in the enlightened
self-interest of the firm. Corporate leaders may prefer to see philanthropy as fulfilling a responsibility that arises because of the special
power and privileges, as well as potential for harm, wielded by business
in society. It seems clear, however, that philanthropy provides tangible
benefits to business. Thus corporate giving, directly and indirectly, enhances firm profitability.

MODELS OF CORPORATE PHILANTHROPY

Several cross-sectional and time series regression models have been
used to test statistically one or more of the three hypotheses on the
motives for giving. In addition, they have assessed the importance of
other factors that could influence contributions decisions, such as industrial sector and market structure, nature of the production process (labor
versus capital intensiveness), and headquarters versus branch plant status. Most models assume that contribution decisions are analogous to a
basic consumption decision and explain variation in giving as a function
of the firm's income and the price of contributions.

In this section, I discuss the major findings derived from studies of
corporate contributions, along with results of associated modeling exer-
cises. This section describes the only major study of corporate giving to
employ individual firm information, which also considers the influence
of locational differences on giving decisions (Maddox, 1981).

Aggregate Models

Income

Most studies assume that contributions are positively affected by the
firm's income, which is also implicitly a measure of firm size (Maddox,
1981, p. 31). Whitehead (1976) hypothesized that elasticities greater than 1
supported the social responsibility motive for contributions and that larger
firms had greater than proportionate responsibilities to the public welfare.

Nelson (1970) suggested that a unitary elasticity of giving in response to income indicated a "scale effect" on corporate giving. Schwartz (1968) argued that inelastic responses would support the notion that contributions were a necessary (rather than a normal or superior) good and were motivated by benefits of through-the-firm giving. Smaller firms would be more likely to be closely held and private, managed by owners or managers holding sizable shares of company stock. Thus, personal giving by owners and managers channeled through the firm would increase total giving of these smaller firms.

On the other hand, inelastic responses were explained by Whitehead as indicating either the existence of scale economies in contributions impact, meaning the return to giving, in terms of profits, increased faster than gift amounts, or through-the-firm giving. His rationale for through-the-firm giving differs from that of Schwartz, however. Whitehead suggested that in larger firms, personal motives of any one officer are less effective in influencing giving decisions and that the costs of making contributions decisions could increase with firm size. Cross-sections studies produced varying elasticities, but there are reasons to conclude that the smaller estimates are questionable (Maddox, 1981). Moreover, there may be misspecification biases, calling certain results into question (such as Bennett and Johnson's [1980], where some key model variables are likely to be colinear).

Price

The deductibility of charitable contributions, in effect, reduces the price of a gift to the corporation. Schwartz (1968) suggested that if firms made donations in an effort to maximize profits, tax savings arising from the deductibility of gifts would not affect the rate of giving, since all other production costs are similarly deductible. On the other hand, if giving was motivated by through-the-firm considerations, then owners and managers would be encouraged to give more with increasing tax rates and price elasticities would be larger.

The reduced price of the contribution is typically defined as the complement to the marginal tax rate, although in some studies average tax rates are used instead. Time series studies capture the impact of price changes and in general show that giving decisions are sensitive to changes in marginal corporate tax rates. Price elasticities are uniformly negative and significant and range from about 1 (Nelson) to over 2 (Schwartz).

Industry Group

Studies that disaggregate data according to industry group indicate differences in corporate giving between groups. Schwartz (1968), for example, found income and price elasticities to vary substantially across industry group. Maddox (1981), on the other hand, found that although income elasticities for manufacturing industries tended to be slightly higher and more reliable than for all industries together, the magnitudes of the differences were not overwhelming.

Market Structure

Johnson (1966), and Johnson and Johnson (1970), argue that the level of competition in an industry will affect the propensity of firms to give. They assume that philanthropy does not indirectly lower production costs. Therefore, in perfectly competitive industries, firms cannot give, because of least cost production pressures. In monopolistic industries, firms need not give. But in oligopolistic, imperfectly competitive, or monopolistically competitive industries, which they term the "rivalry" sector, firms are more likely to give to gain competitive advantage in the marketplace.

Since average firm size tends to be small in highly competitive industries and large in monopolistic industries, but medium sized in the rivalry sector, analyses that only consider size, in terms of income or assets, may make an error in causal logic. Size per se may not be as important as market structure.

The Johnsons' own analyses of the influence of market structure on corporate giving are not sufficiently elaborate to test their hypothesis. Whitehead (1976) and Nelson (1970) included the number of firm employees in their regressions, in an attempt to explore the market structure question. In fact, this is an extremely rough proxy for the level of competition within an industry. Their results were mixed; Nelson obtained positive coefficients, whereas Whitehead's were negative. Whitehead (1976) and Bennett and Johnson (1980) also used the four firm concentration ratio as a measure of market concentration (oligopoly) and market power, which was expected to vary positively with contributions. This variable was positive but insignificant in Whitehead's empirical tests, but negative and significant in Bennett and Johnson's. This is perhaps a result of the very different specifications the two studies employed, rendering their results inappropriate for comparison.

Since Johnson (1966) had predicted that the relationship would be nonlinear, with firms in competitive (and hence unconcentrated) markets and in monopolistic (and hence totally concentrated markets), giving less than firms in the somewhat concentrated rivalry sector, Whitehead divided the sample into low and high concentration ratio groups. Coefficients were negative and positive for the low and high concentration subgroups, respectively, but were not statistically significant (Maddox, 1981).

Employment Factors

Employment patterns have been hypothesized to affect giving patterns. First, Nelson (1970) suggests that firms with large numbers of employees, labor intensive firms, may be more generous than capital intensive firms because they feel more responsibility toward the employees' communities.

This variable then stands as a test of the social responsibility motive for corporate giving. His estimates of employment level coefficients were significant and positive. Whitehead (1976), however, argues that a positive relationship between number of employees and gifts could also support a profit maximization rationale for giving because increased giving would indirectly enhance profits via greater employee welfare and improved labor relations.

In his own equations, the employment variable was positive but insignificant. But Maddox argues that the use of an employment variable to test the influence of giving on profits is not appropriate. Rather, the impact of firm philanthropy on profits should be tested with a profits equation (Maddox, 1981, p. 35). She also questions the utility of Nelson's use of the employment variable to test the social responsibility motive because employment is likely to be related to other measures of firm size, such as net income and assets.

A second use of an employment variable to explain corporate giving is suggested by Bennett and Johnson (1980). They argue that the percentage of the work force of an industry that is unionized is likely to influence levels of giving negatively. Their rationale is that giving may be seen by workers as an indication that the firm has excess profits and if so, that such profits should be reflected in higher wages rather than corporate philanthropy. Unionized employees are hypothesized to have more power vis-a-vis management and to be more successful in exerting pressure on management to increase wages rather than contributions.

In their cross-section regressions for 1967 and 1971, Bennett and Johnson obtained mixed results, with the percentage unionized work force variable being negative and significant as expected in 1967 but positive and insignificant in 1971.

Other Input Factors

Several studies suggest that the level of giving will be affected by corporate decisions about other inputs, besides employment, to the production process. In particular, advertising expenditures, officers' compensation, and dividends have been included in regression models.

Advertising expenditures are hypothesized to be a substitute for giving since giving, like advertising, may be a public relations effort. Alternatively, advertising and giving could both reflect the firm's desire to improve its public image. Some studies of advertising indicate some complementarity (Schwartz, 1968; Whitehead, 1976); in other cases, results have been mixed (Bennett and Johnson, 1980). Officers' compensation could also affect the availability of funds for contributions, as could levels of dividends. Empirical analyses of these relationships are not definitive however (Nelson, 1970; Whitehead, 1976).

Maddox's Individual Firm Model

Maddox (1981) surveyed 166 publicly held firms in ten cities and used data at the individual firm levels to test a set of corporate giving models. The models focus on community level influences on contributions. The cities included in her survey were located primarily in the midwest, south, and southwest, and so are not strictly geographically representative. Firms were selected for the study on the basis of size and fell into one of several industry groups, primarily manufacturing.

The models were designed to test Maddox's theory that corporate contributions enhance managerial utility, which is in turn affected by firm profits and the public image of the firm. Contribution levels are influenced by the ability of the firm to give (e.g., income), community characteristics, and tax considerations. Relevant community characteristics included: (1) population, with firms in larger, more anonymous cities being under less pressure to give; (2) government spending of collective services, which could have a positive or negative influence on giving, since more services could lower marginal operating costs of the firm or imply diminishing marginal returns to the firm's giving efforts; (3) philanthropic expenditures by other firms in the city, expecting a pattern similar to those noted for government spending on collective goods; and (4) the flow of services from local charities in the health, education, and welfare fields that yield increasing returns to corporate gifts. State tax credits for contributions were available in two of the states where surveyed firms were located. This was expected to increase giving rates.

In addition to the impact of corporate income, community characteristics, and tax laws, Maddox argued that the allocation of gifts by multilocation firms would be biased in favor of the city in which firm headquarters, as opposed to plants, are situated. She theorized that executives at the firm's headquarters would be under greater social pressure to give because of the increased visibility of company headquarters to community fund raisers and the operation of executive networks that promote local philanthropy.

One difference of means test and two regression models were employed to test these propositions. The difference of means test explored the hypothesis that the ratio of gifts to employees at the headquarters location would be greater than in branch plant communities. Results indicated that firms were more generous, on a per employee basis, in headquarters communities. They gave on average $216 per employee in contrast to average gifts of $36 per employee in plant communities. But the average aggregate amount given in headquarters communities was not higher than the amount given in plant locations because the number of employees at plant sites was generally much larger than at headquarters. Average contribution to headquarters cities was $456; to plant cities, $456 (Maddox, 1981, p. 157).

Thus from this analysis, it is difficult to argue that differences in the number of headquarters companies across cities will affect their aggregate level of corporate philanthropy. Rather, the total number of workers employed in the private sector would seem to be more critical. However, the results refer to Maddox's entire sample. It is conceivable that headquarters-plant allocation patterns could vary by industry. So cities with differing industry mixes, and mixes of headquarters and plant operations, might receive varying levels of philanthropy.

The first regression model tested the influence of firm income, community characteristics, and tax credits on total giving. The second model was designed to explain the level of headquarters giving on the basis of the firm's total contributions budget and headquarters city specific variables from the first model.

Results from the total contributions model produced income elasticities ranging from 0.67 to 0.8, depending on specification and estimation procedure used. These estimates are thus considerably higher than those derived from previous cross-section analyses. The only other consistently significant variable was population, which had the predicted negative sign.

Results obtained for other variables depended upon estimation technique. In those instances where results were significant, the sign of coefficients supported Maddox's proposition that philanthropic resources of the community encouraged giving. Government funding of collective services was insignificant in all but one regression variant. Results concerning the impact of tax credits and giving by other corporations were inconclusive.

Results of the headquarters giving model were similar, generating income elasticities in the same general range, and they showed the significance of population. The total contributions budget of the firm also had a clear and positive influence on headquarters giving. Like the total contributions model, however, the performance of other community specific variables was mixed.

More generally, measurement problems surrounding the variables may explain these mixed results. For example, giving by other corporations was proxied by corporate gifts to United Way. But corporations typically target only a fifth of their donations to that organization. Similarly, government spending on collective goods was measured by state and local spending on health and welfare although the majority of funding in these areas originates at the federal level. The insignificance of the tax credit variable may likewise be related to the relative unimportance of state as opposed to federal taxation. Last, and perhaps most troubling, since community data on plant locations were not collected, the giving environment of the firm was proxied in the total contributions model, by a weighted average of the city specific variables in the headquarters city and the average from the ten survey cities. This procedure reduces the range of data variation. It also dampens chances for significance and is unlikely to capture the characteristics of branch plant communities located in suburban or rural settings.

A RESEARCH AGENDA

Research on corporate philanthropy provides urban researchers with important background information on the patterns and rationales for business giving. Past studies document variations in giving levels and rates according to firm size and industry type, identify the targets of contributions, and suggest the role of corporate philanthropy in advancing the interests of the firm. Moreover, statistical models of corporate giving behavior support the hypotheses that giving levels vary according to the ability of the firm to make contributions and the existence of tax incentives for giving.

However, the existing base of knowledge about corporate philanthropy is seriously deficient. First, a good deal of the literature is written by business representatives and lacks a critical perspective. Second, much of the data on which aggregate statistics are based suffer from shortcomings (under reporting, bias toward large firms, self-selection of survey responses, large variations in sample sizes). Third, past modelling efforts have been predicated on different economic theories of the firm and have used different proxy measures to test the same hypotheses, so model results are not comparable or inconsistent. Fourth, most studies focus on the economics of corporate giving in a narrow sense. This approach leaves many vital questions unanswered, such as those related to geographical patterns of giving and their implications for the welfare of urban populations. Moreover, questions remain about public policies which define the appropriate roles for government and business in contemporary society.

This review suggests an agenda for future research on corporate giving. It addresses both behavioral and policy oriented questions and is targeted to questions about corporate philanthropy at the urban regional scale.

First, we need stronger information on corporate giving in individual urban areas, as well as comparative metropolitan studies. Also, more knowledge about interregional flows of philanthropic funds, and how local, nonlocal allocation rates vary with firm characteristics, is needed. Only when these types of data are available will we be able to examine the influence of local characteristics on corporate philanthropy or explain variations in giving across metropolitan areas.

Second, a focus on local factors is long overdue. Geographic variations in urban economic and political characteristics need to be investigated further. For instance, does the composition of the business community (cohesiveness, social class mix, extent of interlocking directorates) affect the amount of social pressure on executives to give? Are firms with a long standing local presence and close ties to local government more attuned to giving opportunities and service needs at home, as compared to mobile firms with few local ties? This raises the issues of the impact of mobility rates and their effect on total corporate gifts. Does the geographic structure of markets prompt a differential giving response from companies, with firms buying from local suppliers or selling to local, regional markets more likely to give to community causes? Past work suggests a positive relationship between number of employees and contributions, but does this relationship vary depending upon the types of workers employed (e.g., white collar, blue collar)? Analyses of the linkages between local government spending and corporate giving could be fruitful in increasing our understanding of the roles of public and private enterprise in society. What is the impact of local public goods mix on corporate giving patterns? If research does demonstrate some interdependence between governmental service levels and corporate giving, can we explain any of the interurban variation, either in service or in giving levels, on the basis of this interaction and interdependence? Also, future research would provide insight into the workings of local politics and the role of corporations in this arena. Do executives make contributions to local causes to exert influence on local government, making gifts strategic weapons in the business lobby arsenal?

Some of these questions are vital to public policy. The success of governmental decentralization and privatization rests on the ability of the voluntary sector to provide needed services and on the willingness of the private sector to donate resources to fund these services. Future research on corporate philanthropy can help us evaluate the desirability of redefining the respective roles of governments and markets in the supply of collective goods and to understand the consequences of such a shift for the people who live in the cities and regions of the nation.

ACKNOWLEDGEMENTS

Research support from the National Science Foundation, Program in Geography and Regional Science, is gratefully acknowledged. Thanks are also extended to Julian Wolpert, Thomas Reiner and Annette Rubalcaba for their assistance and comments.

REFERENCES

AAFRC. (1980) *Giving USA: 1980 Annual Report*. New York: American Association of Fund-Raising Council.

Baker, R. P. Jr, and Shillingburg, J. E. (1977) "Corporate charitable contributions," in *Foundations, Private Giving and Public Policy: Report and Recommendations on Foundations and Private Philanthropy, Volume 3: Special Behavior Studies, Foundations and Corporations*, Commission on Private Philanthropy and Public Needs, Chair J. H. Filer. Washington, DC: US Government Printing Office, pp. 1853–1905.

Baumol, W. J. (1970) "Enlightened self-interest and corporate philanthropy" in *A New Rationale for Corporate Social Policy*, edited by W. J. Baumol, R. Likert, H. C. Wallich, J. J. McGowan. Lexington, MA: DC Heath, pp. 3–19.

Bennett, J. T., and Johnson, M. H. (1980) "Corporate contributions: some additional considerations" *Public Choice* 35, pp. 137–143.

Eells, R. (1956) *Corporate Giving in a Free Society*. New York: Harper and Row.

Eells, R. (1968) "A philosophy for corporate giving." *The Conference Board Record* 5, pp. 14–18.

Fremont-Smith, M. R. (1972) *Philanthropy and the Business Corporation*. New York: Russell Sage Foundation.

Galaskiewicz, J. (1982) "Corporate–nonprofit linkages in Minneapolis–St Paul: Preliminary findings from three surveys." Unpublished manuscript, Department of Sociology, University of Minnesota, Minneapolis, MN.

Geiger, R. K. and Wolch, J. R. (1984) "Resource command of voluntary organizations: Group power and governmental prerogatives." Working paper, Planning Institute, University of Southern California, Los Angeles, CA.

Harriss, C. L. (1977) "Corporate giving: rationale, issues, and opportunities," in *Foundations, Private Giving and Public Policy: Report and Recommendations on Foundations and Private Philanthropy, Volume 3: Special Behavior Studies, Foundations and Corporations*, Commission on Private Philanthropy and Public Needs, Chair J. H. Filer. Washington, DC: US Government Printing Office, pp. 1789–1825.

HBSCC. (1953) *Corporation Giving in Greater Cleveland*. Cleveland, OH: Harvard Business School Club of Cleveland, Inc.

IS. (1984) *Dimensions of the Independent Sector*. Washington, DC: Independent Sector. Inc.

Johnson, O. (1966) "Corporate philanthropy: an analysis of corporate contributions." *Journal of Business* 39, pp. 489–504.

Johnson, O., and Johnson, W. L. (1970) "The income elasticity of corporate philanthropy: comment." *Journal of Finance* 25, pp. 149–152.

Keim, G. D., Meiners, R. E., and Frey, L. W. (1980) "On the evaluation of corporate contributions." *Public Choice* 35, pp. 129–136.

Kirschten, D. (1981) "In the eyes of the administration, charity begins with the private sector." *National Journal* 13, pp. 7–9.

Levy, F. K., and Shatto, G. M. (1978) "The evaluation of corporate contributions." *Public Choice* 33, pp. 19–28.

Lippin, P. (1981) "When business and the community 'cooperate.' " *Administrative Management* February, pp. 34–36, 66, 70, 72.

Maddox, K. E. (1981) *Corporate Philanthropy.* Unpublished PhD dissertation, Department of Economics, Vanderbilt University, Nashville, TN.

Moskowitz, M. (1977) "Corporate charitable contributions and corporate social responsibility," in *Foundations, Private Giving and Public Policy: Report and Recommendations on Foundations and Private Philanthropy, Volume 3: Special Behavior Studies, Foundations and Corporations,* Commission on Private Philanthropy and Public Needs, Chair J. H. Filer. Washington, DC: US Government Printing Office, pp. 1827–1838.

Neal, A. C. (1968) "A more rational basis for nonprofit activities." *The Conference Board Report* 5, pp. 5–7.

Nelson, R. (1970) *Economic Factors in the Growth of Corporate Giving.* New York: National Bureau of Economic Research.

Noyelle, T. J. (1983) "The rise of advanced services: some implications for economic development in US cities." *Journal of the American Planning Association* 49, pp. 280–290.

Schwartz, R. A. (1968) "Corporate philanthropic contributions." *Journal of Finance* 23, pp. 479–497.

Troy, K. (1982) *Annual Survey of Corporate Contributions.* New York: The Conference Board, Inc.

Turner, W. H. (1968) "The societal role of the corporation." *The Conference Board Report* 5, pp. 11–13.

Tuthill, M. (1980) "The growing impact of business giving." *Nations Business* 68(10), pp. 66–70.

Vasquez, T. (1977) "Corporate giving measures," in *Foundations, Private Giving and Public Policy: Report and Recommendations on Foundations and Private Philanthropy, Volume 3: Special Behavior Studies, Foundations and Corporations,* Commission on Private Philanthropy and Public Needs, Chair J. H. Filer. Washington, DC: US Government Printing Office, pp. 1839–1852.

Watson, J. H. III. (1972) *Biennial Survey of Company Contributions.* New York: The Conference Board, Inc.

Whitehead, P. J. (1976) *Some Economic Aspects of Corporate Giving.* Unpublished PhD dissertation, Department of Economics, Virginia Polytechnic Institute and State University, Blacksburg, VA.

Wolpert, J., and Reiner, T. A. (1980) "Metropolitan Philadelphia Philanthropy Study." Unpublished manuscript, Metropolitan Philanthropy Project, University of Pennsylvania, Philadelphia, PA.

3 Community-Based Development—Avoiding Resource Misuse and Abuse

Kenneth A. Bertsch

Most corporate contributions officials no longer question the legitimacy of corporate philanthropy. Nevertheless, not too long ago, whether or not corporations should give to charity was very much an open, controversial legal and ethical issue. After all, traditional economic theory held that the capitalist economic engine should be fueled by the pursuit of profits, not the desire to do good deeds. And under common law, corporation managers were not allowed to expend corporate funds for charity unless the company benefitted.

While corporate philanthropists may not question the legitimacy of their project, there still are critics on the left and the right willing to subject corporate charitable largesse to criticism, and these criticisms deserve attention. To begin to satisfy the critics, a company must avoid giving that (1) misuses corporate resources and (2) abuses the corporation's power. Unfortunately, these two directives would seem to require contradictory actions. If you spend money unrelated to corporate interest, you can stand accused of misusing resources; if you make contributions designed to further the corporate interest, you can be accused of abusing corporate power.

The suggestion here is that support for community-based, community directed economic development programs may hold promise for companies that wish to avoid these two hazards, which can act as a sort of psychological jujitsu on the thoughtful corporate philanthropist.

FUNDAMENTAL CONTROVERSIES OVER GIVING

For two reasons, critics generally agree in viewing corporate philanthropy within the context of larger public policy debates. First, corporations are, in the end, creatures of the state, and they function under rules established by the state. Second, because corporate contributions are tax deductible, a large portion of the corporate contributions dollar can be seen as deriving from funds that otherwise would have gone to the government.

The "conservative" critique: For many years, cautious company lawyers warned management against using corporate funds for charitable purposes. In raising the legal questions surrounding such gifts, they frequently quoted the British Lord Justice Bowen's 1883 opinion that "charity has no business to sit at the board of directors qua charity."

The legal and theoretical obstacles to corporate giving were rooted largely in two premises. First, the capitalist economy's "invisible hand" provided for a congruence between social benefit and the pursuit of individual self-interest; the proper *social* role of business was to produce and sell goods and services for profit. In his 1962 book, *Capitalism and Freedom,* economist Milton Friedman wrote that, in a free economy, "there is one and only one social responsibility of business—to use its resources and engage in activities designed to increase its profits so long as it stays within the rules of the game, which is to say, engages in open and free competition, without deception or fraud."

The term "conservative" is appropriate here in some respects, since the desire to confine each political/social/economic entity to the activities appropriate to that entity is, no doubt, a desire characteristic of the conservative psychology. But "conservative" here should not be posed against "liberal," since the position described also can be called a classically liberal approach.

A variant of Friedman's theme is the contention that, because a business is a profitmaking venture geared to the bottom line, it is not well suited to other functions. Henry Ford II asserted that "the corporation is not an all-purpose mechanism; it is not well equipped to serve social needs unrelated to its business operations." Business professor Thomas A. Klein, of the University of Toledo, has written that corporate social spending may "distort social priorities" and that corporations are likely

to be less efficient in social efforts "than are agencies specifically organized to engage in 'social' tasks."

A second premise of conservative critics of corporate philanthropy,
closely related to the first premise, focuses on the corporate structure as
opposed to business per se. This principle is that corporations, as the legal
instruments of shareholders who own them, should not engage in nonbusi-
ness activity. Corporate managers make use of resources owned by shareholders in order to earn a return for those shareholders. In this view, it is
unethical to use those resources for purposes that are not related to making a profit. In *Capitalism and Freedom,* Friedman wrote that:

The corporation is an instrument of stockholders who own it. If the corporation
makes a contribution, it prevents the individual stockholder from himself deciding how he should dispose of his funds. . . . (The) policy . . . of permitting
corporations to make contributions for charitable purposes and allowing deductions for income tax, is a step in the direction of creating a true divorce between
ownership and control and of undermining the basic nature and character of our
society. It is a step away from an individualistic society toward the corporate
state.

Friedman concluded that "the acceptance by corporate officials of a
social responsibility other than to make as much money for their shareholders as possible" is a "fundamentally subversive doctrine."

CONTRIBUTIONS AND CORPORATE POWER

We will see that the wedge that opened the door for widespread corporate donations is the notion that companies have a broad interest in the
welfare of their communities. It is precisely this view that causes concern among progressive corporate critics. To reverse the formulation of
interest, we might say that corporate gifts are not in fact "disinterested."
If such a view is correct, and if contributions give corporations as much
leverage as some executives contend, it is easy to see how corporate
philanthropy would be viewed suspiciously by persons concerned about
excessive corporate power. One critique submitted to the 1975 Filer
Commission on Corporate Philanthropy and Public Needs said that

It is especially inapposite for business corporations to play any role in the philanthropic process. . . . The real problem posed by corporate 'philanthropic'
activity is that corporations are the embodiment of concentrated wealth. As
such, they can hardly be expected to underwrite the political needs of Americans
who wish to redistribute and deconcentrate that wealth.

What makes corporate giving especially troubling in this view is that
it diverts otherwise public money to corporate control, since a large por-

tion—now about one-third, based on new tax rates—of corporate contributions come out of taxes that would have been paid to the federal government. Columbia business professor Richard Eells has called this "a large grant of discretionary authority from society to the directors of corporate business."

Several years ago, law professor Christopher Stone wrote:

If there are social services that are not being adequately performed in the society, and if corporations have excess unexpended earnings at the end of the year, why not raise corporate taxes rather than put ourselves at the mercy of corporate largesse: If we took the latter route, excess monies would be drawn into and disbursed through governmental channels, where they would be subject to the democratic processes of a general electorate, rather than doled out at the whim of nonrepresentative corporate managers.

Among the concerns of critics on the left are corporate attempts to shape ideology through the creation of "chairs of free enterprise" and other methods of influencing educational institutions and "think tanks." Beyond such blatant attempts to gain influence with the corporate dollar, critics on the left lodge a number of specific complaints about corporate giving. Two areas of concern are considered here.

1. Such giving can be used by corporations as a way to evade "real" social responsibilities. Author Milton Moskowitz has called corporate charity "conscience money." In a paper for the Filer Commission, Moskowitz wrote that:

Efforts to reform corporations or change business practices have concentrated on corporate behavior as reflected in day-to-day, ongoing activities. The objective has been to make the corporate animal a socially responsible creature. To zero in on philanthropy and neglect the basic operations of the companies is to beg the question of corporate social responsibility.

The assertion that corporate philanthropy at times is used as a "cover" is supported by observers who see highly visible philanthropic efforts by controversial corporations as public relations gambits. As one social services official put it, "If your image is bad, you buy Shakespeare." In the 1970s and early 1980s, certain oil and tobacco companies in particular were accused of this practice. In a comment she later said was taken out of context, a manager of corporate support programs at Philip Morris told *Fortune Magazine* that, "The people we're interested in impressing are the opinion leaders." Fortune observed that the perception of Philip Morris as a valuable corporate citizen would be useful to the company as legislators consider tobacco subsidies and bans on throwaway bottles.

At the height of the infant formula controversy, Nestle's established a Nestle's Coordination Center for Nutrition. Critics of the company saw this action as a diversion from the infant formula issue. (Nestle's later addressed that issue directly and in a fashion that was satisfactory to its critics.)

Other examples of giving as P.R. abound; perhaps most notable were the fundraising for the 1984 Summer Olympics and the project to restore the Statue of Liberty. These projects pointed to a subsidiary concern— the commercialization of the nonprofit sector. The two fundraising efforts raised substantial corporate cash, primarily through awarding exclusive right to sponsorship and promotion tie-ins in product categories; thus, tobacco, beer and other commercial products, which were officially identified with the Liberty project, and as might be expected, this elicited considerable criticism.

2. Corporations can exercise undue influence over social priorities. Critics say that many of the groups receiving the most support from corporations are more oriented to serving the middle and upper classes than to serving the poor and working classes. Early in the 1980s, social welfare contributions declined relative to arts and education funding. In 1981, Calvin Pressley, Executive Director of the New York City Mission Society, said that the decline in the social welfare share of corporate gifts was symptomatic of a kind of charity "that locks people in place on a social ladder."

International programs may be even more subject to this sort of objection. John G. Sommer, an international development specialist who had worked with the Ford Foundation and Action, said that "philanthropy ancillary to the pursuit of profit frequently distorts local cultures, local values, and the aspirations for equality of opportunity because business gifts more often support causes favored by the elite sectors of society than those principally benefiting the poverty sectors."

Another aspect to this debate involves the relatively heavy weight that corporations are likely to give to sectors of the nonprofit world that are closely and directly associated with corporate needs. Perhaps the best example of "specialized" giving is in higher education, where many corporations support programs closely related to their personnel needs.

Among those who have criticized the effects of this practice are former New York University President John Sawhill, who expressed concern about an apparent "increase in the number of high technology companies that are restricting gifts to business schools, pharmaceutical companies to medical schools, and so on." Sawhill contended that:

This practice implies a view of the university as a collection of separate training schools; it ignores the interrelationship of all areas of knowledge and the wider cultural context in which business and professional activities take place. It is a particularly destructive pattern for the arts and humanities—areas that relate least clearly to corporate interests and yet most vitally to the understanding, creation and preservation of our culture.

Similar criticisms are voiced about the increasing reliance of public television on corporate sponsorship. While direct efforts to shape public broadcasting programming may be rare, the reluctance of companies to finance controversial or experimental programming, and corporate desire for maximum public relations advantage, has contributed to public television mimicking the ratings games played by commercial television, argues *New York Times* television critic John J. O'Connor.

LEGITIMIZATION AND LEGALIZATION OF CORPORATE GIVING

The conservative (or classic liberal) view that extended corporate giving programs are inappropriate dominated legal circles until well into this century, but it left a loophole that has grown large over the years. Even those with a conservative view of the corporate role have allowed that what many call corporate philanthropy may not be altruistic, but may further the corporation's interest, and in that light, from this perspective, such "philanthropy" is appropriate.

In his 1883 decision, Lord Justice Bowen qualified his view on charity's role at the board of directors by stating that "charitable dealing which is for the interest of those who practice it" could "sit at the board." Bowen's qualification provided an opening for the establishment of corporate philanthropy. Late in the 19th and into the 20th century, corporations began to take on certain philanthropic responsibilities that closely related to the corporate self-interest. These ranged from the company town—which blurred the line between public interest and private business interest—to support by American railroads for The Young Men's Christian Association movement. As business professor Frederick Sturdivant writes, "The YMCA movement needed physical facilities and the railroads needed a moral, healthful environment for traveling employees."

Courts supported this kind of corporate philanthropy, on the grounds that such gifts directly benefitted the company. Corporations generally trod a narrow path in such matters, however, and many declined to make contributions where the benefit to the company was not clear and direct. In World War I, patriotic calls were made for support of the war effort, and support for the Red Cross in particular. Because of continued legal uncertainty about contributions, the Red Cross asked companies to declare an extra dividend and send it to stockholders with an urgent plea that it be turned over to the Red Cross.

The momentum of corporate giving that picked up in the war years continued through the "welfare capitalism" days of the 1920s, particularly as the Community Chest movement grew—from 40 such organizations in 1919 to nearly 350 by 1929. Another legitimizing factor was the states' explicit legalization of corporate contributions, beginning with Texas in 1917.

In 1935, the federal income tax deduction for business contributions was enacted, further validating corporate giving. But while the deduction and patriotic calls to contribute during World War II increased gifts, legal clouds remained until 1953, when the New Jersey Supreme Court delivered a landmark judgment on A. P. Smith Mfg. Co. v. Barlow. In this case, the corporation sought to prove that its $1,500 contribution to Princeton University was not ultra vires (beyond the powers) of the corporate charter, as certain stockholders claimed. While the court held that a common law did exist barring corporate charitable expenditures unless the corporation benefitted, the court applied the rule very broadly with this ringing statement:

The contribution here in question is towards a cause which is intimately tied into the preservation of American business and the American way of life. Such giving may be called incidental power, but when it is considered in its essential character, it may well be regarded as a major, though unwritten, corporate power. It is even more than that. In the Court's view of the case, it amounts to a solemn duty.

The Smith decision was upheld by the U.S. Supreme Court, which dismissed an appeal for want of a federal question. The precedent has represented an enduring victory for those who saw a broader corporate social role than that promoted by Lord Bowen. The "direct benefit" rule of old clearly applied no longer, for while two New Jersey statutes explicitly authorized limited corporate donations, the court based its decision on a broad view of corporate self-interest rather than the state laws as such.

NAVIGATING BETWEEN "MISUSE" AND "ABUSE"

The legal rationale for corporate giving now is well established and protective of a broad array of philanthropic activity. The business philanthropist has little to fear from court challenges to her charitable prerogatives. Nevertheless, companies also may wish to maintain giving programs that keep shareholders and corporate skeptics at bay. The difficulty, as suggested earlier, is that the two kinds of criticism—"misuse" of (shareholders') resources and "abuse" of corporate power—seem to suggest contradictory approaches.

While tension between the two criticisms no doubt exists, there are channels for pursuing charitable programs that avoid the shoals of misuse and abuse. One of those channels, as a number of companies have shown, is the support for community-based, community directed economic development programs. Local economic development and economic stability is manifestly in the interest of most corporations. Secondly, while fixation on issues of material development and productivity growth comes under attack in some quarters, there remains broad support for attempts to address uneven development. (Pope John Paul II, for example, has criticized a tendency to equate economic development with "progress," but has strongly endorsed efforts to address unequal development.)

A model for corporate supported community development efforts is provided by the Local Initiatives Support Corporation (LISC), a national nonprofit enterprise that helps selected local organizations draw new private and public resources into their efforts to revitalize neighborhoods. LISC, begun in 1979 by the Ford Foundation and six companies (Aetna, Atlantic Richfield, Continental Illinois Bank and Trust, International Harvester, Levi Strauss, and Prudential Insurance), is assisting local organizations in lower-, working-, and middle-class neighborhoods in designing, capitalizing, and managing significant housing and commercial developments.

Another model is the Enterprise Foundation, founded by James Rouse of the Rouse Co. The foundation, which is supported both by foundations and corporations, was established to refurbish slum housing for the poor, while giving residents shared title to their apartments to resist eviction in "gentrifying" neighborhoods. Both LISC and the Enterprise Foundation attempt to empower communities, though the Enterprise Foundation clearly includes an individual emphasis (by empowering the apartment dweller) as well. While both these efforts, to the degree they are successful, have broad social effect, they gain that effect through the empowerment of others, not through direct enhancement of corporate power. While we should not underestimate the difficulties and complications involved here, the clear goal of providing power resources to heretofore less powerful communities and groups provides a valuable framework for providing assistance while limiting business direction and control.

A number of corporations are making concerted efforts to support empowerment of less advantaged communities. To take just three examples, Atlantic Richfield, Dayton–Hudson, and Gannett have demonstrated some of the possibilities for individual corporation action.

Atlantic Richfield, an original sponsor of LISC, has made a particular effort to cultivate nontraditional, grassroots community groups. In its 1984 annual report, the Atlantic Richfield Foundation placed these efforts within minority communities squarely within the framework of corporate self-interest: "Corporate and national self-interest requires that the present majority population address the needs of minorities." Arco's focus on small community groups is reflected in the relatively small size of most Arco donations. Only 54 grants in 1984 were larger than $50,000; 1,019 were for $50,000 or less, including 400 between $5,000 and $10,000.

Dayton–Hudson, the retail chain, makes a priority of supporting community-based social action organizations and programs that enable socially disadvantaged adults or young people to attain self-sufficiency, rather than encourage dependence on community services or income subsidies for long-term support. In 1984, some 40 percent of Dayton–Hudson's substantial contributions budget supports such efforts. Among specific programs of particular interest was a program, launched in 1980, to develop and promote Hispanic leadership in a number of cities in the southwestern United States.

Gannett, the newspaper chain and publisher of *USA Today,* sponsors a Community Priorities Program (CPP). CPP projects "are designed to address individual communities' most pressing problems," reports the Gannett Foundation, which spent $2.5 million on such projects in 1984. While these projects extend well beyond the "economic development" arena, they illustrate an effort to rely on communities' leadership. According to the Gannett Foundation:

The community problems identified under the CPP program are determined through an ascertainment process that brings together community leaders and citizen opinion to determine major local needs.

Efforts like these are not new. Certainly the concerted effort by insurance companies to respond to the urban problems of the 1960s also demonstrated both the possibilities and the hazards of corporate philanthropic support for community-based economic development. Despite the difficulties involved, this contributions strategy has proven attractive to business philanthropists seeking to maximize the impact of their corporate contributions dollar, while satisfying both shareholders and critics of corporate power that the contributions dollar is being wisely and justly spent.

NOTES

This chapter is excerpted, with permission, from two previously published Investor Responsibility Research Center publications: *Corporate Philanthropy* (© 1982) and *Corporate Giving in the Reagan Years* (© 1985). The Investor Responsibility Research Center is an independent, not for profit corporation that conducts research on contemporary social and public policy issues and the impact of those issues on major corporations and institutional investors.

4 Community Development: Alternatives to Traditional Models

Ritchie P. Lowry

In part, the United States is in trouble because we have permitted many local communities to slide into social and economic decline. One reason is the traditional view that the philanthropic and public worlds have little connection to the for-profit, private corporate world. It is generally believed that the business of business is to make money, not to resolve social problems. The latter is the business of philanthropies and the public sector. For example, economist Milton Friedman has preached that the only proper goal for business is to maximize return for the shareholders. In the Bible, Jesus instructed a young wealthy man seeking salvation that it is easier for a camel to pass through the eye of a needle than for a rich man to enter the kingdom of God.

This historic tension between the philanthropic and for-profit worlds is not only unwarranted, it is also destructive. It makes a necessary and creative marriage between the two to bring about needed social and economic changes all but impossible.

THE CHALLENGE TO NONPROFITS

That nonprofits face increasing problems is reflected in reports that giving is diminishing because of changes in the tax laws, the stock market mini-crashes of 1987, 1989, and 1990, and a struggling economy (Putka, 1987; Sit, 1987). In 1992, *Business Week* magazine reported that Aetna Life & Casualty, a company with a long record for philanthropic giving, had slashed its budget for these purposes by $3 million since 1990, down 21% (Therrein, 1992). More illuminating was a study of what corporate codes of ethics emphasize as more or less important in terms of company social goals. In 1987, *The Wall Street Journal* reported a study of 202 corporate ethical codes for managerial conduct in terms of those issues mentioned most of the time, contrasted to those issues mentioned the least (Warzman, 1987).

Mentioned over 75% of the time were proper relationships with the government, good customer/supplier relationships, avoidance of political and other conflicts of interests, and honest books and records. All of these issues were seen as directly related to the bottom line, since violations could lead to government fines and controls, bad public relations, and dissatisfied customers. In contrast, not mentioned over 75% of the time in the codes of conduct were social issues that the public would consider most crucial—for example, environmental practices, civic involvement, and community action. These types of issues, which are included in the goals of philanthropy and community economic and social development, were not mentioned at all in over 75% of the 202 codes.

What this study suggests is the need for a new paradigm or perspective that no longer separates the economic (making money) and social (improving the quality of life) aspects of development.

A NEW PARADIGM AND MODEL FOR COMMUNITY DEVELOPMENT

The traditional perspective that sees social concerns as unrelated to profits stands logic on its head. The growing "socially responsible investing" movement provides an alternative view (Lowry, 1982 and 1991). Socially concerned investors argue that companies with positive and supportive employee, customer, and community-based programs and practices are likely to be rewarded financially by productive and loyal employees, satisfied customers, and public good will.

There is no better example of the principle that making a profit can be intimately related to the improvement of social conditions than developer James W. Rouse. Throughout his life, Rouse successfully combined business acumen with a social concern. His real estate firm has refurbished city centers, such as Boston's Faneuil Marketplace, Philadelphia's Gallery at Market East, and Baltimore's Harborplace, and constructed the racially integrated town of Columbia, Maryland.

In the 1960s, Rouse became involved with the Church of the Saviour, a Washington (D.C.) inner city congregation interested in prison work, children's programs, and refugee problems in Thailand. In the 1970s, members formed Jubilee Housing, Inc. to purchase and renovate rundown apartment buildings. Rouse borrowed $750,000 and bought two buildings. The day after Jubilee took control of the dilapidated tenements, local government agencies filed notices of over 900 housing code violations. However, within three years, all the violations had been corrected, primarily with the use of volunteer help. In 1981, The Enterprise Foundation was started by a group headed by Rouse. The Foundation was committed to working with the very poor to help them bring their unfit housing up to livable conditions, and the philosophy of grassroots help, utilizing the resources of the residents and people in the local community, was also important here. The goals were to develop solutions to problems by providing job training and placement, health services, and childcare and recreation, and to improve the overall quality of life.

By 1982, half the goal of $15 million to support this work had been received from corporations (such as American Telephone & Telegraph and Atlantic Richfield), foundations (Ford, Andrew Mellon, and Charles Stewart Mott), and individuals. The Enterprise Development Company was formed as a for-profit, tax-paying real estate company, wholly owned by The Enterprise Foundation. Early projects included a retail center in Richmond, Virginia, and a waterfront marketplace in Toledo, Ohio. The public benefits sought included revitalization of city centers, increases in tax revenues, new jobs (half filled by unemployed and predominantly African-Americans), and minority owned businesses in the centers.

THE SPINOFF MODEL

What Rouse did was use a nonprofit foundation to spin off a for-profit company. This spinoff model was also used by the Institute on Man and Science in Rensselaerville, New York. For several decades, the Institute engaged in community renewal projects involving housing and a full range of physical, economic, and social development programs in economically depressed areas. For example, Stump Creek, Pennsylvania, was built in 1922 and prospered until 1940, when the mine vein began to run out. By the 1970s, Stump Creek had only 150 residents and was quietly dying. The Institute began a five-year project to renew deteriorating homes, revive the lost sense of community, create a local self-government, and transfer ownership and control to the residents.

The Institute purchased the entire town for $150,000 and raised $1 million from two New York City foundations, a planning grant from the Pennsylvania Department of Community Affairs, the Appalachian Regional Commission, and the Federal Housing Assistance Council, and a 40-year loan from the Farmer's Home Administration. Residents were helped to repair roads, install a new water system, and renovate homes. A blueprint, "The Stump Creek Papers," was worked out with community residents describing town self-governance, land use, social and cultural affairs, and transfer of home ownership to charter residents.

This type of experience led the Institute to believe that a housing product was needed that could meet two needs: ease in self-help construction and reduced home heating and cooling costs of no more than $200 anywhere in the United States. The result would be a package that could be erected into a house by no more than three people with average do-it-yourself skills in 15 working days. After consultation with experts, the Institute designed the necessary manufacturing equipment, developed a business plan, and founded Pond Hill Homes Ltd. From 500,000 to 1 million shares of common stock were issued at $5 per share to raise the required capital for machinery, equipment, and supplies and to develop marketing plans, establish regional dealerships, and continue work on product improvement.

INNOVATIVE CORPORATE COMMUNITY PROGRAMS

The nonprofit/for-profit connection can also run in the opposite direction. More for-profit corporations are finding innovative ways to combine doing business with philanthropy, particularly philanthropy that contributes to community development. By the mid-1980s, British clothes retailer Marks & Spencer was already spending $4 million each year on charitable activities. Director David Sieff persuaded board members that these activities could be made even more meaningful by having each of the company's 250 stores choose at least one local community project to support with cash and employee time. The parent company allocated cash according to the size of the stores, which roughly reflected the size of the communities served. In each case, the staff of the stores were asked to match the company's donations. Although the company's headquarters helped with advice, the decision on how to spend the cash rested with each local store.

A U.S. company with the same goals was the Massachusetts-based Norton Company. Throughout the 1980s, the company had a corporate code of ethics and, from time to time, published "Norton Social Investment Reports." The company's 1982 Social Investment Report listed about 600 organizations in 28 states, the District of Columbia, and Canada that received $200 or more from Norton. The company also involved employees in the philanthropic process and encouraged local community participation by inviting requests for needed funding. To these examples can be added community-based banking.

THE COMMUNITY-BASED BANKING MODEL

One of the persistent problems faced in local community development is that those who need the developmental programs the most usually lack the one thing that is necessary—capital. Therefore, they often turn to large foundations and corporations, wealthy individuals, and banks or insurance companies. However, for a variety of political, social, and economic reasons, the competition for these resources can be severe. In addition, grants from these sources often come with strings attached, strings that make the local community residents more dependent upon the granting source. For these reasons, the idea of community-based banking is beginning to spread.

The best known case of a successful community-based bank is South Shore Bank of Chicago. From the 1950s and 1960s to 1973, the South Shore district changed from a predominantly white ethnic community to 95% African-American. Between 1969 and 1979, median family income fell from 10% above to 15% below the average for the city of Chicago as a whole. Families living below the poverty level, abandoned buildings, and general deterioration in the overall quality of life characterized the community. In 1972, Ronald Grzywinski, a socially concerned banker, stepped into this cauldron and, with a group of concerned investors, purchased the community's struggling bank from a parent company that wanted out.

The new owner went into the community to ask for mortgage applications, loans for struggling merchants, and personal loans. The year before its purchase, South Shore Bank had made only two loans to local residents. Yet, in 1976, the new management made 65 loans to more than half of all those who applied. Complete rehabilitation and redevelopment of the district was also necessary. The fact that banks cannot initiate large-scale projects or invest equity capital had often been used as an excuse for them not to become involved in community development. South Shore got around this problem by helping organize three separate companies under one holding company: a real estate development company to rehabilitate residential and commercial properties for rental or sale, a neighborhood fund to provide equity capital and loans to minority businesses, and a neighborhood institute to promote job training and placement and low-income cooperative housing.

Financial solvency and recovery did not come easily for the bank or for the South Shore neighborhood. In the early 1970s, the bank's profits were in the bottom 25% for U.S. banks and much of the main street of the South Shore district was lined with abandoned and absentee owned buildings that had become locations for vandalism, arson, and drug dealing. At this point, the bank and its affiliates targeted their resources for rehabilitation. By 1988, the bank was able to say that South Shore Bank had enabled "a cadre of ma-and-pa rehabbers to restore over 4,500 units" of living space in the once dying community. Development deposits at competitive market rates had been purchased by individuals, churches, and other groups interested in community development, and these deposits, which came from outside the immediate neighborhood, made up 40% of all the bank's deposits and constituted a $59 million portfolio.

The South Shore success story encouraged others. In 1989, Vermont National Bank, the second largest bank in the state, became the first large commercial bank to offer a Socially Responsible Banking Fund. It provided an opportunity for small investors to open IRA, savings, money market, and checking accounts and to purchase certificates of deposit, knowing that the Fund's loans would be targeted for affordable housing, education, small business development, agriculture, and environmental and conservation projects. In 1990, Community Capital Bank in New York City opened its doors for business. Like South Shore, Community Capital was a full service bank that targeted local community development and rehabilitation projects throughout the city.

SUMMARY

The false dichotomy between social and economic goals has impeded the ability to create productive and lasting community development programs. This analysis has considered examples of both nonprofit and for-profit organizations and businesses that have combined the making of money with support for community development programs in innovative ways. The underlying principle in all of the examples and models is the idea of socially responsible investing. As Severyn Bruyn (1987) has pointed out, descriptively speaking, social investing is the allocation of capital with the purpose of achieving greater economic return. Normatively speaking, it is the allocation of capital to improve the overall social and economic wellbeing of people.

In addition, the examples used indicate an attempt to maximize participation and involvement in community development programs. Corporations have involved employees in targeting needed programs. Both for profits and nonprofits have used the self-help resources, as well as economic resources, available from the people for whom the projects were designed to assist. What these experiences suggest is that both the society and the economy possess vast untapped resources that traditional dependence upon philanthropic grants or government intervention do not.

REFERENCES

Bruyn, Severyn. *The Field of Social Investment*. Cambridge University Press, 1987.

Lowry, Ritchie P. "Doing Good While Doing Well." *The Futurist,* 16 (April 1982), 22–28.

———. *Good Money: A Guide to Profitable Social Investing in the '90s*. W. W. Norton & Company, 1991.

Putka, Gary. "With Wall Street Doing Less Well, Donors to Charity Do Less Good." *The Wall Street Journal* (November 13, 1987), 41.

Sit, Mary. "Charities Face Downturn." *The Boston Globe* (December 10, 1987), 57.

Therrein, Lois. "Corporate Generosity Is Greatly Depreciated." *Business Week* (November 2, 1992), 118 & 120.

Warzman, Rick. "Nature or Nurture? Study Blames Ethical Lapses on Corporate Goals." *The Wall Street Journal* (October 9, 1987).

5 Corporate Philanthropy: A Strategic Approach to the Bottom Line

Timothy S. Mescon, Donn J. Tilson, and Robert Desman

Charitable contributions have been called the oldest form of corporate social behavior. They are time honored and, in many corporations, represent a respected tradition of investing a share of company profits in the community.

Many companies with a strong sense of corporate social responsibility, however, are turning away from traditional giving and toward more market driven, strategic, bottom line approaches to philanthropy. They are linking their charitable efforts to community and economic development projects that permit them to aggressively publicize their giving and sponsorships. This new style of philanthropy seeks a tangible return on contributions. In this chapter the growing movement toward professionalizing the corporate gifting function is examined.

PROFESSIONALIZING THE GIFTING FUNCTION

As some CEOs take a harder and more professional look at corporate gifting, their firms are developing cost benefit analyses to determine the long term returns on their social investments. Shell Oil has identified several social performance planning areas in its strategic management plan and has assigned vice presidents to each area. These officers are responsible for goal setting, strategic planning, and coordinating activities in their respective areas and are held as accountable for their performance as are their functional counterparts.

The intent is to take a more proactive role in meeting public needs. In the long run, by incorporating social performance programs into strategic plans and using them as communication bridges to community representatives and advocates, the expense of reacting to organized opposition can be reduced.

As a consequence of reduced federal social funding, some companies report that requests for their help have tripled. While business has increased its charitable support, it has been unable to offset the shortfall. Requests for contributions are, thus, as carefully analyzed as any other business expenditure and donations are targeted to achieve maximum benefit for the company. Gifting decisions are being driven as much by corporate strategic plans and objectives as by vital community needs.

Evaluation is also becoming an increasingly more important part of corporate largesse. Companies are judging their giving by how well corporate philanthropic and business objectives are met. George Weissman, Chairman of Phillip Morris, admonishes, "Our business activities must make social sense and our social activities must make business sense."

GIVING BY OBJECTIVES

A professionally run corporate giving program requires strategic plans, goals, and objectives that are reviewed regularly. Criteria are developed to select deserving, worthwhile areas of involvement, and priorities are established to determine funding levels. Qualified in-house staff or competent external consultants are used to bring expertise to the process. A winning corporate giving program demands personnel as accomplished at funding as the professional fundraisers with whom they interface.

Structurally, these programs are typically managed by public affairs, public relations, corporate communications, government relations, or community relations offices. Companies intending to emphasize their philanthropic activities should consider creating a specialized Community Development function at the vice president level of the organization.

Those in charge of corporate gifting need not be housed in the corporate headquarters. In fact, there are advantages to locating them near seats of government. Such arrangements can be conducive to creating public–private partnerships with State and Federal programs, and in the case of global companies, with international projects such as those affiliated with the United Nations, World Bank, U.S. Aid, and other international development agencies.

COMPETITIVE EDGE

Good deeds are being measured, by many firms, in terms of their contribution to the company's competitive position. At American Express, contributions are treated as a marketing tool. Giving is tied to sales promotions. An Amex marketing executive explains that "the wave of the future isn't checkbook philanthropy. It's a marriage of corporate marketing and social responsibility."

An objective in Southern Bell's 1985 Florida Public Relations Plan calls for the Corporate and External Affairs Department to "work hand in glove with marketing to, ultimately, increase revenues for our company." In addition to developing the usual product and services promotional materials, Bell's Corporate External Affairs Department actively supports marketing and sales efforts by funding special events.

SPECIAL ECONOMIC AND COMMUNITY DEVELOPMENT PROJECTS

Company creativity in linking marketing to special events is becoming increasingly more evident. Typically, such programs are found in the arts, sports, or entertainment. These same approaches, however, might be applied with equal success in community and economic development.

The unprecedented growth of special event sponsorship reflects the growing recognition of the importance of strategic giving. Sponsorship of sporting events, concerts, and festivals has become a major industry. Experts predict that, during the decade of the 1990s, special events promotion will be the fastest growing segment of corporate promotion campaigns.

Special event sponsorship, or event marketing, seeks to link a product or service with an attractive leisure pursuit. Art Stevens calls this "brandstanding" and argues that it "creates for the brand an aura of excitement, interest, reliability, and renewed vitality."

Special events can be integrated into a variety of marketing campaigns. Ideas can be tested, just like new products, and used to bolster local marketing thrusts or broadened to support regional or national promotions. Several examples illustrate how special events can be used as marketing tools to integrate corporate objectives with social needs.

General Wine and Spirit Company "adopted" the American bald eagle to promote its Eagle Rare Bourbon and to demonstrate its social responsibility. The company developed a brochure and an information clearing house on the eagle and supports emergency centers that treat injured birds and return them to the wild. Eagle Rare Bourbon has received very favorable mention from the media covering these activities.

The Metropolitan Life Insurance Company sponsors and organizes health fairs in large urban centers such as New York. Booths are operated by volunteer health professionals qualified to provide health and medical information. The fairs draw extensive local media coverage and Metropolitan receives sponsorship credit.

General and Metropolitan do not represent unique cases. Wrangler Jeans, Kentucky Fried Chicken, and Marriott Corporation have gone so far as to designate employees as full time special events managers for sponsored activities. Even some public relations firms have created events marketing divisions. And, while each company is seeking positive media coverage for its involvement, the media are co-sponsoring their own programs to reach their own audiences.

Among the more common special media events are jazz festivals, summer pops concerts, and dance-a-thons. The next logical step is for companies and consultants to hone their expertise and expand their imaginations so these same techniques may be applied to support community and economic development needs; especially in chronically distressed areas.

Sports Sponsorships

Long the darling of consumer product advertisers, sports are now drawing sponsorship interest from companies wishing to reach target audiences during leisure time. Sports event sponsorships tripled in the late 1980s and have created a need for specialized public relations as an integral part of the sports promotion/marketing strategy.

Be they national, international, or local, sponsored sports events are as varied as the sponsors who support them. The National Hula Hoop Contest; Ken-L Ration Kids' Dog Show; USTA Michelob Light League Tennis; Burger King Pitch, Hit and Run Youth Skills Program; and the Pepsi Cola Hot Shot Basketball Program are among the more popular sports events benefiting from corporate sponsorship.

There is equal variety in the degree to which companies involve themselves in these programs. Event direction/coordination may come from marketing or public relations departments, full-time staff or outside consultants. Some firms evaluate proposals and provide publicity, but contract with professional promoters to produce events. Others undertake the entire event from concept development to production using in-house resources. Still others team their managers with representatives from the organization that benefits from the event. Sometimes, as in the case of charity fundraisers, such as bike-a-thons and walk-a-thons, company employees participate in the event or act as volunteers in support roles.

As with other special events, sports sponsorships offer cost effective exposure for a product, associate a company or product name with a specific event, and provide companies with high visibility; especially if the event is national or international in scope and it features sports superstars or public personalities. All of this contributes to bottom line performance. Similar approaches can work with certain economic development projects.

National Events

While some programs require only nominal funding, others may represent a considerable financial commitment. National events can cost upward of $125,000 per year, with the majority of expenses incurred for administration and operations. Still, some companies see the benefits as far outweighing the costs.

Duncan's Yo-Yolympics and World Junior Frisbee Disc Championships are hosted by municipal parks and recreation departments. Participating communities benefit from company sponsored youth sports programs that they might not otherwise be able to afford. Duncan harvests an enhanced corporate image, heightened consumer product awareness, and increased sales to would be Yo-Yo and Frisbee champions.

National events, coupled with local activities, offer extensive media exposure and positioning in important markets. Fleischmann's margarine sponsored both the U.S. Cross-Country Ski Team and regional, family oriented, cross-country skiing competitions. Ski Team members wore blazers bearing Fleischmann's logo during television interviews, news releases emphasized cross-country skiing as a wholesome family sport, and the company's product was characterized as a healthy food.

Local ski event winners were publicized in a media campaign that focused on each community market where competitions were held. Major media campaigns promoted regional competitions and publicity was provided to local and national media. Regional winners competed in a national finals events. Fleischmann's received considerable publicity for their sponsorship in the national media as well as in the large New York and Boston markets.

From the sponsor's perspective, success measures may take numerous forms. Among the most common are: the extent of media coverage, the number of program participants, the number of affiliated host organizations (i.e., parks and recreation departments), and sales volume increases. Some companies conduct pre- and post-event awareness studies to determine the effects of their sponsorship on product recognition, corporate image, and various other public relations objectives.

Culture and the Arts

Examples of other ways in which companies can use sponsorship strategies for community and economic development are provided by the arts. According to the Business Committee for the Arts, company sponsors provide approximately $500 million annually to support cultural programs. This represents a four-fold increase between 1980 and 1990.

As public funding for the arts declines and costs rise, the pressure for company support is intensifying. Exxon and Phillip Morris, both major arts sponsors, report significant increases in the number of requests they receive for contributions. Companies that have been traditionally large contributors to the arts have been forced to examine their gifting practices with a more critical eye. The most agreeable projects are those that offer the greatest return for the sponsors' dollars.

Affiliation with the arts can be used to promote a firm's image and to penetrate key market segments. Cater Hawley Hale Stores, Inc. repositioned its gifting practices away from a broad range of charities and toward a concentration on the arts. The arts patron well represents the upscale consumer the company wants to reach. SCM Corporation concentrates on museum exhibitions. Company executives unabashedly admit a purely economic motive. They estimate the company would have to spend $51 million per year on advertising, for five years, to reach the same SCM customers they now access through the $200,000 per year they spend on museum sponsorships.

AT&T hitched its image building campaign to sponsorship of the American Orchestras on Tour Program. "There is a higher percentage of the types of people we want to reach in the arts," notes Vice President Edward Block. "You think in terms of what it costs you to reach whatever kind of person you're trying to reach, and clearly our support of orchestras is a very attractive business proposition."

An overt commitment to culture has the power to impress . . . particularly those who have an interest in culture. After arranging to sponsor the Houston Symphony for a performance in New York City, Bankers Trust flew a group of important clients from Houston to attend. After introducing key clients to its new midtown Manhattan office, United States Trust Company escorted them to Carnegie Hall for a company sponsored chamber ensemble concert.

Sensing corporate America's newfound interest in the arts, arts organizations have changed their traditional solicitation practices . . . they have stopped asking for charity and started selling utility. PACE, Performing Arts for Community and Education, Inc., no longer asks for corporate handouts. Instead, they offer to name various events after the corporations who agree to sponsor them. Testimony to the increasing importance of name identification in arts sponsorship, PACE has gotten Southern Bell and Citicorp to underwrite two of its programs. Citicorp also signed on to become official sponsor of the Tampa Orchestra's Pops concert series, now the Citicorp Superpops, to reach the orchestra's audience. The average Pops concert ticket holder has an annual income in excess of $50,000.

In exchange for name identification on its sponsored events, Merrill

Lynch offers arts groups sponsorship packages ranging from $5,000 to $50,000. These packages may also include season ticket purchases, program advertising, local publicity, and special events. The Pittsburgh Symphony availed themselves of this program and now perform the Merrill Lynch Great Performers series.

Charlotte, North Carolina–based NCNB Corporation, assumed sponsorship of the Florida Performing Arts Touring Program almost immediately upon entering the highly competitive Florida banking market. Performing Arts Touring Program publicity touted NCNB's support and explained that "the goal of the arts program, like NCNB, is to be 'in your neighborhood.' " Recognizing the value of arts sponsorship for gaining visibility and name recognition, NCNB outgave the donations of ten other banks to develop a performing arts center in Tampa. The new facility was christened the NCNB Performing Arts Center.

Since 1940, Texaco has sponsored the radio broadcasts of the Metropolitan Opera. The company limits its corporate message time to less than two minutes per broadcast and only briefly mentions its petroleum products. Texaco's understated advertising, coupled with over 50 years of continuous sponsorship, has paid large dividends. Market research indicates that significant numbers of listeners make a special effort to buy the company's products, and Texaco holds two and one-half times its normal market share among motorists who regularly listen to the broadcasts. The bottom line is that opera fans appreciate Texaco's sponsorship, and they are willing to express their gratitude at the gas pump.

While some companies, like Texaco, prefer subtle institutional advertising, others, like American Express, opt for product/service promotion. Amex calls its approach "cause related marketing." The objective is to increase the use of American Express products and services, while supporting local causes.

By 1981, American Express was contributing $7.5 million per year to worthwhile causes through its foundation. At this point, marketing executives felt they could boost credit card sales by tying use to philanthropic activities.

The company embarked upon a philanthropy-as-marketing strategy that paid two cents to the San Francisco Arts Festival each time a customer made a credit card purchase. Within three months, the Arts Festival received $100,000 in contributions as a result of cardholder activity. Since that time, American Express has extended its cause related marketing approach to 50 markets and now supports such local institutions as the Dallas Ballet, Fort Lauderdale Symphony, Greater Miami Opera, and the San Jose Symphony.

While their promotions have generated much needed funding for local causes, American Express executives insist that their main objective is to increase company sales and bottom line performance. In the San Jose Symphony campaign, for example, the promotion generated $30,000 in card related contributions and an additional $205,000 from the publicity. Simultaneously, card usage and new applications increased by 25 percent.

No matter what the cause or location, the formula is always the same: an advertising blitz pledging a contribution to a local charity for each American Express card use or new application. The company has spent over $3 million on local television, newspaper, and point-of-purchase advertising with the funds coming from promotion budgets. No funds have been shifted from the philanthropic foundation to support cause related marketing activities. "By giving people a local cause to rally around," says Jerry Walsh, Senior Vice President and architect of the campaigns, "we hoped to spark cardholders into using their cards for local purchases. We're giving away money, but we're doing it in a way that builds business."

The same logic seems to hold true for national fund drives. A $4 million nationwide advertising campaign for the Statue of Liberty restoration project in 1983 "made people feel good about American Express," according to Ogilvy and Mather, the company's advertising agency. The public saw American Express as a responsible, public minded, even patriotic, corporation. With a penny pledged for each credit card purchase and a dollar pledged for each new member, the campaign raised more than $1.7 million. As was the case with Texaco, Amex's good deeds did not go unrewarded. Card usage increased 20 percent over the same quarter in the previous year (exceeding forecasts of 18 percent), and new cardholders increased by more than 45 percent during the promotion.

Other firms have had equal success with cause related marketing. Southern Bell offered to donate 50 cents for every Custom Calling Feature sold during July 1985, in the Melbourne–Titusville area of Florida, to raise funds for a young boy in need of a liver transplant. The campaign raised $2,500 in a community where the sales of electronic telephone features averages $3,000 per month.

Similarly, when Barnett bank opened a new branch office in San Marco, a Jacksonville, Florida neighborhood of 1920s era homes, it offered to donate $1 to the San Marco Preservation Society for each $100 in deposits received during its first week of operations. The branch established itself as the fastest growing office in the system when it logged $1 million in deposits within a week.

American Airlines gave the Dallas Symphony $5 for each passenger who flew their newly inaugurated Dallas–London route within a six-month period and $3 to the Fort Worth Symphony for each route segment flown by Fort Worth members of its frequent flyer program. Chesebrough–Ponds pledged 5 cents to CARE, up to $100,000, for every coupon it redeemed during a special newspaper promotion that offered 15–20 cents off Ponds' products.

Variations of cause related marketing are evident in several publicity campaigns. Verbatim Corporation, a computer software manufacturer, produced and promoted a guide to summer camps offering computer instruction for distribution through the American Camping Association. In similar fashion, Atlantic Richfield subsidized the production of 200,000 guides to Los Angeles distributed by the city's tourist bureau. In both cases, the printings put the sponsors' names in front of thousands of potential customers with little investment.

American Express took the publishing approach one step further by underwriting the printing of a cookbook featuring recipes from 16 Broward County, Florida restaurants that accepted "the card." Cardholders who dined at any of the restaurants received a free cookbook. When cardholders charged their meals, a percentage of the sale was donated to the Museum of Art in Fort Lauderdale.

By supporting worthwhile charities through "cause related marketing," several companies have demonstrated that good citizenship can also be good business. Charitable donations need not siphon off profits. If targeted wisely, as part of a well conceived marketing plan, contributions can actually improve bottom line performance.

While such programs are growing in popularity, many companies still approach gifting in traditional fashion. Some obviate strategic considerations by limiting their vision to acts of sheer benevolence . . . after all, is it really charity if it is profit motivated? Still, the data suggest that when the company profits, the charity profits more than it would under other circumstances. Furthermore, cause related marketing does not preclude traditional gifting, it augments traditional gifting.

Other companies have more generalized objectives such as increasing visibility in the marketplace or enhancing the corporate image. As a consequence, their contributions produce no readily measurable results.

Yet to be explored are the potentials of economic and community development programs as beneficiaries and profit enhancers. Might cause related marketing assumptions hold equally true for project or program related marketing strategies?

GIFTS AS PROMOTION?

While profits derived as a consequence of corporate gifting provide a nice measure of philanthropic success, image oriented philanthropy is not without some merit. Companies that prefer good citizenship gifting over philanthropy-as-marketing are beginning to promote their charitable giving more heavily. This shift to a position of high visibility is also part of the new strategy. The objective is to make consumers more aware that the company is putting money back into the community that supports it.

New York advertising executive Stephen Arbeit contends that such giving, when properly promoted, has a positive effect on public perceptions of a business and can produce marketing gains. "With products exactly alike and prices the same," says Arbeit, "consumers are basing their buying decision on their attitude toward the company itself." They ask themselves, "Is this a good company? Does it care about me, my family, and my community?" Companies that make highly visible charitable contributions in the community demonstrate their corporate sense of social responsibility to consumers. They also enhance their position in the marketplace even though this is not their primary motivation.

McDonald's pet philanthropic project, the Ronald McDonald Houses, contributes to the company's bottom line in spite of its altruistic intentions. For every McDonald's that has run a promotion for its Ronald McDonald House in a particular market, sales in that community have increased significantly. Consumers perceive McDonald's as a good corporate citizen and a company worthy of their business.

Sponsoring special event sports and arts programs is becoming increasingly more important. Companies support their marketing efforts with their charitable contributions. Few companies give quietly and most actively seek public recognition for their donations.

The new directions in gifting programs can be used even more broadly than current practices suggest. Economic and community development are not priorities for many companies who prefer to support more traditional cultural, educational, and charitable causes. Still, as corporate giving increases and gifting becomes a more popular and sophisticated strategic tool, niche philanthropy may be the only option for firms wishing to retain their distinctive charitable images. Only those companies dedicated to anonymous benevolence will be content to become lost in the crowd. As a consequence, new causes might be sought with the same zeal as new products. This, in turn, may lead corporations into nontraditional areas of giving.

The management of philanthropic activities, in many organizations, is as much a legitimate business function as quality assurance or auditing. Beyond simply accounting for the potentially large sums of money that flow through gifting channels lies the not so simple task of qualifying worthy recipients. Even the most purely charitable donor must be concerned that funds are not squandered, or worse, are not directed to causes that oppose the best interests of the company or community.

At the opposite extreme lie the strategic implications of gifting. Corporate philanthropy, if properly managed, can be an effective marketing tool. It can enhance image and increase a firm's "touch factor" with clientele. It can promote name recognition and facilitate market penetration. It can engender customer loyalty and improve bottom line performance. As such, it deserves as much specialized and professional attention as marketing and public relations.

Furthermore, as those requesting funds become more numerous and sophisticated, those providing charitable contributions must posture themselves to be equal to the task. Priorities must be determined, recipients researched, funding levels decided, and impacts analyzed.

If gifting is integrated into a larger marketing or public relations strategy, philanthropic activities require even more specialized handling if they are to be successful. Projects and programs must be coordinated across functional departments and between the organization and representatives of the groups receiving the benefit. Activities may range from assessing tax effects to graphics production, media relations to logistics, generating volunteerism to outcome measurement. In brief, a sound gifting program demands professional direction. It is no longer a spot to place managers who have outlived their usefulness as operating or staff personnel.

Finally, the full potential of philanthropy as a vehicle for community and economic development has yet to be explored. Untapped marketing applications notwithstanding, healthy communities breed and support healthy businesses, and this fact alone warrants giving the gifting function special consideration.

6 Strategic Philanthropy and Partnerships for Economic Progress

James E. Post and Sandra A. Waddock

INTRODUCTION

Social partnerships have become one of the organizational fads of the 1980s. The concept of partnership is ubiquitous, producing a host of local community coalitions, statewide business government collaborations, and federal or national commitments from the public and private sectors. By one count, more than 6,000 social partnerships have been formed in the 1980s to combat crime, drugs, poor housing, hunger, gaps in education, economic development problems, and lack of job skills, among others. Rhetorically and philosphically, as well as in action programs, the idea of partners for social progress has flourished in this decade.

In the arena of economic development, several distinct types of partnership have developed. One type brings a broad representation of societal interests together to discuss, for example, extending earlier efforts to build job skills among high school dropouts, underachievers, the unemployed, and underemployed. The best known example of this type is the federally legislated Job Training Partnership Act, which mandates the creation of private industry councils (PICs) comprised of private and public sector representatives to provide direction to community efforts in job training for the disadvantaged.

A second example of partnership is designed to stimulate economic development through changes in the physical infrastructure of society by focusing on projects in housing, commercial construction, and urban revitalization. These partnerships are exemplified by the Committee for Economic Development's recent emphasis on using partnerships to develop state and local economies and by urban development in such cities as Baltimore, Minneapolis, Pittsburgh, Portland (Oregon), and Boston.

Other partnerships focus on meeting the needs of an industry or other interest group or a region by bringing together a federation of organizations to discuss and develop programs to deal with the specific problems of the region. Included in this category are partnerships between an industry group, such as a trade association of small machine shop owners, who band together to develop a mechanism for meeting their industry's needs for unskilled machinists.

The final type of social partnership that exists in the economic arena revolves around the development of specific programs that meet the specific objectives and needs of the participating organizations, even while they may have broader societal implications. The partnership entered into by the Massachusetts General Hospital and Hoechst to perform basic research activities represents such a partnership.

In general, social partnerships are social problem solving mechanisms that deal with very large, complex phenomena, which other scholars have variously called "messes" (Ackoff, 1975) or metaproblems (Chevalier, 1984). Essentially, these are problems that are too large or complex or require too many resources to be successfully resolved by a single organization. The partnership derives from the active involvement of multiple organizations from more than one economic sector, who engage in collaborative problem solving around issues that concern all participants but on whose resolution none of the participants' goals may directly focus.

From the perspective of corporations, there are a number of reasons for becoming involved in social partnerships. Personal values of leaders or an emerging "vision" about a common problem are one source of motivation that is rooted in organizational and societal values. A second source of motivation derives from pressures from stakeholders, internal and external, to do something about a problem. This pressure can result from participation in an interorganizational network or from the recognition of a common crisis or problem needing resolution. A third motivation comes from a requirement to participate in a given activity deriving, for example, from legal mandate such as the "tying" of attractive commercial development projects to less attractive neighborhood development activity. Finally, incentives can be provided that promote the interaction of organizations through external brokers, such as funding agencies or political maneuverings that provide tax or other financial incentives for acting in a certain way.

PARTNERSHIPS AND PHILANTHROPY

Some observers view the participation of private sector enterprise in partnership as part of their philanthropic endeavor or program of social responsibility; yet there are features of social partnership that distinguish involvement in them from pure philanthropy. Social partnership rests on the fundamental tenets of partnership, that is: (1) *active involvement* as well as *contributions of resources* from participants are required so that participants can legitimately be considered partners, unless one partner is to contribute resources only and be considered a silent partner, and (2) *benefits to all partners* (although not necessarily the same benefits) are to be expected as a result of their contributions and efforts (Waddock, 1987). The "social" in social partnership implies that the activities involved are part of the *social or public policy agenda* (Waddock, 1987) insofar as they can be expected to contribute to the common good. The expected benefits, however, mean that social partnerships do not represent giving in its purest form; a return or benefit is an important aspect of the involvement for all partners.

When these "conditions" of partnership are met, and a partnership actually exists, then the contributions to a specified partnership can be viewed through a philanthropic lens. Increasingly, corporate giving is being perceived as a significant element of corporate strategy as well as part of the corporation's responsibility to the society in which it exists. The development of the concept of strategic philanthropy highlights the increasing attention that is being paid to the role of philanthropic endeavors in strategic management of the firm, while at the same time demanding that care be paid to developing appropriate definitions of partnerships as strategic and philanthropic endeavors.

The expectation of benefits to be derived for public, nonprofit, and private sector partners in a social partnership places the social partnership squarely in the realm of *enlightened* self-interest (Bowen, 1956; Walton, 1965), as opposed to purely economic self-interest. Thus, for some corporations that are deeply cognizant of their social role, participation in social partnerships may be considered as part of their corporate strategy and, even more centrally, as part of the increasingly common political strategies that corporations are pursuing (e.g., Mahon, 1989). For others, notions of corporate giving may be rooted in deeply

held personal values that push philanthropic activities in certain directions. A distinction must therefore be drawn between the concepts of
strategic philanthropy and *philanthropic strategy*. By dissecting the
meaning of each of these phrases, then weighing them in relation to the
concept of social partnership, it will be shown that two quite different
thrusts have been given to the strategy/philanthropy relationship.

Philanthropy connotes giving, whether that giving is direct dollar contribution, donation of time and effort, in-kind goods or service, or equipment. Partnership, on the other hand, requires "giving" of resources but
with the expectation that returns will be generated from those resources.
Benefits may be direct or indirect (c.f., Astley & Fombrun, 1983; Troy,
1985); however, they are frequently more explicit than the reputation as
a good corporate citizen, the good will, or the improved community relations expected as a result of more "pure" forms of philanthropy (the
Conference Board, 1987).

Additionally, there is a passivity to much corporate philanthropy that
derives not so much from the sometimes extensive effort that is put into
reviewing and evaluating proposals for grants or responding to requests
for help, but from the fact that the proposals are typically generated
without the active involvement of the philanthropic institution. The latter may supply guidelines or interest areas within which funding or other
support may be requested but generally does not become involved in the
grantees' day-to-day activities. Participants in partnership, in contrast,
do become involved in the strategic decision making for, and sometimes
the implementation of, the partnership's activities because they are partners in a developmental process as much as they are donors. Since they
expect benefits from the partnership, partners have much more incentive
than donors, who may desire good will or better community relations,
to become involved.

STRATEGY AND PHILANTHROPY

Generally speaking, strategic thinking is holistic insofar as it involves
thinking about the direction of an enterprise; it is integrative in that it
involves pulling all of the disparate pieces of an entity into a coherent
whole and placing that enterprise in an external (environmental) context.
The formulation and implementation of strategy, whether done formally
or informally, provides guidance and direction, gives participants a
sense of the mission of the enterprise, and develops a shared sense of
values or organizational culture. Thus, strategic thinking involves the
recognition of larger patterns (c.f., Simon, 1987; Andrews, 1987) of relationships among the elements of an environment, so that the organization pursues a set of goals and directions that make sense in light of the
environment it faces.

Philanthropy, viewed strategically, involves a recognition that it is not enough to "give" of a company's resources to achieve a status of being "socially responsible." Laudable as giving for its own sake may be, corporations have other, primarily fiduciary, responsibilities to their shareholders, (as Milton Friedman [1970] is fond of pointing out). Others argue (Freeman, 1982) that there are equally important responsibilities to other stakeholders, such as employees, customers, and society as a whole. These stakeholder responsibilities have helped legitimize philanthropy and defend the arguments of critics of corporate social responsibility.

Applied to philanthropy, the term strategy involves a recognition that greater impact can be derived from limited corporate resources by allocating those resources effectively so that they can be "leveraged" in light of the corporation's overall strategy, a concept increasingly well accepted by corporate givers (Troy, 1985). From society's perspective, the social partnership as philanthropy represents a positive sum solution to what might otherwise be a zero sum competitive game. The positive sum solution arises from the ability to think about the interaction of organizations in society in cooperative and competitive ways, ensuring that they work toward goals that are coherent and focused on achieving resolutions that positively impact both the corporation and the broader society in which it exists. In this sense, social partnerships tap into what scholars of strategy have termed synergy; that is, two or more organizations working together in partnership can provide a better solution to a social problem than could both working separately.

There are two ways of looking at the strategy/philanthropy nexus. The term *philanthropic strategy* implies that certain fairly well defined and focused goals have been established for a giving program and that specifiable means have been identified to achieve those goals. A strategy, that is, has been worked out for a giving program, within the context of certain interest areas of an organization that may or may not be directly related to the enterprise's own goals and strategy; indeed, that may be based on the values of certain individuals within the firm. Very well defined programs for supporting the arts or human service organizations may be supported by corporate giving programs, for example, with well defined philanthropic strategies. Phillip Morris' support for the arts illustrates such an approach.

The second concept, *strategic philanthropy,* is a much broader one that takes into account the strategic thrust of the enterprise as a whole and attempts to use the philanthropy programs within the enterprise as one element or means by which the overall strategy will be achieved. Giving is tied to the larger purpose of the organization's economic and social mission; philanthropy is one, increasingly important, part of that strategy. Phillip Morris' donations to minority organizations, for example, supports a political strategy that recognizes the higher rates in the minority population.

A Framework

Social partnerships are primarily devoted to improving local and regional economic situations, although sometimes, as the Japanese experience with the Ministry of International Trade and Industry (MITI) illustrates, the concept can be applied at the national level as well through industrial development and trade policies. Difficult issues of industrial policy surround attempts to establish cooperative relationships between the typically adversarial private and public sectors in the United States when issues of national concern are involved and sometimes even when more local issues are the subject of partnerships.

The mechanisms and programmatic thrusts chosen to implement social partnerships for economic development range widely. They may include quality improvement training programs aimed at developing greater productivity and quality and therefore more jobs; technological innovation through cooperation between universities and businesses; specific training programs to meet employer needs; small business and technology incubators; and major urban redevelopment projects. Although developing social partnerships almost always involves one or more specific programs that address a problem, the partnership can be dominated more by substantive issues or by process issues; that is, developing and working through the interaction and relationships or partners, depending on the type of partnership (Waddock, 1987; Epstein, 1979).

Philanthropy can be viewed as having both costs and benefits, each of which can be either direct or indirect. Direct benefits include solutions to immediate problems with largely tangible or immediately recognizable gains, most of which fall in the economic realm. Indirect benefits are more social and long term in nature, relating to attitudinal change and having to do with reputation, image, and goodwill, as well as relations among interacting organizations. Costs can also be split along direct and indirect lines, with direct costs being largely measurable by economic indicators, such as dollar value for donations, equipment, or services rendered, and indirect costs being the less easily measured or intangible costs of executive time, advice and input, some opportunity costs, and costs to reputation, goodwill, or image.

Arraying these direct and indirect costs and benefits in a matrix enables transactions among interacting organizations to be classified into four catagories (Figure 6.1). The first is contractual relations, in which benefits and costs are direct, and the interaction is based primarily on economic reasoning; the outcome for both parties is, it is to be hoped, a

Dominant Costs

	Direct	Indirect
Direct (economic benefits)	**A** Contractual relations; Pure economic reasoning; (Programmatic partnerships)	**C** Strategic philanthropy; Normal rules of investment; (systemic partnerships that deal with tangible parts of the infrastructure)
Indirect (social benfits)	**B** Philanthropic strategy; (doing good for its own sake) (Federational partnerships)	**D** Social welfare thinking; Long term good of society (Systemic partnerships that deal with less tangible parts of the infrastructure)

(row label at left: **Dominant Benefits**)

Type of cost:	Tangible; measurable	Less tangible; less quantifiable;
Primary benficiary	Participants;	Society;
Free riders	Few or none;	Numerous;

Figure 6.1. A Framework for Assessing Strategy and Philanthropy

relatively well balanced exchange transaction (i.e., the transaction results in a zero sum solution). The second is "pure" philanthropy or what has been termed above philanthropic strategy, where costs are direct and benefits in a net loss of dollar value, while the potential gains are intangible. From the recipient's perspective, there is a net gain without having to give up equivalent resources (i.e., a lose/win situation). Participation is based on concepts of indirect benefits to participating organizations, resulting from improvements in social conditions and enhancements to goodwill for the participants.

The third category is what has been called above strategic philanthropy, where costs are indirect in that major commitments tend to be as much noneconomic as economic, and benefits to participants accrue because enterprise goals are being enhanced. Good is done, that is, to achieve organizational (economic) goals. In the short term, the result might look like a positive sum solution to the "giving" parties since there is little direct outlay and some directly beneficial gains. From the recipient's perspective, it is a positive sum solution; hence it can be classed as a win/win or positive sum solution for both parties, at least in the short term. The dominant current example is the cause related marketing efforts initiated by American Express, in which a portion of profits from increased credit card usage are donated to a local charity. The normal rules of investment are followed in this situation, in that economic gains for the "giving" organization derive from exchanges or transactions that would probably not have taken place without the program in place and the recipient benefits from the increase in transactions. The programs are strategic in that they further the (largely economic) goals of the donor organization, while simultaneously creating direct benefits for recipients in the form of increased donations. At least in the short term, this is a win/win or positive sum solution although, as the cause related marketing example illustrates, there may be a longer term negative backlash associated with using social programs for direct economic gain.

The fourth category involves indirect costs and indirect benefits; it represents a "pure" form of social welfare thinking, where the major benefits for contributing organizations are intangible, involving improved interorganizational relations, changed attitudes, and a better society. The benefits to recipient groups follow much the same pattern, in that improved social conditions may enable social service organizations to better achieve their goals (or have less to do so), although immediate, tangible results may not be present. Figures 6.2 and 6.3 illustrate the expected benefits and costs of engaging in these forms of interaction from the perspective of decision makers in "giving" organizations, depending on whether the major benefits or costs are expected to be in the economic or social realms.

	Dominant Areas of Benefits From Interaction	
	Economic	Non-economic
Direct	Return on investment	Image/reputation
Type of Benefits		
Indirect	Stock price improvement;	Better social environment

Figure 6.2. Benefits from the Philanthropic Organization's Perspective

Dominant Areas of Cost

	Economic	Non-economic
Direct	Tangible; money; time;	Intangible; Direct expenditures to promote philanthropic objectives
Indirect	Opportunity costs;	Goodwill; reputation; Possible backlash; Disappointment when stakeholder expectations are not met;

Type of Costs (row label spanning left margin)

Figure 6.3. Dominant Areas of Cost for the Philanthropic Organization

THE ROLE OF SOCIAL PARTNERSHIPS
IN PHILANTHROPY

Using Figure 6.1 as the basis, one can compare the expected outcome of a number of different types of social partnerships. Thinking of partnerships not as pure philanthropic endeavors but along much the same lines as outlined in Figure 6.1, three distinct types of social partnership, one of which has two major forms, can be distinguished and placed in each of the cells (Waddock, 1987). In cell A can be found what are termed programmatic partnerships, which involve direct benefits to partners and largely direct giving. These partnerships are dominated by a product/program/outcome orientation (Epstein, 1979), as are the partnerships found in cell B, which are termed federational partnerships because they typically involve the coming together of a group of interested parties into a federation that attempts to get its needs met through the social partnership, although benefits to any individual participant may be indirect or diffused throughout the group. Giving tends to be quite direct in both programmatic and federational partnerships.

Two forms of systematic partnership are found in cells C and D. These are broad based partnerships that attempt to deal with systemwide problems. In cell C are partnerships for which benefits to involved parties are direct and usually tangible, such as changes in the network of interrelations among organizations, changes in the political infrastructure, or changes in attitudes (e.g., less stereotyping). In both types of systematic partnerships, the free rider problem exists, as the primary long term beneficiary of the effort is society, rather than participating organizations. Each of these partnerships will be discussed in more detail below and examples of each will be developed.

Programmatic Partnerships

Most programmatic partnerships involve organizations that come together, not entirely out of altruistic reasons (although often there is some
altruistic reasoning involved in the decision to enter into a social partnership, as opposed to a purely economic contract), to engage in a relationship from which both directly benefit. The form is often of a contractual nature in which partners agree to exchange services and
"contributions" in return for expected benefits. The private sector orga-
nization(s) benefits from having its needs quite directly met and the public or nonprofit sector organization from being better able to fulfill its
social mission through the interaction. Outcomes tend to be specific to
the involved organizations and directly meet their needs, say for employees skilled in a new technology or other area of education.

One example of a programmatic partnership occurred between a community college in Massachusetts and General Motors Corporation, that
was sponsored in part by Massachusetts' Bay State Skills Corporation,
a quasi-public corporation in the business of fostering partnerships. General Motors approached Quinsigamond Community College with the idea
of establishing a partnership that would retrain a group of workers
whose jobs were expected to be eliminated by automation. Using the
partial funding provided by Bay State Skills, the partners established an
upgrade program specifically geared to meeting the GM workers' identified needs and giving them skills that would make them employable in
the future. GM's costs were directly related to the training being provided and the benefits, of course, were readily measurable, in the form
of retrained employees who would not be laid off as a result of internal
changes. As the college's representative to the partnership indicates, "It
wasn't something that [the General Motors people] were doing for enrichment. It was something that the union and General Motors felt that
these people had to do in order for them to survive; because when they
start using robotics and computerization in the plant, you have to have
people who can handle it."

Programmatic partnerships like this one, in one sense, are fairly simple in that they can be organized as an ordinary contractual relationship.
Contributions (often monetary, as well as advice, participation, and
facilities and equipment usage) from partners and the expected gains can
typically be clearly spelled out for both sides. They do require thinking
in terms of socially responsible behavior, as opposed to a narrow bottom
line orientation.

Federational Partnerships

In cell B, the typical partnership is the "federational" partnership, in which industry, interest group, or regional representatives form a group that interacts to have its collective needs met, although individual partners may benefit only indirectly or in the long term. For corporate participants, benefits are often rather less tangible and may be related to goals of social responsibility, community relations, and general attitudinal change, rather than strict economic goals. Costs to private sector participants are likely to be tangible in that direct monetary or measurable contributions may be required to make the partnership work. Benefits to the public sector or agency partners, as a result, may be quite direct.

One example of this type of partnership is the Chicago-based organization called Second Harvest. More than 250 corporate donors, most directly involved in the food production and distribution industry, donate surplus food and other grocery products through Second Harvest to a network of nearly 200 food banks in the United States. Essentially, Second Harvest serves as a distribution vehicle through which excess but perfectly usable food products can be channelled to groups that serve needy individuals. Second Harvest's stated "goal is to feed the hungry by soliciting surplus food and grocery products from America's industry and distributing these donations to a nationwide network of certified food banks. The food banks, in turn, distribute the food to community charities, day care, senior centers, and church groups with feeding programs for the needy."

John H. Bryan, Jr., chairman and chief executive officer of Sara Lee Corporation and an active partner in the Second Harvest program, in a recent speech, described a program of what we have termed the philanthropic strategy for Sara Lee. This philanthropic strategy focuses on target areas as a means of meeting Sara Lee's social responsibilities; matching grants for direct employee contributions in areas of the employee's choice and programs directed at aiding the disadvantaged. Participation in Second Harvest is one of the latter activities. These activities represent a fulfillment of the social responsibilities of Sara Lee as they are developed by executives within the firm. They do not directly enhance the firm's economic goals, but they reflect an integrated approach to the achievement of economic and social performance objectives.

Serving in the central "broker" or catalytic role, Second Harvest has been responsible for creating the network of private sector food industry organizations that has become involved in donating their surpluses, overruns, and mislabeled products. In the same speech, Bryan recently cited four major motivations and expected benefits for corporate involvement in such programs: (1) meeting individual motivations of altruism; (2) tax incentives provided for donors; (3) corporate support of communities in which plants exist, thereby improving local social and economic conditions; and (4) enhancement of the corporation's public image.

Costs of participation in such a partnership for corporate partners are direct in that financial contributions, product contributions, and equipment contributions are critical, although other less tangible contributions of employee time or management time on boards (i.e., Second Harvest's board or the boards of local community food banks), as well as in-kind service related to public relations, advertising, and image development, are also present. Clearly, in a partnership such as Second Harvest, the primary benefit is the tangible donation of food products to the needy. The benefits to corporate participants are related to the goals articulated through a philanthropic strategy; that is, benefits are expected in the long term for the image and reputation of corporate participants, for improved employee relations, and for improved community conditions. The overriding emphasis, however, is on the notion of doing good for its own sake, rather than for the direct expected returns to the firm.

To summarize, in cells A and B, cost is directly borne by the participating organizations. Benefits are direct in programmatic partnerships and less so in federational. The more direct the benefits, the more short term and specific in orientation are the partnerships. More diffused benefits, as in cell B, pick up some free riders who may benefit from the efforts of the involved group, although the group as a whole is expected to benefit more than organizations not directly involved. These conditions can be contrasted with those in cells C and D, where the primary costs to participating organizations are indirect in nature.

Systemic Partnership: Tangible and Intangible Infrastructure

In cells C and D can be found two forms of what have elsewhere been termed "systemic" partnerships (Waddock, 1987), in that they attempt to deal with fairly large scale, intractable, systemwide problems of the sort that were earlier referred to as metaproblems (Chevalier, 1984) or "messes" (Ackoff, 1975). By their nature as complex issues that span the activities of multiple organizations, the problems with which systemic partnerships deal are usually resistant to solution by single organizations. Cooperative endeavors may be the only feasible way of resolving these issues, among which might be included urban redevelopment, economic development for a reason, job training for the disadvantaged, improving education at all levels, and industry/national competitiveness generally, to name just a few areas. In the past, individual organizations or governmental agencies have attempted to solve these problems, often with relatively little success.

Social partnership and other forms of collaboration are increasingly being seen as potential solutions to these difficult problems, which involve multiple constituencies, have many manifestations, and cross the boundaries of single organizations. Systemic partnerships hold the potential for resolving such "metaproblems" (Chevalier, 1984), rather than either the programmatic or federational forms that have been described above. From the perspective of corporate givers, participation in systemic partnerships probably involves both indirect and direct costs, with the indirect costs of executive time commitment, input, and advice just as important as the very likely direct contributions accompanying the less direct inputs. Because they involve the establishment of new relations among organizations that otherwise tend to interact infrequently and who also may have widely divergent goals, systemic partnerships are dominated by the processes of interaction and engagement more than the specific product or programmatic outcomes associated with programmatic and federational partnerships (c.f., Epstein, 1979).

Systemic partnerships are primarily concerned with enhancement of an interorganizational infrastructure. There seems to be a continuum of involvements, ranging from dealing with attitudinal change to the creation of a network infrastructure between organizations. Developing a safer community through improved lighting or rebuilding the physical infrastructure of a deteriorated downtown (as was done in Baltimore, Boston, and Seattle), through the interactive efforts of the private sector developers, city government, and other stakeholders, represents one type of systemic partnership dealing with the infrastructure. Other systemic partnerships can develop around economic incentives provided through political or governmental actions to enhance the likelihood of interaction and may involve a combination of monetary and physical resources. For example, the establishment of small business incubators by providing a tax break as well as short term sites for new ventures reflects such a systemic approach. Systemic partnerships that involve broad social problems, like job skill training of the disadvantaged or the physical infrastructure that directly affects businesses, can have quite direct benefits for participants. Improved urban conditions, for example, can make it easier to recruit qualified individuals to downtown businesses. As Figure 6.1 indicates, such partnerships can manifest the strategic philanthropy of corporate givers, following the normal rules of investment. "Giving" is done in the hopes that relatively direct benefits will be received from the interaction, in the form of improved business conditions, a better local economy, and particularly, a more coherent physical infrastructure.

Improvements in the Saint Johns Business District in downtown Portland, Oregon, as reported by Barbour (1982), represent one such systemic partnership. A coalition of seven neighborhoods came together in 1976 to focus on revitalization of the business district, with the expressed purposes of "improv[ing] the appearance, traffic circulation, the economic performance of the Saint Johns business district as both a commercial and neighborhood center" (Barbour, 1982, p. 212). The focus of the development activities was physical improvement, as well as economic and educational development. But the partnership, which included the government agency, the Portland Development Committee, the Bureau of Planning, neighborhood groups, and local business interests, realized that "physical changes alone will not solve the problems facing the business district. In order to create a stronger commercial center, it is equally important to improve management of business operations and to promote and provide new opportunities for private investment. The city wanted to maximize the benefits of the physical improvements by coordinating them with the activities designed to increase the economic strength of the commercial center" (Barbour, 1982, p. 212).

As a result of the multiyear partnership efforts in Oregon, numerous improvements were made in the physical environment of the Saint Johns area, which directly benefitted the local businesses, as well as residents, and made the city a more attractive place in which to live. Costs involved were, to some extent, out of pocket for the businesses but also involved a great deal of active involvement in the processes of decision making around improving the city's environment.

Partnerships that Focus on Network Infrastructure

Purer forms of social welfare thinking are involved in systemic partnership that have less tangible and longer range benefits, for example, the economic development programs in West Virginia with which C&P Telephone, a Bell Atlantic Division, is involved. Specific objectives of that partnership, as stated in a flyer released by the partnership, are to "provide leadership in changing attitudes and perceptions towards the state's business climate . . . create an awareness and acceptance by all stakeholders . . . that economic development benefits everyone, coordinate with the West Virginia Roundtable . . . to support programs with financial and human resources." To develop their involvement, C&P has formed an Economic and Community Development Council that organizes their resources on a statewide basis. The ultimate purpose of their participation is related to improving the economic climate, so that there will be a stronger business base paying taxes, and otherwise providing funds and resources for community development. A very long range consideration in attempting to improve the business climate is that there may be more customers for the phone company if business conditions improve. Direct ways of measuring this improvement, however, are difficult to find.

In addition to partnerships in business retention, C&P has become deeply involved in fostering partnerships within the educational systems throughout the state. In about two and one half years, more than 240 partnerships between schools and businesses have developed, in part because of the facilitative role that C&P has played. C&P itself has employees directly involved in 20 partnerships. For C&P partnerships represent an organized way to share resources and concerns between schools and businesses in a way that will enhance the education that students receive. Like the business retention program, involvement is primarily through the volunteer efforts of individuals located at all levels of the firm. Resource costs for both of these partnerships are derived primarily from employee donations of time and, for the corporation, from providing release time to employees who are engaged in partnership activities. While some dollar contributions have been made, C&P considers its contributions of employee time (and some use of facilities) to be far greater and more significant than any dollar contributions made. As with other systemic partnerships dealing with attitudinal and interorganizational relationship changes, the benefits expected from C&P's participation in the schools and in the business retention program are indirect, long range, and relatively unmeasurable. The basic motivation for the business retention program derived from a recognition within the company that although internal costs might be cut to reduce expenses, the company's telephone lines were a long-term fixed investment that was not readily transportable. To enhance business opportunities, C&P needed to find a way to affect the business conditions in the communities where it operated such that they remained stable, and if possible, grew so that a future customer base would be available. With this recognition came the additional awareness that one of the primary things that West Virginia had to "sell" to retain its job base was the positive lifestyle and quality of life.

This realization led C&P to become involved in improving the schools. School improvement partnerships tied individual businesses to school involvement. C&P employee volunteers showed great willingness to offer assistance to help the schools improve certain aspects of their educational programs—areas in which employees had expertise that may or may not be tapped on the job. The approach C&P uses is one of "can we help you?" rather than "let us tell you what you are doing wrong." C&P representatives believe this is the only partnership approach that can work. Issues of mutual mistrust of the motives of both parties must be overcome before the partnerships can begin to work; however, C&P believes that when care is taken to maintain the "let's help" attitude, rather than a more critical one, this trust building process is shortened.

The company's involvement at the policy level is that of setting an agenda and permitting employees to use some of their work time for involvement in the schools. The company does not necessarily allocate dollar resources to the schools or community agencies.

Two types of benefits are expected from these partnerships. First, C&P management believes there is an improvement in employee satisfaction that results from employees being able to employ talents that they might not otherwise have used, in their connections with the schools. Employees feel that their skills, which may not be directly used on their jobs, are being put to good use in their school relationships and, as a result, feel better about working for the company. The second and even longer term benefit is that graduates of the schools will be better equipped to deal with the world they will face. In the long run, C&P hopes the company will benefit from a better prepared work force.

In one sense, the corporation views its role, much as was suggested above, as leveraging limited resources for the long-term betterment of society but with results that may be neither direct nor identifiable for the corporation. As Tom Terry, Manager of Business Development for C&P, put it, "Long range, you're developing a future employee body that is better educated and able to understand what will be needed in the future. . . . But we have always gone in with the attitude that we are not here to run your schools but to help you."

A central characteristic of successful social partnerships is highlighted in the development of numerous business-school partnerships in West Virginia. Social partnership, when it works, is a local phenomenon that addresses the needs of a local community or group and is not imposed by a central authority. C&P's role is a carefully defined facilitative role that brings together local groups to determine what their needs are, both in the schools and in business retention. It is key, however, that the partnerships remain in control of the local groups. One result of the partnerships that have now sprung up throughout the state, facilitated in part by the learning that has evolved from the C&P experiences, is the change in attitude between members of the organizational systems involved. Corporation is becoming a more familiar approach to problem solving.

Like other systemic partnerships, the C&P partnerships have spawned other partnership experiences, including efforts to provide management training by C&P for teachers and, conversely, bringing teachers into the corporation to help parents teach their children how to study. By leveraging their resources and using primarily human resources, C&P has performed the catalytic role of bringing together numerous other businesses with schools and drawing other partners into the economic development process.

POLICY IMPLICATIONS

This chapter has reviewed three significant trends, each with important public policy implications. The first trend is a more strategic approach to philanthropic activity. This behavior, reflected in the actions of foundations, charitable recipients, and donors, reflects a larger trend toward the focused use of resources. To the extent that it promotes efficiency, minimization of transaction costs, and enhancement of charitable ends, it is a trend with positive economic effects.

The second trend is the strategic use of philanthropy by for-profit participants. "Charity sells," as one of the consultants told us. The growth of cause related marketing highlights the opportunity that is seen by market hungry executives, ever on the lookout for new ways to segment the populus into consumer clusters and to reach them through whatever appeals will loosen their purse strings. Beyond the market effects, of course, are the political dimensions of this "charity sells" attitude. When companies promote charitable activity for the purpose of building political capital in a community or among a grassroots constituency, they have created an asset for the political arena.

The third trend involves the proliferation and successful incubation of intersectoral partnerships. Business, government, and non-profit organizations dance in new, and still often unfamiliar ways, in order to address a social, economic, and political policy agenda speckled with intractable problems. This paper has reviewed the various types of partnerships—programmatic, federational, and systemic—in terms of costs and benefits to the participants. But the theory and practical understanding of partnerships and interorganizational, multi-sectoral arrangements are too new to permit definitive conclusions. They may be, as their supporters claim, the light for a new world of institutional cooperation. But it is also possible that they may be the institutional hegemony that their detractors fear.

From a policy perspective, there are at least four questions that deserve more careful and extensive attention. These questions reflect the diverse perspectives that can be applied to strategic philanthropy and to the role of partnerships as the means through which economic development goals can be achieved.

1. *Do social partnerships represent a fad or a genuine shift in the American ideology?* This question points to the significance of the partnership phenomenon but leaves open the possibility that this may constitute more form than substance. More than a decade has passed since George Lodge's *The New American Ideology* (1974) first proclaimed the need for American society to pass from a mostly individualistic to a communitarian society if pressing problems were to be addressed effec-

tively. Lodge articulated what many others saw as the harmful and costly adversarial relationship between business and government and presaged what Bellah et al. (1985) would identify as the tension between individualism and communitarianism in the individual consciousness of modern Americans. The cross-currents of a culture seem to be reflected in this dialogue about individualism and community, and we must leave to historians the verdict on the present conflicts. Philanthropy has both benefitted and responded to these currents but may well have been transformed in the process. Pristine detachment from social issues and the intractable social ills is no longer possible, and partnerships demand and require participation of foundation leadership, as well as corporate and community entities. Thus, philanthropy itself may be caught up in the passage through these value conflicts and conundrums.

2. *Does the evident effectiveness of partnership arrangements provide a compelling case for their extension and endorsement as instruments of public policy?* Whether on the basis of demonstrated effectiveness, or the political cachet of the idea, partnerships have been roundly endorsed as problem solving techniques by virtually every presidential candidate. In the fall of 1987, for example, a Democratic presidential forum on social policy led each of the Democratic candidates to warmly endorse and signify how they would apply the partnership concept to policy problems. Throughout the 1980s, the approach has been applied by governmental leaders at the federal, state, and local levels, but on a largely voluntary basis. Only in a few instances, such as the Job Training Partnership Act, have partnerships been mandated by law. Presumably, however, the political leaders contending for the presidency would attempt to devise more persuasive arguments for motivating reluctant partners to participate. In the absence of clearer results from participants, this trend toward mandatory partnership involvement may have the character of a shotgun marriage.

3. *Who is to make social policy? Are partnerships a politically legitimate means for addressing political issues?* The political appeal of the partnership approach cannot, by itself, be sufficient reason to cede social policy decision making to a cohort of public and private sector leaders, however well-intended they may be. One of the telling criticisms of expanded corporate social responsibility in the past has been the inappropriateness of managers making decisions that have traditionally been—or should be—reserved to elected political leaders. That criticism, which has foundations in addition to the narrow economic fundamentalism of Freidman, Hayek, and Buchanan, reaches new levels of complexity when addressing such economic issues as international competitiveness, the collaborative design of economic policy, and the shape of economic development in a community.

4. *Do partnerships represent an economically efficient means of pursuing appropriate economic policy objectives?* To our knowledge, there are still insufficient analyses of the transactions costs of public–private partnerships. To the extent they have been assessed with care, it is to evaluate what possibility of success might exist in their absence. In areas such as economic development, therefore, the weight of the evidence seems to favor partnership approaches. Yet, as we have discussed above, it is imperative that direct and indirect costs be understood, calculated, and weighed in advance. The process cost of managing social partnerships is noteworthy and is largely absorbed by participants under current arrangements. These expenses are properly attributed to social beneficiaries of partnership projects, but the current calculus provides no efficient way to do so. This represents a major challenge for economists, accounting theorists, and policy analysts.

CONCLUSION

This paper has reviewed an important development in the political and public policy landscape of the 1980s, the creation and extension of social partnerships. Their potential for contributing to economic progress seems considerable but is by no means certain. One problem is the relative dearth of systematic knowledge about the various types and forms of partnership; another is the unanswered questions pertaining to the legitimacy of the partnership approach. Our purpose has been to focus primarily on the former, by articulating a rather full framework for analyzing partnership activity and composition. The latter problems, however, bearing as they do on the legitimacy of the partnership approach, require serious policy debate and discussion.

REFERENCES

Andrews, Patti N. (1987) "Public Affairs Offices in Large U.S. Corporations: Evaluation, Structure, and Development." Unpublished doctoral dissertation, Boston University, Boston, MA; University of Michigan Microfilm series.

Barbour, George P. (1982) "Portland Oregon: A Balance of Interest in Public–Private Cooperation," in R. Scott Fosler and Renee A. Berger, *Public–Private Partnership in American Cities: Seven Case Studies.* Lexington, MA: Lexington Books.

Bellah, Robert, et al. (1985) *Habits of the Heart: Individualism and Commitment in American Life.* Berkeley, Los Angeles, CA: University of California Press.

Bowen, Howard R. (1953) *Social Responsibilities of the Businessman.* New York: Harper.

Freeman, R. Edward. (1984) *Strategic Management: A Stakeholder Approach.* Marshfield, MA: Pitman, Inc.

Friedman, Milton. (1970) "The Social Responsibility of Business," *New York Times Magazine,* September 13, 1970. Reprinted with commentary in Thomas G. Marx, ed., *Business and Society: Economic, Moral, and Political Foundations.* Englewood Cliffs, NJ: Prentice-Hall, 1987.

Lodge, George. (1974) *The New American Ideology.* New York: Alfred A. Knopf, Inc.

Mahon, John. (1989) "Corporate Political Strategy," *Business in the Contemporary World* (Autumn), pp. 52–60.

Petersen, George, and Sundblad, Dana. (1994). *Corporations as Partners in Strengthening Urban Communities.* New York: The Conference Board.

Selznick, Philip. (1992) *The Moral Commonwealth: Social Theory and the Promise of Community.* Berkeley, Los Angeles, CA: University of California Press.

Troy, Kathryn. (1985) *Studying and Addressing Community Needs: A Corporate Case Book.* New York: The Conference Board.

Waddock, Sandra. (1986) "Public–Private Partnerships as Social Product and Process," in J.E. Post, ed., *Research in Corporate Social Performance and Policy,* vol. 8. Greenwich, CT: JAI Press, pp. 273–300.

Walton, Clarence. (1967) *Corporate Social Responsibilities.* Belmont, CA: Wadsworth.

Part II
Philanthropy and Community-Based Development

7 Community-Based Development—Lessons Learned

Virginia Hodgkinson

The impact of federal budget cuts in community-based economic development and low-income housing change during the 1980s led to some creative experiments in the private nonprofit sector to alleviate the growing need for low-income housing and economic development. The purpose of this chapter is to identify what has been learned in some of these projects and to propose what kinds of efforts and resources are needed to replicate, expand, and build upon the successful models that emerged.

In 1987, the Council for Community-Based Development estimated that foundations gave 2.4 percent of their total grants, about $68 million. They estimated that among the ten largest foundations, grant support had increased 54 percent from 1982 to 1987. After surveying 5,000 independent, corporate, and community foundations in this study, the Council found that 196 foundations had provided grants to community development organizations and that one-quarter of these foundations had started funding such programs since 1982 (Peirce and Steinbach, 1990).

Recently, the Council on Foundations and the Ford Foundation commissioned three separate studies to determine the level and kind of social investments in foundations, community foundations, and corporations. In the foundation study, the author selected a sample of 50 private foundations from around the country. The foundations had to have engaged in at least one program-related or social investment project. For the purpose of this study program, related or social investment programs related only to projects with charitable purposes that were designed to improve the economy of a locality or region through the use of program related loans, loan guarantees, equity investments, linked deposits, or recoverable grants. Foundations can use both their annual funds available for such investments or choose to use some of their assets for such purposes. When they do, they are able to return the repayment of loans or grants to their assets and thus get more use out of their funds. The sample included foundations of all sizes, ranging from under $1 million to over $4 billion (Council on Foundations, 1989).

Foundations have been allowed to use their assets for program related investments (PRIs) for charitable purposes, since the Tax Reform Act of 1969 specifically exempted these types of investments from its regulations on assets relating to the tax-exempt status of foundations. The author of this study interviewed representatives of these 50 foundations to identify foundations involved in social investing, to determine the kinds of problems foundations had with such programs, and to identify perceived problems or obstacles that might prevent foundations engaging in social investment. The Ford Foundation has been most active in this program. From 1968 to 1989, it had approved 230 program related investments, totalling $175 million (Ford Foundation, 1990).

The study found that the most common forms of program related investment were low or no interest loans, loan guarantees, linked investment, or recoverable grants. Most of these loans were given for mortgage financing and predevelopment costs of housing and commercial development projects. A foundation can make a loan directly with a variety of payment methods, as well as interest payment arrangements. In many cases, the foundation serves as a guarantor on a loan or a line of credit given to a nonprofit organization by another financial institution. Such methods allow a foundation to leverage its support to generate more investment funds from other sources. This practice also serves as an incentive for financial institutions to make loans. Linked deposits are similar, where the foundation makes a deposit to an account in a financial institution to persuade that institution to support a particular project. The foundation may put the money in a no interest account to assist the financial institution to make below market rate loans or, if it gets a return, allow the institution to borrow from its account. Equity investments involve buying stocks in small business or buying office buildings to lease to nonprofit organizations at below market rates. Recoverable grants are made from the foundation's grantmaking budget, rather than from its assets. These grants are no interest loans that revert to grants if they are not paid back (Council on Foundations, 1989).

Many foundation representatives reported that the major impediments with PRIs were the foundation's lack of experience with the available instruments for program investment and investing in business ventures themselves. Other foundations mentioned that community economic development was not part of their mission. Those foundations that did engage in such program related investments found them on the whole to be good investments. They mentioned that, in most cases, loans were paid back (Council on Foundations, 1989).

COMMUNITY FOUNDATIONS

In a second study of community foundations commissioned by the Council on Foundations and the Ford Foundation, the authors interviewed officers from 42 community foundations and found that 32 of these foundations were engaged in some type of program related investment. Fourteen of these community foundations invested in program related investments by investing a portion of their assets, and 21 had invested in community development by using the "recoverable grant." Several community foundations had used the program related investment as a fundraising strategy, either by actively raising funds to establish a loan fund or making loans based on a donor's initiative. Both large and small community foundations were engaged in social investing. The sample of community foundations that were interviewed had assets ranging from $1 million to over $500 million (Council on Foundations, 1988).

CORPORATIONS

The third study commissioned by the Council on Foundations and the Ford Foundation reviewed social investing by corporations. Corporations use the term "social investment" to mean giving below market loans or making loan guarantees and equity investments in high risk projects. The authors of the study were optimistic that more corporations could engage in a range of investment options available to them. Social investing by corporations started in 1967 as a response to urban riots. In 1967, the $2 billion Urban Investment Company was started in which 160 health and insurance companies participated over a period of five years. Under this program, over 100,000 housing units were built and 60,000 jobs were created. As part of that effort, the Center for Corporate Public Involvement was also created to serve as a clearinghouse on information and guidance about social investment programs. Most insurance companies funded social investments from the corporation and not from their foundations. The authors found that these companies set aside a certain amount of money each year for high risk projects having "social relevance." Investments are typically made in mortgages for low-income housing, business development, job creation and retention, and minority business investment, among others. The investments range in size from a few hundred thousand dollars to several million. Many corporations make loans with below market interest, and some also subsidize the development plans of community and neighborhood organizations (Council on Foundations, 1989).

In this same study, the author found that investments by banks in urban and neighborhood redevelopment was a more recent phenomenon. Of the five banks that the author interviewed that had social investment programs, two had set up affiliate banks for social investing purposes. The banks both make loans and use the recoverable grant to provide up front money for planning. The loan funds available in these five banks ranged from $3.35 million to $65 million (Council on Foundations, 1989).

Corporations have been provided with further incentives to invest in community development over the last four years as a result of the Low-Income Housing Tax Credit, established by the Tax Reform Act in 1986. This legislation allows investors to take up to 9 percent of related costs as a credit against their annual tax bill, which with other provisions allows a return on investment of 18 to 20 percent (Ford Foundation, 1990). The Council for Community-Based Development estimated that 54 corporate foundations made grants to community-based development groups in 1987 (Ford Foundation, 1990). More recently, corporations have been making investments through intermediary organizations, such as LISC and the Enterprise Foundation, and Fannie Mae, the federal national mortgage association for support of low-income housing using the investment advantages provided by the low-income housing credits. Other corporations, such as Brooklyn Union Gas, Levi Strauss, and the First National Bank of Chicago have supported community development in communities in which they were directly involved (Council on Foundations, 1989).

The Ford Foundation estimated that $2 billion was invested in community development by foundations, community foundations, insurance companies and other corporations, and individuals from 1970 to 1990 (Ford Foundation, 1990). While slow to get off the ground, the federal Low-Income Investment Tax Credit is starting to generate real money for investment in low-income housing. In 1987, LISC started a subsidiary company, the National Equity Fund, to adapt financial instruments for use by community development corporations. In its first three years, NEF raised $141 million from 58 corporations and created over $370 million for low-income housing. It also created another affiliate to create a secondary market for funds and increase the dollars available. This affiliate, the Local Initiative Managed Assets Corporation (LIMAC), started in 1987, raised about $11 million from corporations and foundations to buy loans. As of 1989, a new IRS ruling will permit LIMAC to be the first nonprofit corporation to offer market rate securities, which will be backed by public pension funds and community development loans. Since LISC was founded, it has attracted funds from over 600 foundations and corporations to LISC projects in over 30 cities. Their total investment of $300,000 million generated another $1.3 billion from public and private sources to invest in community economic development. They created over 21,000 housing units and 6 million square feet of commercial and industrial space (LISC, 1990).

Another major intermediary, the Enterprise Foundation, was started by James Rouse in 1981 and has helped to build or renovate 14,500 units of housing for low-income people. The Foundation, with $28 million in 1990, gave out $2.8 million in loans and $6.6 million in technical assistance to nonprofit housing groups in that year (*The Chronicle of Philanthropy*, April 1991).

Although there is no definitive number of intermediary organizations, as of 1987, there were more than 100 such intermediary organizations at the national, regional, and local levels. In addition to intermediary organizations to serve as both brokers and lending institutions, more than 150 directors of community development corporations have received training from the Development Training Institute. It provides a one-year training program in business and real estate development, finance, management, and planning for leaders at the local level. Money for the Institute comes from several foundations and the Economic Development Administration of the federal government (Peirce and Steinbach, 1987).

In 1991, six major foundations and a major corporation pledged $62.5 million to LISC and the Enterprise Foundation to revitalize inner city neighborhoods. This project, the National Community Development Initiative, hopes to generate another $500 million in additional support from banks, corporations, local foundations, state and local governments, and $100 million already pledged by the Federal Home Loan Mortgage Corporation (Freddie Mac). It is estimated that this single project will equal one-sixth of what the federal government spends annually ($3 billion) on block grants through the Department of Housing and Urban Development. It may represent a significantly higher proportion of the annual amount into low-income housing, since HUD does not know the proportion of the $3 billion that is dedicated to low-income housing (*The Chronicle of Philanthropy*, March 12, 1991).

Another major movement to provide low-income housing is the coalition of churches involved in saving low-income communities by renovating and building new housing units. A few of the earliest efforts are the East Brooklyn Churches/Nehemiah Project, the Southeast Bronx Community Organization, the Mid-Bronx Desparados, and the Jubilee Housing; all are representative of community development efforts led by local churches. In each case, a single member of the clergy or a coalition of clergy developed projects to rehabilitate or rebuild housing.

A study from the National Center for Charitable Statistics (NCCS) at the INDEPENDENT SECTOR reveals that circa 1988, there were approximately 5,000 organizations in community improvement, housing construction, and rehabilitation. The total expenditures were $2.5 billion in 1988. Total assets were $2.5 billion. All forms of public support, including grants and loans from private and governmental sources, was $1.8 billion (Hodgkinson et al., 1992).

To determine the effectiveness of the community development movement, several questions need to be addressed:

1. What is the character of community development organizations and how are they staffed?
2. Can these organizations help to eradicate poverty, build effective businesses, and create more jobs?
3. Can these organizations meet the needs for housing among low-income individuals and families?
4. Have we learned some lessons from this movement that should lead to changes in public policy relating to housing, job training and development, and economic development in depressed areas?
5. How can this movement be more effectively and efficiently financed to meet the needs of moderate and low-income neighborhoods?

The factors that determined the success of CDCs were good construction, resident participation, good project management (both while constructing and management of property after construction), the location of the project, and the clustering of projects over time. For housing, local government support, advocacy and the provision of social services to residents were also considered important (Vidal, 1989). These findings were generally confirmed by another study commissioned by the Community Development Research Center, which evaluated the factors that were necessary to develop business enterprise development in severely distressed communities.

It seems that community development organizations could go a long way toward establishing a permanent housing stock for low-income families should there be adequate public and private investment available. However, the needs far outstrip the current investment available. Studies have shown that subsidized low-rental housing fell in constant dollars by \$2.3 million annually from 1974 to 1987, and unsubsidized units fell by \$3.3 million during the same period (Apgar, 1991; Leonard, 1989). The annual estimated cost to meet our current needs for public housing, preservation of subsidized housing, production of new low-income housing, and restoring the Community Development Block Grants is estimated at \$11.4 billion. Even if we accept the highest estimates, less than 10 percent of the current need is met annually. And these figures do not include subsidies for low-income families, education and job training, child welfare, and health. These together represent an estimated need for \$40.7 billion, excluding care for the elderly (Center for Community Change, 1990). While nonprofit community organizations could probably more effectively meet the needs of low-income communities, they cannot do so at the current level of investment.

Over the past quarter century, several lessons have been learned about effective investments in eradicating poverty. Neighborhoods with organizations providing for advocacy, community development, and a range of necessary social services can have a decided impact on community development, job creation, and economic development. These results are even more dramatic in those organizations with stable leadership and where housing is managed by nonprofits. What this lesson tells us is that building community leadership and community capacity to achieve economic development is far more likely to succeed than to allow outside organizations and developers to determine the future of a community.

A second lesson is that community development does not come without training leadership and building the capacity for community investment. In this, the development of intermediary organizations and training institutes has been the key in insuring wise investments at the community level. Without such organizations, experience in developing capital investment at the local level probably would not have been possible.

A third lesson is that to preserve a permanent reservoir of well maintained housing—either rental or owned—it must reside in the nonprofit sector regardless of the source of investment, public or private. Much of the crisis in housing is caused by allowing developers to take back the land and buildings they invested in twenty years ago. Not only was such housing not maintained on the whole, but investors made money initially and have the land and buildings after twenty years. Such public policy merely exacerbates current need, does not support local leadership and control, and puts the ownership and the major earnings in the hands of investors who have no motivation to maintain the property. When housing is in the hands of community development organizations, and housing is managed by tenants, not only is the housing maintained, but it is more likely to be designed to meet the needs of the community.

The establishment of land trusts allow low-income families to own their own homes and build up equity, but when they sell, they must sell back their home to the land trust with a small increase in the selling price. Such practices allow low-income housing to remain in a permanent pool.

A fourth lesson is that investing in low-income housing by corporations and foundations, through intermediary organizations and aided by the federal government, has led to a good return on investment, but the assets for the most part remain permanently in the community. Therefore, the investment is a permanent investment and not one that has to be continuously remade on a twenty year cycle.

Finally, it would seem that if food and shelter are the basics of survival, a permanent investment in low-income housing held in trust and under the management of local nonprofit organizations provides the best solution for more permanent social progress. For example, if we were to take the lessons we have learned as a nation, we might consider investing in a permanent revolving fund for low-income housing. It would involve both rental housing and home ownership. Over the next fifteen to twenty years, by expanding investment by government, the private sector, and foundations, we could set a goal to establish a permanent revolving fund for such housing. It would involve greatly expanding the number of both intermediary organizations and neighborhood organizations. Increased funding to the Neighborhood Reinvestment Corporation could provide the impetus to such an expansion. Continuation of the Low-Income Housing Credit could expand corporate and other individual private investment in building a permanent pool of low-income housing, as well as the new HOME program.

Theoretically, if the private sector and individuals could invest $5 billion a year and the government $15 billion a year over the next ten to fifteen years, a permanent pool of well maintained housing for low-income families could be created. Part of the interest from investment funds could be used to rehabilitate and maintain current housing, or to invest in the building of new housing. Such a program, like Fannie Mae in mortgages, would result in enlightened social policy by marrying the best of capitalism with social investment. Grant support for job training and some support of operations, particularly in new community development organizations, would still be necessary during and after this period. But as neighborhoods become more successful over time, earned income increases as a proportion of total revenue (Vidal, 1989). Such a revolving fund would gradually eliminate the massive needs for annual appropriations for public housing. It would also demonstrate a nation's commitment to securing basic shelter as the foundation for more permanently attacking the causes of poverty. By assuring ownership, the maintenance of ownership, and management in the nonprofit sector at the local level, such a policy will better assure the development and training of local leadership to maintain quality housing. Developing a revolving fund from both public and private sources will assure a permanent fund not as subject to the vagaries of government appropriations.

To increase private investment from $500 million to $5 billion annually, the Low-Income Housing Credit would have to be maintained for at least a decade. More foundations and corporations, as well as pension funds, should be encouraged to put their investment dollars in intermediary organizations and particularly LIMAC, which is allowed to offer market rate securities. Increasing such social investments by corporations, as the Council on Foundations studies of both foundations and corporations suggest, will involve a rather massive public education campaign to inform both corporations and foundations of legitimate social investment opportunities. Such programs offer these institutions the best in enlightened self-interest, a good social investment, and a safe return. If government were to consider returning to its previous annual $15 billion dollar investment for a ten-year period, it could set up a fund more like Social Security, to assure a permanent pool of investment dollars for maintaining and building new housing. It would involve a one-time major commitment, rather than a long-term major commitment. Having housing maintained by the nonprofit sector would lower the long-term costs of public bureaucracy and assure a more continuous development of local leaders and managers.

In conclusion, while the situation is grim and the needs greater than before, promising programs have been tested. What is needed is vision and commitment from the public, private, and nonprofit sectors, to expand these programs and create a permanent housing pool as the first step toward creating the social environment for more permanent and successful economic development in chronically distressed communities.

REFERENCES

Against All Odds: The Achievements of Community-Based Organizations. Washington, DC: National Congress for Community-Based Development, 1989.

Bendick, Marc Jr., and Egan, Mary Lou. "Business Development in the Inner City: Enterprise with Community Life." Published paper from study prepared for the Community Development Research Center at the New School for Social Research, New York, 1990.

Cook, James. "Priming the Urban Pump," *Forbes* (March 13, 1987), pp. 62–64.

DePalma, Anthony. "Tax Credits Produce Housing for Poor," *The New York Times,* January 17, 1988.

Findu, Alan. "Nonprofit Community Groups Rebuild Housing in the Bronx," *The New York Times,* March 11, 1990.

Goldman, John J. "Bronx Reborn: Housing Emerges from Ashes," *Los Angeles Times,* March 27, 1989.

Goozner, Merrill. "Housing Group Rebuilds Areas from Within," *Chicago Tribune,* October 9, 1989.

Goss, Kristen A. 'A Big Push to Receive Inner Cities," *The Chronicle of Philanthropy,* March 12, 1991.

Greene, Elizabeth. "Enterprise Foundation Seeks to Reconstruct America," *The Chronicle of Philanthropy,* April 23, 1991.

Hodgkinson, Virginia Ann, Weitzman, Murray S., Toppe, Christopher M., and Noga, Stephen M. *Nonprofit Almanac 1992–1993: Dimensions of the Independent Sector.* San Francisco: Jossey-Bass Publishers, 1992.

Kuttner, Robert. "A Blueprint for Affordable Housing," *Business Week,* August 31, 1987, p. 18.

Local Initiatives Support Corporation, *News,* 1991.

Marble, Melinda. *Social Investment and Community Foundations.* Washington, DC: Council on Foundations, 1989.

Marble, Melinda. *Social Investment and Community Foundations.* Washington, DC: Council on Foundations, 1988.

Peirce, Neil R., and Steinbach, Carol F. "Doing Well by Doing Good: Social Purpose Investing," *Letter.* New York: The Ford Foundation (Summer 1990), pp. 10–11, 16.

Peirce, Neil R., and Steinbach, Carol F. *Enterprising Communities.* Washington, DC: Council for Community-Based Development, 1989.

SEEDCO. *Religious Institutions as Actors in Community-Based Development.* New York: SEEDCO, 1988.

Skloot, Edward. *Social Investment and Corporations.* Washington, DC: Council on Foundations, 1989.

Vidal, Avis C. "Community Economic Development Assessment: A National Study of Urban Community Development Corporations, Preliminary Findings." Unpublished report. New York Community Development Research Center, Graduate School of Management and Urban Professions, New School of Social Research, New York, 1989.

"What's Ahead for Housing Legislation," *The LISC Link* 1(2) (Spring 1990), p. 4.

8 Community Organizations as Housing Developers

Phillip L. Clay

In the past five decades, we have made significant progress in improving housing and living conditions in urban neighborhoods. When the Depression began, in 1932, one-third of Americans were ill-housed. That was down to 5 percent in 1980.

Despite significant progress, millions still live in inadequate housing, and a greater number live in neighborhoods experiencing social and economic crisis. Many neighborhoods still lack vital retail services or job opportunities critical for community viability and self-help initiatives (DHUD, 1984; Levitan, 1985; Struyk et al., 1983; Nenno and Sears, 1985).

In recent decades, the "war on poverty," Model Cities Programs, and community development, under CDBG, have not achieved for every family a decent home in a suitable living environment. Nor have they made all families self-supporting and all neighborhoods economically viable.

Federal initiatives and support, that defined urban policy for 40 years, declined in the 1980s. Responsibility for community and neighborhood development shifted to local government and the nonprofit sector. These local units had to set goals, design programs, raise and allocate money, and take the heat for shortcomings in their programs. And they had to advocate for the poor against a Federal administration that sometimes tried to reverse progress.

Some communities have been more capable than others in filling the void left by federal withdrawal, and some states, like Massachusetts, Maryland, and New York, have also been more active and generous than others. But in every case, even in states where there were organized efforts, helping poor communities has become more difficult.

Progress in the 1980s slowed considerably. The decline in federal assistance, and the emergence of a more significant local role, raised questions about government, volunteer, and self-help efforts, and about the future of community-based organizations.

It's now clear that the community-based organization (CBO) is a key player in neighborhood economic development. There is considerable literature on these organizations. It is not heavily analytical, but it is substantial and growing (Mayer and Blake; National Commission on Neighborhoods, 1979a; Bratt et al., 1983).

In this chapter, we focus on their role in economic development, and we examine their potential for increased responsibilities if greater philanthropic resources were made available.

WHAT COMMUNITY-BASED ORGANIZATIONS CAN DO

What are these organizations best at? And what have they demonstrated a capacity to do? Here is some of the record of success.

They:

1. Develop and manage housing and other physical facilities.
2. Support small business development and, in some cases, cooperative enterprises.
3. Organize and coordinate activities of constituent organizations and provide technical assistance.
4. Enter into partnerships with public and private organizations for development projects.
5. Provide social, educational, and other services to support economic and community development.
6. Advocate for neighborhood interests.
7. Serve as development entities and designated developers for neighborhoods.
8. Provide jobs and mobility opportunities for neighborhood residents and serve as a conduit for funds, including those from government, foundations, and private corporations.

The scale of projects and the level of activity in cities vary. Nevertheless, there is sufficient success to demonstrate that much can be accomplished successfully by community-based entities.

WHAT COMMUNITY-BASED ORGANIZATIONS CANNOT DO

Just as community development organizations have demonstrated success in some functions, in others there is a demonstrable lack of success. For example, community-based organizations have not been able to consistently attract private financial resources. They haven't been able to make themselves independent and self-sufficient or generate capital within a neighborhood for internally generated economic development projects.

Likewise, they have not been able to serve as a "government" or a general purpose public service manager for neighborhoods. They have not been able to achieve the scale, breadth of competence, support, or authority required to perform this function. They only had limited success in tenant management of public housing projects or in managing municipal services, such as park maintenance. They have not shown a capacity to address massive poverty. They have only been able to produce limited results.

CBOs have an admirable track record in developing housing units or creating jobs, but their accomplishments are small given the scale of the problems in their communities. They are most effective where there is talented indigenous leadership, not where poverty is at crisis level, nor where the underclass is pervasive. In those cases, they show greatest success when managed by professionals from outside the neighborhood.

CBOs may do well, but they are not a substitute for formal official organizations that build neighborhood capacity; nor do they really empower. They serve, rather than develop, the community. There is nothing wrong with this service role, but it should be understood for what it is and not romanticized.

Despite these limitations, community-based organizations are still significant, and they are an important component in a network of public and nonpublic organizations that philanthropy can look to for community economic development.

It goes without saying that not all CBOs are the same. Many are fledgling with no staff, no obvious community support, and only casual and minimal operations. At the other extreme is the growing, but much smaller, number that have staff, a steady though not permanent source of operating dollars, access to capital, and the goodwill of local residents, government, and private contributors.

The most sophisticated are in northeastern and mid-western cities.

But they are building experience and capacity across urban America. To understand and to help them achieve their goals, we need to understand the differences among them. This requires some analytical scheme, and such a scheme will help corporations, foundations, governments and others determine the kind of support they need.

This chapter identifies the stages of organization development. This was first undertaken by Mayer and Blake in 1980. This chapter revises and elaborates upon their scheme.

STAGES OF ORGANIZATIONAL DEVELOPMENT

This scheme simplifies reality. Not all CBOs go through the stages neatly. Circumstances sometimes allow CBOs to skip or combine stages. Indeed, some are "born mature." They have a defined mission, experienced staff, adequate operating and capital resources, a professional and active board, and community support.

They can do major projects right away. The Boston Housing Partnership is an example. It was set up with major funding and the mandate to rehabilitate 800 units within two years. Its board includes senior officials in the private, public, and community sectors. Its staff has prior experience in housing development.

This mature and mainstream character, and the organization's ability to act, were the result of clear and sophisticated planning. The scheme concentrates on organization characteristics, but the evidence is that the executive director is the key to success.

Finally, the stages reflect the environment. We have seen the emergence of creative financing, greater flexibility in use of federal resources, flexibility about what kind of organizations do community development, increased focus on small business development, increasing corporate support, increasing use of partnerships, gentrification, prevalence of low-cost development opportunities, etc.

If the environment changes further, the process and pace of development in distressed areas might also change. For example, greater support of community-based organizations could help them develop faster, and more might survive. But adverse events or a general decline in support could likewise make it harder for them to accomplish much.

Stage 1: Formal Establishment and Advocacy

Most start as informal advocates for improved conditions. This advocacy sometimes leads to mobilization and focused intervention. Focus on housing and economic development and project implementation is unusual in this stage.

But if development is on their agenda early, CBOs typically go through basic common steps to prepare. They incorporate, raise funds, and either hire staff or sign on volunteers. Not all even make it to this point, but formal organizing to become development oriented may come early or after years in a nondevelopment status. Many, that think initially in project and development terms, actually do not go forward. They become nondevelopment, advocacy, or public interest organizations. Timing and opportunity are important determinants.

Stage 2: Project Development

When a CBO has a development focus, it organizes for project implementation. It hires professional staff, obtains non-profit tax status, installs or changes accounting systems, obtains office space, and puts together a development team. The CBO may also change its name, define and publicize its development interests, and target geographical areas.

They also have typical troubles in early projects. These include resolving the conflict between their capacity and the expectations of their constituents, matching limited staff resources to complex and sometimes unexpected project tasks, fundraising without a track record, resolving political issues within the community and between organizations, and working out the relationship between the staff and the board.

If successful, this stage sees the implementation of the first "major" project. Typically, it's small—rehabilitating a small multifamily structure or launching small commercial enterprises. This first project fully invests the organization. The project becomes the basis for identifying this CBO as an entity to be reckoned with.

Visible success, if not impact, is critical in this stage. Failure to complete the project or to have some success, however defined, may abort development or at least impair it substantially.

Stage 3: Building a Track Record

With a successful project, the CBO typically tries to build on the success by completing additional projects and establishing itself as a "can-do" organization. The expansion is typically with the same type of project, although successive efforts may be bigger or more complicated.

The organization may also expand by doing a project in other areas. The success draws more attention and increases its confidence. A growing "track record" supports staff expansion and broadens the funding base. Success also allows the organization to build connections with institutions that will be important in later stages.

The evolving organization often has to address some of the same problems as in Stage 2, but with higher stakes. Failure to address crises may retard needed growth, expose the organization to risks that later prove too great, or provide negative or mixed messages to outsiders.

Sometimes the organization is unable to build this track record in a timely or convincing manner. When this happens, the organization remains at stage three for an extended period, often making false starts or trying new but modest initiatives.

While this futile effort to grow may result from internal problems, it may also result from limited resources or opportunities that would allow it to repeat earlier success.

The organization in Stage 3 is often still staff centered, but increasingly the board sees the success and potential impact of the organization and seeks to exert more control. This control or influence often involves personnel matters and project selection. This is also the stage at which the capacity of the board becomes an issue. Many organizations begin to make changes in their board, for example, by increasing the number of nonresident members or outside professionals. Earlier emphasis on neighborhood resident members only diminishes. Residents are sometimes relegated to "advisory boards" or "consumer panels."

Stage 4: Institutionalization

Once the CBO has developed a strong track record, it moves to institutionalize itself and become an advanced community-based organization. The track record may be reflected in any of the above, including number of projects completed, size of projects, or complexity of efforts. Often advanced community organizations are marked, not only by the number of projects, but also by the complexity, incorporating as they must creative financing, using an unskilled labor force, building on difficult sites, incorporating social as well as economic goals, managing relations with fickle funding sources, entering into partnerships, or using multiple funding sources.

Beyond this, they must overcome the normal small business risks and housing risks that call for the poor produced only with deep and multiple subsidies.

In Stage 4, CBOs:

1. Develop internal and external networks that are accepted and deferred to by other organizations.
2. Obtain legal authority, such as designation as a developer for a particular area by the local government.
3. Have a more solid funding base (i.e., United Way, Community Development Block Grant allocation, more favorable line of credit at lending institutions, or affiliation with national organizations such as Local Initiative Support Corporation, Neighborhood Reinvestment Corporation, or a partnership with a corporate foundation).
4. Initiate or participate in partnerships.
5. Provide technical assistance and consulting services to other organizations.

6. Have a larger and more professional staff that includes not only development but administrative staff.

7. Obtain more stable resolution of lingering conflicts and difficulties faced in Stage 2 and a stable management of those issues through formal bylaws, contracts, etc.

For the advanced community organization, the board takes on a more substantial role. The composition reflects a resolution of issues, such as local versus nonlocal residents, professional versus nonprofessional members, authority of the board versus staff, the process of project selection, and control over external relationships. This stage is also characterized by delegation of responsibility within the board for such matters as fundraising, external relations, program expansion, community relations, and personnel policy.

Despite the advanced status, however, these organizations typically do not have independent control over a large amount of capital. They must go to subsidized or preferential sources for development capital.

Foundations and local government are anxious to collaborate and give preference to these advanced organizations. They often seek out a mature CBO to assist. A major issue in strategic planning for the successful and mature CBO is how to manage the growth and keep perspective on limitations.

Stage 5: Consolidation

The final stage is really not a new stage so much as an elaboration of advanced status. At this point the organization deals with how it faces new opportunities and how it addresses problems. Organizations at this stage are able to expand and/or contract or change directions without compromising basic integrity.

Few organizations that have reached this status disband; they typically have holdings or assets to manage. At some level they may be self-sustaining and able to survive on investments, fees, contracts, and profits. They have developed mechanisms to solve problems which would be fatal if experienced in Stages 1, 2, or 3.

Not all organizations that start on the road toward development make it to Stage 5, or Stage 4, for that matter. Those that do have a substantial investment of trust and resources in the organization on the part of residents and others.

TECHNICAL ASSISTANCE

One crucial question for advocates of community-based organizations is how to increase support for community-based organizations generally.

Mayer has identified the kinds of support that make a difference (Mayer and Blake, 1980; Mayer, 1984).

Critical to success, according to Mayer, is a source of early financial support that provides flexibility and the promise for continuing support. In addition to funding, organizations also need help in proposal writing, project packaging and management, professional services, architecture, accounting, engineering, planning, and legal assistance.

CBO's also benefit from assistance in bookkeeping, and in internal organizational issues like board and staff training. Assisting community-based organizations has always been a problem. There are no perfect assistance models, though each approach has good points.

National Organizations: Several organizations assist community-based organizations. Some, such as the Neighborhood Reinvestment Corporation, which developed the NHS program, have a model of neighborhood-based development including commercial revitalization. They attempt to replicate these (Clay, 1981).

They assist financially. And they help the staff, both at startup and through later stages. Other assistance provides a loose affiliation which comes with various types of assistance over an extended or indefinite period. Examples include Local Initiative Support Corporation (LISC), the Enterprise Foundation, and the Partnership Institute.

LOCAL COMMUNITY DEVELOPMENT ASSISTANCE ORGANIZATIONS

These are organizations (in some cases formerly advanced neighborhood-based community organizations) that provide assistance to organizations on a city or regional basis. Sometimes they perform specific functions such as financial consulting or more generalized support. These organizations act as a specialized staff to augment and develop capacity. The funding often comes from foundations or from local government. The Greater Boston Community Development Corporation is one example.

Joint Development: A third type of assistance is the joint effort of the community-based organization and private developer. The relationship provides certain mutual benefits including, potentially, the transfer of skills to the CBO. The CBO is able to apply their on-the-job training and "track record" in a later project. Joint development, in contrast to the types of assistance mentioned above, involves the CBO as a partner, more or less equal, depending on the project and its own stage of development.

Consultants: Consultants represent another form of technical assistance. As individuals or in firms, they are retained to perform functions deemed critical to the success of the organization or the implementation of specific projects. They may also train staff to perform these functions.

Each of the forms of assistance has strengths and weaknesses. There is a good argument for having all of them available in a given community since they respond to different circumstances. Future research will help us better understand the ways these various models work, and how we might make better use of them.

Further research will also help us better understand aspects of the various kinds of assistance—project assistance, strategic planning, training of staff and board, financial analysis, fundraising, project management, market analysis, etc.

EVALUATING COMMUNITY DEVELOPMENT ORGANIZATIONAL POTENTIAL

To progress toward increasing organizational capacity, we need to have a way of assess organizational growth and strength. Below are some questions that help assess organizational capacity.

Internal Characteristics

1. Does the organization have an Executive Director who is credible, committed, and competent?
2. Does the staff have the right combination of skills in community organizing and administration, as well as development, to match the growth stage of the organization and to make the transition to the next stage?
3. Is there support and commitment to professional development for the staff and training for the board?
4. Is the staff free to devote time to development work, or are they overloaded with activities that distract them from these activities?
5. Is there a division of responsibility between the staff and the board that reflects the strengths, weaknesses, responsibilities, and expectations of each?
6. Does the organization have credible project management and fiscal control systems?
7. Is there evidence that the organization learns from experience and adapts its activities to reflect the lessons of that experience?
8. Does the organization show evidence of having an effective process for dealing with the inevitable crises in an organization?

Program Characteristics

1. Has the community-based organization identified a problem that is amenable to neighborhood organization intervention?
2. Can the project(s) they select show progress in a reasonable period of time?
3. Is there a strategic plan that reflects how the community-based organization will choose projects and build a track record?

4. Is the strategic plan reasonable, given the available and potential resources available?

5. Has the organization put together the resources for implementation? Are backup systems in place?

6. Are the board and community involved in an ongoing planning process?

Local Economic and Political Environmental Characteristics

1. Has the organization made studies or consulted social, demographic, and economic data on the market and on the issues of interest to it?

2. Do activities relate realistically to the economic, housing, and market conditions in the neighborhood? Is there a strategy for "swimming up stream"?

3. Has the organization evaluated the cost, time, and other factors in working in the neighborhood? Does its budget reflect the environment in which it operates?

4. Has the organization dealt with racial, ethnic, and other issues within the neighborhood and similar issues between the neighborhood and others, including institutions and government?

Relations with the Community and Outside Actors

1. Does a community-based organization have roots in and the support of its community? Is there visible evidence of that support?

2. Is the community-based organization credible with its peer organizations?

3. How does the community-based organization handle conflict with community and peer organizations?

4. Is the community-based organization effective in dealing with local and state officials? Is there evidence of this effectiveness, such as grants, designation status, etc.?

5. Is the community-based organization effective with local financial and business leaders and organizations, either generally (i.e., lines of credit, grant support) or for particular projects (joint development)?

6. Does the organization have the support and respect of foundations, churches and other benefactors, including potential sources of technical assistance?

These questions may be used both by staff and others in learning about organizations. The more questions that can be answered in the affirmative, the greater the chance that the organization will mature as described in earlier sections of this chapter.

THE ROLE OF COMMUNITY ORGANIZING

Thus far, we have not mentioned community organizing. For many years community development was principally community organizing and the advocacy associated with it. For a variety of reasons, including specifically the desire of community-based organizations to have a direct role in shaping the physical and economic future of their neighborhood, organizations have been turning away from advocacy and towards development. The CBOs described in this chapter are the ones that took this route.

The pursuit of development by community-based organizations is encouraged by most local government officials, who see the potential of community-based development and who want to develop a less combative relationship with citizen organizations. Such self-help is also consistent with prevailing political sentiments. Since few local governments have much in the way of direct development capacity and because of the political pressure to moderate the sometimes negative attitude towards private development, local governments have become one of the major boosters of community-based development. While the tension between what the city wants the private sector to do and what community-based organizations want to do (or influence) is not settled, and the details about how to best accomplish this role are not standard, a role for the community-based organizations as key players, as well as key resources, is secure.

This still leaves open the question of the advocacy role in what are increasingly development oriented organizations, and how the capacity which community-based organizations need to have is, in effect, obtained. The latter question is addressed in the section above. The former question, on who organizes and advocates, is addressed by other participants at this conference.

FINAL OBSERVATIONS

This chapter summarized information that can help us put in perspective the growth and development of CBOs, and the evolving role they play in community development. We've identified a number of areas where the organizations can be effective, discussed the stages through which they grow, and outlined the characteristics of those organizations that appear successful. We have also provided a list of questions that would allow you to evaluate organizations as they grow. What is clear from all of our experience in this area is that organizations run a high risk of failure, or aborted success, if they are left to their own devices.

Each stage (and the transition to the next) is marked by an attempt to establish legitimacy and respond to the social, political, and institutional environment. All three must respond positively to what the organization presents and, in most cases, must take some active step to allow the organization to move to the next stage.

While it is not expected that every single organization reaches the mature status, it is important that we develop mature capacity in every neighborhood. This capacity means that there will be a number of organizations around, with some more advanced, broad scaled, and development oriented than others. But the efforts to promote this capacity require us to be generously supportive of initiatives that emerge in communities, so that we have a broad range of organizations available.

Efforts such as the Partnership Institute, and other national efforts to support local community-based development, represent important contributions to this goal of supporting the emergence of community development capacity and become an important way to identify and support a strategy by which these organizations can flourish.

REFERENCES

Bratt, Rachel et al., *The Private Sector and Neighborhood Preservation*. Medford, MA: Tufts University, 1983.

Clay, Philip. *Neighborhood Partnerships in Action*. Washington, DC: Neighborhood Reinvestment Corporation, 1981.

Committee for Economic Development. *Public–Private Partnership in American Cities: Seven Case Studies* New York, 1982.

Department of Housing and Urban Development. *The President's National Urban Policy Report*. Washington, DC, 1984.

Levitan, Sar A. *Progress to Aid the Poor* Baltimore: Johns Hopkins, 1985.

Mayer, Neil. *Neighborhood Organizations and Community Development: Making Revitalization Work*. Washington, DC: The Urban Institute, 1984.

Mayer, Neil and Jennifer Blake. *Keys to the Growth of Neighborhood Development Organizations*. Washington, DC: The Urban Institute, 1980.

National Commission on Neighborhoods. *People Building Neighborhoods: Final Report*. Washington, DC: U.S. Government Printing Office, 1979a.

National Commission on Neighborhoods. *Neighborhood Case Studies*. Washington, DC: U.S. Government Printing Office, 1979b.

Nenno, Mary and Cecil Sears. "Rental Housing; Outlook for the Low Income." in *Journal of Housing* (September–October, 1985), 174–76.

Struyk, et al., *Federal Housing Policy at President Reagan's Midterm*. Washington, DC: The Urban Institute, 1983.

9 Philanthropy, Community Development Organizations, and Economic Development

Raphael Thelwell and Jerome Smith

PROBLEMS FACING LOW-INCOME COMMUNITY ECONOMIC DEVELOPMENT

Increasing Poverty Concentrated in Ghettos

The official definition of poverty, used in Figure 9.1, reflects the successes and failures in the fight against poverty.[1] The striking success in cutting the rate of poverty in half between 1959 and 1973 is apparent, as is the failure to make significant progress since then.[2] It is understandable that poverty might increase following the deep recession of 1982. However, it is disappointing that the longest economic expansion since World War II, which followed the 1982 recession, failed to improve on the previous low poverty rate of 1973. Economic development discussed in this chapter is targeted to the 31.5 million people that were in poverty in 1989, a population that has grown by 37 percent since 1973.

The prospect for economic development in low-income communities

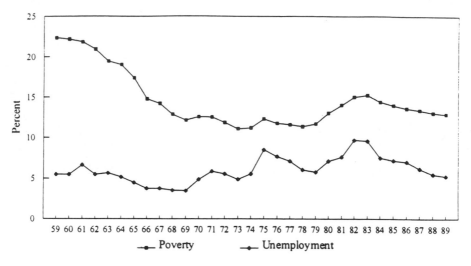

Figure 9.1. Poverty and Unemployment Rates (Census, Consumer Income, P-60, No. 168)

is not bright. Poverty will undoubtedly increase during the recession, and our ability to help decreases as receipts of the federal, state, and local governments decline in response to a failing economy.

This growing poverty population is concentrated in low-income communities as a result of segregation by income, race, and national origin. For example, in 1989, 40 percent of the white poverty population lived in poverty areas in central cities. The percent of the black and Hispanic poverty populations living in central cities' poverty areas was 70.9 and 61.8 percent respectively.[3] These low-income ghettos suffer from under investment in health, education, and training and are experiencing increased welfare dependency, crime, and more female-headed households. These social dysfunctions tend to perpetuate themselves by inhibiting the potential of children. They greatly increase the prospect of adult poverty and of being trapped in a similar ghetto. This environment sometimes nurtures a fatalism, spawned of helplessness, which focuses on day-to-day survival, destroying the motivation necessary to change conditions—motivation for change, the genesis of economic development.

Negative Feedback

There are strong feedbacks which exacerbate and perpetuate the poverty of low-income community residents. For example, ghetto conditions reinforce the propensity for the majority population to correlate the characteristics of social dysfunction of poverty communities with race and national origin, thereby encouraging discrimination in hiring which institutionalizes continuing segregation in low-income minority ghettos.

Local Expansion in Opposition to National Policies to Restrict Growth

A review of the Economic Report of the President during the 1980s documents the use of tight monetary policy to successfully slow economic growth to avoid inflation on several occasions. As a result, community economic development must occur in an environment in which experienced workers are being fired and previously successful businesses fail. The slow economic growth and recessions of the 1970s and 1980s are particularly hard on fledgling attempts at community economic development. The same factors that make starting small businesses so hazardous also exact their toll on community efforts at economic development. While statistics are not available, the impression is that the failure rate of Community Development Organizations (CDOs) are below that of small businesses.

Structural Changes in the Economy

The changing structure of the economy, as a result of an expanding service sector with low paying, low value added jobs, makes economic development more difficult. The trend toward lower wages has been exacerbated by low productivity and the increasing ability of multinational firms to increase profits by shifting economic activity to low cost areas, restricting upward mobility and making entry to the labor force more difficult. In addition, areas with low-income communities, i.e., central cities, are losing jobs at a faster rate than they are gaining them. Finally, the effect of national, state, and local taxes has shifted the tax burden to people with lower incomes. The combination of these changes has shifted the income distribution so that the percent of the total income received by the poorest 20 percent of households was 13.6 billion dollars less in 1989 than they would have received if they had been able to maintain their 1973 share of income. The richest 20 percent of households had an extra $109.1 billion in 1989 income over their 1973 share, with $95.5 billion coming from the reduced share of the middle 60 percent of households.[4]

Reduced Federal, State and Local Assistance

The inequality is even greater when adjustments are made for the changes in noncash benefits in health, employment, and other low-income discretionary programs. In fiscal year 1990, Budget Authority for these programs was $45.8 billion, or 52 percent, lower than the inflation adjusted 1981 level.[5] The tax revenue of federal, state, and local governments, major supporters of community economic development, is closely related to income which declines in a recession. When government revenue falls, discretionary expenditures for the disadvantaged are cut—just when the need is the greatest.

This chapter outlines the problem of economic development in low-income communities as promoting economic well-being in high risk communities, with a large if not growing poverty population, that are receiving less governmental help. The remaining portion of this chapter explores how the effectiveness of self-help community groups, CDOs, can be improved to serve as an engine of economic development.

CDOs RESPOND TO THE NEEDS
OF LOW-INCOME COMMUNITIES

CDOs represent a growing nationwide movement that is rooted in the American tradition of people organizing to improve their social and economic well-being. They are community centered, nonprofit organizations that now account for a significant portion of current efforts to meet the needs of low-income communities. CDOs began with the civil rights and anti-poverty movements of the 1960s. The objectives of the 1960s, embracing broad approaches to address the many needs of the poor, have been replaced by more limited, quantifiable objectives.[6] In addition, confrontational processes have been replaced by cooperative efforts[7] (Vidal, p. III-6). These 1960s organizations were few, perhaps no more than 100.[8] Subsequent growth of CDOs fits no simple pattern since it arose from many sources; i.e., groups fighting redlining, urban renewal and highway development that divided neighborhoods, factory closings, the fight for women's rights, food distribution, health and drug counseling, enhancing culture and the arts, etc. The first census of CDOs, published in *Against All Odds* (hereafter referred to as the Census), estimated that in 1988 there were between 1,500 and 2,000 organizations with a primary commitment to the production of housing and/or economic development.[9]

In addition to the Census, the *Community Economic Development Assessment* by Vidal was used to estimate the measurable economic development outputs of CDOs in 1988. Between 38,490 and 51,320 housing units per year were produced by all CDOs. The average rate of production was 25.7 units per year, by each CDO. Approximately 4,780 square feet of commercial/industrial construction was the average output per CDO, which would provide between 7.2 and 9.6 million square feet per year for all CDOs. The provision of venture capial for business enterprises was quite small per CDO: only $9,200. In 1988, between $13.8 and $18.4 million in venture capital was provided.

FACTORS INFLUENCING THE OUTPUT OF CDOs

Non-Profit, Self-Help Organizations with Community-Building Objectives

The objectives of CDOs are in sharp contrast to the profit maximizing objectives of for profit organizations—the alternative means of providing public or subsidized services to disadvantaged communities.[10] Data on the relative costs of nonprofit and for profit delivery systems is not available to evaluate at this time.[11] At a minimum, the "bribe" necessary to entice for profits to provide goods and services in low-income communities is saved. Neil Mayer makes this case as follows:

Created and controlled by community people themselves, [CDOs] need not be "bribed" or cajoled into choosing troubled neighborhoods in which to pursue their efforts. Their projects are more likely to be designed to serve current residents than to produce only physical revitalization that benefits richer households and institutions at the expense of the local inhabitants. Ideally, [CDOs] also bring special knowledge of and sensitivity to neighborhood needs to their work, by virtue of their own local origins. And, for that reason, they have a greater capacity to involve neighborhood people in revitalization activities—a key to the health of any neighborhood (Mayer, 1985, p. 3).[12]

Management by the Community

There is appreciable community representation on the staff and board of directors (Vidal 1989).[13] As a result, they have a direct understanding of problems, objectives, and opportunities and a high level of self-motivation to solve their own problems. Above all, CDOs represent a means of self-actualization and the ability to make significant changes in their lives—motivation for change and participation in change are necessary conditions for community economic development.

A Holistic Framework for Addressing the Many-Faceted Problems of the Poor

CDOs provide a framework for planning, developing, and managing the wide variety of categorical programs addressing the problems of the disadvantaged that are concentrated in these communities. This holistic community plan is increasingly important because the legislative and executive branches of government are organized along functional lines, an arrangement which forces them to address the problems of the poor as a part of their major concern for housing, energy, education, health, social services, etc. Most organizations, when faced with a cross-cutting problem of this nature, find it necessary to assign responsibility for its solution to a single person. That type of cross-cutting responsibility has evolved at the community level. CDOs frequently combine affordable housing, for example, with advice and social services that are sometimes necessary to have the tenant become a productive part of the community. However, as Shiffman and Motley point out, the categorical interests of their funding sources tend to restrict objectives to a single program requirement. In addition, holistic approaches result in greater than expected payoff from the beneficial interactions of individual programs.

Skill at Raising Resources in High Risk Situations

CDOs have exhibited flexibility and patience in developing approaches and solutions to their problems. In the process, unused and underutilized human resources in the community are tapped. This contributes to the development of future leaders (Census, pp. 3–4).[14] CDOs undertake community development that is too risky for conventional developers (for example, housing for single parent and large families) and frequently requires complex partnerships and financing arrangements—with unmeasured but high transaction costs.[15] Political skills are honed since practically every successful project requires political support.

Small Scale

CDOs were started by an individual or small group and have remained small, with median organizations having a full time staff of seven: five professionals and two assistants. The average number of professionals is ten, with nine clerical or manual supporting staff, indicating the presence of a few very large CDOs and the existence of the very large number of small groups (Vidal, Table III-2).[16] The Census reported that 44 percent of CDOs had five or fewer staff members, and 76 percent had less than 20.

The small scale of operation for CDOs is also reflected in their relatively small budgets. CDOs engaged in housing rehabilitation had a median budget of around $200,000, 32 percent had annual budgets under $100,000, and 79 percent were under $500,000. Vidal's sample of CDOs, engaged in a broader scope of economic development, had a median budget of about $700,000, with 37 percent with budgets under $500,000 and 75 percent under $2,000,000 (Vidal, Table III-2).

These small organizations, managed by a single individual or by a small group, lead to an informal management style not found in institutionalized management.[17] The Vidal survey reported that only nine out of the 130 groups in their survey had institutionalized management, and another 38 had "somewhat institutionalized" management (Vidal, p. III-6). As a result, many CDOs are very fragile, depending, as they frequently do, on a single person.

Managerial skills of the leader and staff are sometimes inadequate for the difficult task they face. Table 9.1 quantifies the opinion of observers in the Vidal survey that the principal constraint for about 60 percent of the CDOs with which they worked was insufficient resources. The second most serious constraint was inadequate organizational skill, which afflicted 20 percent of the CDOs. The articles of incorporation, which dictate a minimum organizational structure and create an immortal legal entity, do not assure the strong, self-perpetuating organizational structures needed for fiduciary responsibility and future expansion. Effective management and control is needed for that. Others have pointed out that trained people to staff CDOs are scarce, hindered by low salaries and the absence of a good career ladder. The feeder system from the Peace Corps, CETA, and VISTA has been all but eliminated in the last ten years (Peirce).

Success depends on stable leadership, with an ability to develop a clear strategy with supporting plans and the drive to complete projects

Table 9.1
Percent of CDOs for Which Constraints Are of Major Importance

Constraint	Housing Development (113)[1]	Commercial/Industrial Development (73)	Business Enterprise Development (62)
Organizational Characteristics			
Staff Development	21	18	21
Leadership and Organizational Skills	16	15	18
Local Environmental Conditions			
Community Support	5	6	5
Weak Local Economy	15	25	21
Good Projects Not Available	8	7	7
No Local Problems	0	4	3
Resources			
Insufficient Public Subsidies	64	51	54
Insufficient Overhead Support	60	56	40
Reluctant Commercial Lender	37	39	48
Insufficient Local Govt Support	27	16	11
Source: Vidal, Table V-5 [1] ( ) is sample size			

and deliver on their commitments. Management skills in general and those required for project selection strategies, planning, and control of projects are teachable (Vidal, p. III-5, IV-18 and Tables V-1 and 2).[14]

With success and increasing experience, these CDOs grow large enough to handle projects with increasing efficiency. Success provides feedback, which strengthens CDOs. It elicits better financial support from enhanced visibility and reputation and improves rapport with the community—all of which strengthens the staff and organization. Constraints on success are critically influenced by environmental conditions, such as the strength of the local housing market and economy, which was discussed earlier. In addition, there is a constant struggle for overhead funding for predevelopment work and subsidies for housing.

Experience

Output as a measure of effectiveness has proven to be a function of size, experience, and clarity of objectives, as reflected in Table 9.2. For example, CDOs with more than 16 years experience constructed an average of 49 units of housing per year, which is over 50 percent greater than the average production of 32 units per year by CDOs with up to seven years of experience.

FUNDING CDOs

Allocation of Funds

Salaries are by most standards modest. Executive Directors of CDOs with median experience of seven years received a median salary of $37,000, which was 23 percent above that of the next highest paid staff member (Vidal, Table III-8).[14] Organizations that pay below the median find it difficult to obtain talented and well trained managers.

Source of Funds

The general climate for charitable giving is influenced by the rate of economic growth, the marginal tax rate, and the value of charitable deductions. Social choice since the "War on Poverty" has favored private, rather than public, organizations as the source of funds for nonprofit organizations, culminating in Bush's "thousand points of light." Public, rather than private, funding is the case in many other developed countries. Thus, it seems that the U.S. is experimenting with delivering services to the poor through voluntary contributions which are not primar-

Table 9.2
Effect of Organizational Characteristics on Annual Production per CDOs

Characteristic	Housing Units Constructed	Commercial/Industrial Sq Ft Constructed	Business Enterprise Venture Capital Invested
Size Annual Budget			
$0 - 250,000	15 (4)[1]	10,486 (5)	0 (0)
$250,001 - 750,000	27 (32)	8,339 (13)	$17,864 (3)
$750,001 - 2,000,000	25 (28)	16,406 (15)	$44,687 (2)
Over $2,000,001	39 (26)	13,450 (13)	$194,085 (4)
Importance			
Major	31 (80)	14,033 (30)	$188,029 (7)
Minor	31 (7)	13,352 (9)	$30,080 (2)
Experience			
0 - 7 years	32 (42)	9,648 (29)	$55,625 (3)
8 - 15 years	23 (43)	9,345 (17)	$21,797 (2)
Over 16 years	49 (12)	36,550 (5)	$197,324 (5)
Leadership Stability			
Stable	30 (84)	13,243 (41)	$144,186 (8)
Unstable	34 (22)	5,862 (7)	$21,797 (1)
Neither	17 (4)	12,476 (3)	$0 (0)
Strategy			
Clear	32 (47)	18,761 (20)	$145,867 (7)
Not Clear	22 (50)	7,941 (31)	$58,672 (3)
Source: Vidal, Table V-3 & 4. [1]( ) is sample size			

ily focused on the poor. It remains to be seen if this approach has reduced the accountability of the public sector and shifted the costs to the wealthy. While it is difficult to get comparative financial information of uniform quality for CDOs, Table 9.3 was prepared from a sample of 121 CDOs (Vidal p. III-10). The median budget of CDOs was $705,750 (Vidal, Table III-2).

Government: The government is a major source of funding for CDOs,

Table 9.3
Sources of CDOs' Unearned Income, by Age

Source of Income	Mean Percentage of Unearned Income	Percent of CDOs with Source Type[1]	Mean Percentage of Unearned Income — Age (in years)			Amount of Unearned Income — Age (in years)		
			0-7	8-15	16+	0-7	8-15	16+
Federal Government[2]	33	78	38	36	22	$249,424	$323,052	$583,127
Foundations	14	63	19	13	10	83,817	74,813	164,733
Local Governments	11	36	11	9	14	182,648	257,912	424,646
State Governments	9	45	6	8	12	36,368	70,368	400,856
Corporations	8	59	9	8	7	95,935	54,026	183,570
Banks	7	32	9	6	8	223,323	49,272	126,585
Passive Investments	4	42	1	3	9	3,639	16,524	98,740
Intermediaries	3	30	4	3	1	32,308	25,793	30,019
Dues, Memberships	2	25	1	2	3	4,001	5,628	63,095
Other Charities[3]	2	19	1	3	1	13,114	13,034	69,190
United Way	1	17	0	2	2	0	9,102	25,615
Other Sources	10	19	1	8	20	4,892	33,837	1,052,515

[1] Includes 116 CDOs with a median budget of $705,750 and a mean budget of $2,404,638. [2] Includes federal funds to cities, e.g., CDBG, UDAG. [3] Includes religious organizations

Source: Avis C. Vidal, Community Economic Development Assessment, Tables III-10 and 11 (revised).

with the federal government being the principal source, supplying 33 percent of the unearned income for 76 percent of the CDOs that have this type of income. Program levels reflect the public's attitudes. Those attitudes seem to be influenced by the surplus of the 1960s, which saw the inception of CDOs, by the scarcity of the 1970s, which halted any expansion and resulted in efforts to maintain their real level, and by the deficits and laissez-faire approach of the 1980s, which sanctioned neglect (Shiffman & Motley, p. 5). The United States General Accounting Office "identified 46 federal programs—administered by 9 cabinet-level departments and 7 independent agencies—that support public–private partnerships. The Department of Housing and Urban Development (HUD) administers more of these programs (19) than any other agency. Among these programs, 20 were designed to address housing purposes; 25, community development purposes, and 1, both types of purpose" (GAO, September 1989). A table of these programs identified by agency, purpose, type of support, mediating agents, target population and their special identifying characteristics, as well as their appropriations and obligations for Fiscal Year 1988, is included as an Appendix.

In 1987, an Executive Order supported the concept of CDOs, requiring all agencies to encourage individuals, families, neighborhoods, communities, and private associations "to achieve their personal, social, and economic objectives through cooperative effort." [15] This order also gave state governments more latitude in using federal money, by directing federal agencies to refrain from establishing uniform national standards and to afford states the maximum administrative discretion.

Large federal budget deficits and the success of CDOs have stimulated interest in CDOs as a vehicle for leveraging limited federal funds to combat growing economic problems and to maintain needed housing and community development programs. Jack Kemp, while Secretary of HUD, championed public–private partnerships as a way to address housing and community development problems. This approach has been enacted in The Housing and Community Development Act of 1989 to address the diminishing supply of affordable housing. This Act legislates "nationwide a cost-effective community-based housing partnership." The Community Housing Partnership section sets aside no less than 15 percent of the funds to be appropriated "for investment only in housing to be developed, sponsored, or owned by community housing development organizations" (U.S. House, 101-943, p. 38). This Act also gives nonprofits the right of first refusal on properties being disposed of by the Federal government. Preferred positions for nonprofit community organizations also appear in the Financial Institution Reform, Recovery, Enforcement Act of 1989 and the Affordable Housing Program.

Corporations: Funds from corporations account for only 8 percent of their unearned income for CDOs. The real value of corporate giving has grown from $1.3 billion in 1980 to $2.3 billion in 1987—an average growth rate of 7.5 percent a year, well above the 2.8 percent rate for GNP.

Financial Intermediaries: CDOs have benefited from a new type of financial intermediary created to provide a means for raising funds from contributors that would like to make a well managed investment in low-income economic development. These financial intermediaries have a thorough understanding of CDOs and their problems and provide a way in which contributors with very little knowledge of the activities of CDOs can feel that their funds are being used wisely and in a way that spreads the risk of funding a specific project with a particular CDO. For example, the Local Initative Support Corporation (LISC) has leveraged $300 million into $1.3 billion in 21,500 housing units and 5.5 million square feet of commercial space, for 662 CDOs.[16] The Enterprise Foundation, since its inception in 1982, has raised over $90 million which has renovated over 5,000 units of housing and has another 3,500 under development. In addition, they have found employment for 12,700 people (Peirce, pp. 25–33). These intermediaries are able to tap funding sources that might not be available otherwise.

Payroll Deductions: CDOs have not made much progress in tapping the resources represented by automatic payroll deductions. The contributions from United Way are very small: 1 percent.

Community Investment Act: The Community Investment Act of 1977 has supplied $5 billion to CDOs (Peirce p. 23).

FOUNDATION SUPPORT

Size of Contribution

After governments, private foundations are the next largest contributor, providing 14 percent of the unearned income to 63 percent of the groups (see Table 9.3). Corporations and Corporate Foundations provide 8 percent of the income to 59 percent of the CDOs. Foundations and corporate foundations together contribute 22 percent of the unearned income to CDOs. The support of both the federal government and foundations is a relatively larger share of the income of young organizations. Foundations, corporations, and corporate foundations contribute 19 percent of the unearned income to young organizations. However, 51 percent of all foundation support went to older organizations and 26 percent to the younger ones. These percentages must be viewed cautiously because of the intentional over representation of older CDOs in this sample.

The contributions of a sample of foundations to economic development are reported in *The Foundation Grants Index* annually. Unfortunately, the grants are not classified according to economic development. We used, as a proxy for economic development, the sum of grants for

business and employment, urban and rural development. The sample reported on provided some insight into the funding of CDOs from the perspective of foundations. However, as seen in Table 9.4, only $2.6 of $5.9
billion in foundation funds in 1987, about 45 percent, have been accounted for in this sample. However, a large sample (473 foundations in
1987) which includes the 100 largest foundations reliably measures the
modest portion of all grants, between 5 and 7 percent of the total, that
has been directed to economic development (see Figure 9.2). Business
and employment received the largest amount of funds, with urban and
rural development following in that order. Funding for urban development was the most variable, losing about one-half and one-third of their
share of funding in 1981 and 1985 and doubling their share in 1982 and
1984. Nevertheless, while foundation support for economic development
represented a small proportion of their total giving, that support was the
second largest source for funding for CDOs.

The share of foundation funds going to economic development is
growing. Economic development share grew at 11.5 percent, between
1980 and 1987, while the total grew at only 11.5 percent. These growth
rates are well above the 2.7 percent rate of increase in real GNP, and
the 1.4 percent increase in the poverty population highlights the growing
support of foundation funding.

A more detailed analysis of foundation funding for community-based
development over the 1983 and 1987 period also reached the conclusion
that a larger proportion of foundation money is now going to community-based development. The increase is the result of additional foundations deciding to include community development in their grants and not

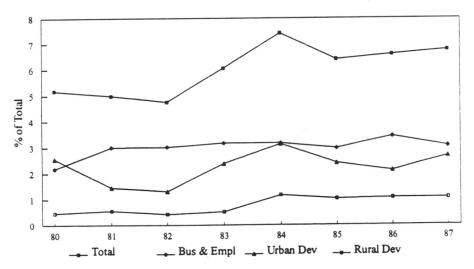

Figure 9.2. Economic Development % Total (Source: The Foundation Grants
Index)

Table 9.4
Distribution of Foundation Grants by Subject

Dates	Private Philanthropy Funds in billions[1]		Foundations in thousands[3]					Foundations Number of Grants					
	Total All Giving[2]	Foundations Total	Total Sample of Foundations	Economic Development				Total	Economic Development				
				Total	Bus&Empl	Urban	Rural		Total	Bus&Empl	Urban	Rural
80	48.7	2.8	1,190,800	61,634	25,875	30,300	5,459	21,590	1,339	810	445	84
81	55.6	3.1	1,257,056	62,694	37,486	18,157	7,051	22,322	1,121	692	340	89
82	59.8	3.2	1,490,246	70,667	44,858	19,485	6,324	27,121	1,566	1,066	388	112
83	64.7	3.6	1,792,519	108,393	56,472	42,589	9,332	32,165	2,401	1,485	767	149
84	70.6	4.0	1,646,711	122,142	51,792	51,333	19,017	34,040	2,556	1,464	848	244
85	80.3	4.9	2,013,401	128,524	59,700	48,230	20,594	36,320	2,886	1,634	958	294
86	91.9	5.4	2,216,647	145,891	75,723	46,721	23,447	40,546	3,211	1,882	1008	321
87	97.8	5.9	2,588,996	175,092	78,861	68,867	27,364	43,032	3,460	1,983	1,098	379
88	103.9	6.2	2,873,000	222,832	75,693	101,619	45,520	43,066	3,329	1,700	1,184	445

[1] Giving USA, provides the most comprehensive estimate of philanthropy funds. The principal source is the data from the Internal Revenue Service. In 1987 their records covered 24,000 foundations.

[2] Total of individuals, foundations, corporations and charitable bequests.

[3] Source: The Foundation Grants Index, 18th Edition, Tables 4 and 6. Sample of 473 foundations in 1987.

from foundations giving larger shares to CDOs. The potential for growth in this area seems to be large because only 43 of the 100 largest foundations supported community-based development in 1987. Unfortunately, CDOs are not well understood by foundations (Weinbaum and Talton, 1989).

Disproportionate Effect of Foundations

Foundations provide seed money to fund the new, innovative, and sometimes very successful programs for social change. For example, the Ford Foundation's early support helped start the movement, and it continues to be the major donor, supplying over 30 percent of all foundation grants in 1987. The Local Initiative Support Corporation (LISC) was spun off by the Ford Foundation and was still supported by a $5.5 million grant in 1987. Foundations continue to be the pacesetters, and the Lilly Endowment, in partnership with Ford Foundation, is using LISC to administer grants to 28 inner city churches, allowing them to undertake economic development projects. In general, among CDOs, progress has been greatest in those communities that have CDOs with long and continuing philanthropic support (Peirce). Foundations are a part of innovative partnerships in several cities. (Mayer, p. 13; Leigh, p. 27).

The National Committee for Responsive Philanthropy (NCRP), based on an in-depth analysis of six of the 300 "oldest and most experienced" community foundations, believes that these foundations operate "at too great a distance from their communities' most serious problems . . . and do not consider the leaders of the disadvantaged groups as partners in a common enterprise" (p. 3). The study, while not on economic development, seems relevant because it suggests a failure of these foundations to involve communities in optimizing the distribution of foundation funds.

Taxes and Philanthropy

A significant portion of all charitable giving is influenced by preferential tax treatment.[17] Charitable paternalism is legitimized by the tax code. The tax codes, unlike some federal programs, do not apply a "means test" to charities. An opera company and homeless soup kitchen are treated the same. Private and not public choice dictates the distribution of these tax expenditures. Hence, the causes of the wealthy and not necessarily the needs of the poor are the principal beneficiaries (Odendahl, 1990, p. 3). In 1989, NCRP reported that 6 of the largest community foundations, out of approximately 300, a rapidly growing segment of philanthropy, are not serving the disadvantaged very well. There are 309 community foundations, which provide $316 million in grants from

$4.78 billion in assets (p. 1). fifty-three percent of these grants were discretionary. Of the discretionary funds, 42 percent were grants to the disadvantaged. The fastest growing foundations had more nondiscretionary funds and poorer performance with the disadvantaged.

OPPORTUNITIES AND RECOMMENDATIONS

As the unique ability of CDOs to empower residents of low-income communities and to serve as a catalyst for economic development become more widely recognized, it provides an opportunity for foundations to finance activities to make CDOs more effective. The following section describes how relatively small investments can be leveraged into large social improvement.

Encourage Holistic Approaches to Problems of Low-Income Economic Development

A serious deterrent to low-income economic development is the fragmented approach imposed on CDOs by narrow planning and funding requirements of the major governmental programs providing aid to people with low-incomes. Fragmented approaches occur at the governmental level because low-income programs are planned and funded as a by-product of departments and agencies pursuing other goals. CDOs are adversely effected in several ways. First, there is evidence that the synergistic effect of managing those resources in a coordinated way is lost. For example, funding for a program aimed at specific needs, such as housing, does not permit diversion of funds to provide for a community environment that will insure the continuing value of that housing investment or for services to maintain them. Economies are possible, for example, in using subsidized labor in training programs to build housing. Frequently, the health, education, welfare, training, job opportunities, and personal safety of the residents need attention, as do their housing needs. Addressing the many causes and results of poverty, for example, in terms of the planning and funding requirements of each narrowly defined federal program is a large burden for CDOs. Foundations should continue to encourage innovative approaches that supplement housing expenditure, for example, to impact employment, education, health, etc.

Because federal programs frequently force state, local, and private activities to structure their programs along the same lines, changes at the federal level will be reflected in changes at many other levels as well. Therefore, the benefits are large if holistic planning and funding could be imposed on the federal efforts. It is recommended that foundations prepare the guidelines for a strong coordinating responsibility at the federal level to provide a holistic framework for low-income programs in general and economic development specifically.

It is also recommended that new national efforts to stimulate economic development include specific programs to address the problems of low-income communities in a holistic framework. It is possible that a Poverty Czar may be needed to reconcile the anomalies of current programs that work at cross purposes.[18]

Develop Local Institutional Arraingments to Better Support CDOs

At the local level, fund efforts create a formal partnership of government, industry, financial institutions, etc., to support the operation of CDOs. While the creation of a more stable and dependable development fund is a critical activity of such groups, improving communication and providing advice and access to other resources of the larger community is also very important. These local development partnerships become an umbrella organization to support efforts for low-income economic development and provide a vital communications and support link between the larger community and CDOs.

Increase Output by Creating More Organizations

This initiative is necessary to improve the sagging growth rate of CDOs in the 1980s and meet the expected increase in demand of the 1990s. It is necessary to tap the resources, membership base, and organizing skills of traditional organizations with long standing commitments to help low-income communities to aid in developing new CDOs. For example, recent efforts by the Lilly Endowment to interest and then help religious organizations assume a developer's role should be extended to other groups. Foundations might offer inducements to the NAACP, Urban League, universities and community colleges, and civic and professional organizations to assist in the development and support of CDOs. Establishing new CDOs is risky. Partnerships with these older organizations both reduce and spread these risks.

Provide a Sound System for Planning and Controlling Funds

Like many small activities, guidance in handling money in a way that meets the standards of prudent financial management and control is necessary if scandals are to be avoided. The growing reliance of government on CDOs can be destroyed with a few well publicized scandals concerning the misuse of public monies. Funding should be provided for accounting systems, computers, and technical assistance in their proper use by all CDOs with such a need.

Improve Funding Mechanisms

Economic development requires funding for operating, project planning, and development. CDOs have the greatest difficulty in obtaining grants for general operating expenses and expenses of preparing project plans necessary to obtain development funds. Foundations should consider funding necessary to establish operating methods for the following.

Development Fees: A self-perpetuating funding mechanism for nonprofits that rewards success is necessary; for example, providing CDOs a development fee to pay for operating expenses of these nonprofit organizations. The fee would have a reasonable maximum of, say, no more than 5 percent. This method of funding would provide discretionary funds that could be used to pay for operating overhead and predevelopment expenses. The study should examine the various procedures used by federal, state, and local governments and foundations to define recoverable costs in a way that would provide for overhead which included the forward planning necessary to attract new projects.

Wide Use of Payroll Deductions: Effective mechanisms to tap automatic payroll deductions for charitable giving should be established. CDOs do not receive a significant share of automatic payroll deductions. Studies should be funded to develop a means of more effective use of the donor option or some other means to capture for CDOs a share of this growing source of funds (Henry and Paprocki).

Multi-Year Funding: Prepare foundation strategic plans, in cooperation with the leaders of disadvantaged groups and, where possible, in conjunction with other foundations and donor groups, to focus on a multiyear approach for economic development. This recommendation complements the earlier recommendation for the development of holistic plans which will necessarily cover a longer period of time.

Innovative Financing: Encourage wider use of low-income tax credit to attract equity capital; secondary market for project loans; and new and expanded sources of savings and loan financing. There need to be studies of ways of simplifying the complex sources of financing required for development projects. In addition, there is a significant untapped source of funds that can be reached by the CDOs themselves.[19]

Change In Tax Policy: The provision of the tax law could be changed to give preference to donations to programs that are targeted to the poor.

Additional Federal Funding: Even a modest growth in federal funds could have a major impact (Mayer, p. 17). Funds and technical assistance to help present CDOs expand their development activities would be a cost-effective way to build on proven capacity. In addition, a program level of between 34 and 45 million could provide $50,000 for between 675 and 900 existing CDOs not presently acting as developers. Developing new CDOs at a rate of 3 percent a year and at a cost of $50,000 of operating expenses per year would require between 2 and 3 million dollars in the initial year and increase at a 3 percent rate in subsequent years. Any development would have to match funding made available for economic development projects.

Increase in the Annual Output of Existing Organizations

In addition to expanding the effort by increasing the economic development activities that CDOs are presently engaged in and increasing the number of CDOs, there is an opportunity to make each CDO more efficient in doing the things that it is now doing. For example, increasing the average output of CDOs from the current average of 13.86 units per year to the average of CDO developers of 25.26 units per year, an 82 percent increase, translates into between 17,000 and 22,800 additional housing units each year. A goal of this magnitude, while ambitious in its assumptions of additional resources, is modest in the possibility of tapping the capabilities of CDOs, since it assumes output rates below the 30 to 34 units a year estimated in the Vidal study.

Staff Training: The clearinghouse could also provide needed *technical assistance* by developing a resource network to handle the unusual problems that always occur. This type of effort should be institutionalized as a separate organization or as a special emphasis of Small Business Development Centers. Assistance is also needed to show CDOs the best way to take advantage of private, state, local, and federal programs. It would be possible for such a group or groups to develop *training material* and programs to facilitate the training of community people for a career in CDOs. The early involvement of institutions of higher education in developing programs, and perhaps offering degrees in community management, should be considered—with scholarships that would be doubly useful in providing opportunities for deserving low-income people, while directing current scepter expenditures to a needed area. The donation could be made to serve a third purpose if institutions with large minority populations that are now facing enrollment declines benefited from that attendance. On-the-job apprentice training with successful CDOs would provide additional resources to successful CDOs while building capacity for new CDOs. Mayer reports on the importance of experience in increasing the success rate of CDOs and the effectiveness of the donated resources that they use (p. 7).

Economies of Scale: Additional efforts should be made to develop ways in which the most capable CDO in a particular type of economic development could expand to their most efficient scale of operation by serving as subcontractor to CDOs that are less productive in those activities.[20] Fully utilizing a CDO's experience and reputation that is the result of a record of successful economic development is the simplest way to get additional funding necessary to undertake new projects and avoid the inefficiencies associated with inexperienced and understaffed CDOs. A large city may need only a few large efficient organizations with a track record that will make financing easier with specialization in housing, another in a particular type of commercial space, etc. Hence, optimizing the size of a few successful CDOs specializing in different areas of economic development should receive greater attention. The political problems of such arrangements are very large. However, if each neighborhood CDO could control the funding of its project, some compromise to achieve greater efficiencies might be possible.

Promotion of Macro Growth Policies

Provide fiscal, monetary, trade, and sectorial policies that are more conducive to economic growth and greater economic opportunities for the disadvantaged. A grassroots educational program to stress the importance of economic policies on issues of local economic development would be a first step. Public opinion would then be prepared to support policies that gave greater priority to long and short term employment issues. These policies certainly ought to be combined with countercyclical programs to promote economic growth in low-income communities that are hardest hit by unemployment.

Programs to Influence Public Policy

There is a need to fund activities to translate what is being learned by CDOs into governmental policies and programs. For example, if a more effective approach to the problems of poverty is developed through the diverse approaches being used by CDOs, that story must be spread among the CDOs and passed on to our legislators. Finally, effective anti-discrimination programs to share more equitably in the benefits of economic growth with minorities in business formation and employment need to be supported.

NOTES

We are appreciative of the suggestions provided by Avis Vidal and Renee Berger.

1. The current definition of poverty is based on money income before taxes and not on disposable income. The poverty income is adjusted for the size and

composition of the family. It is computed as three times the cost of a minimum adequate diet. That proportion reflected the distribution found in the budgets of low-income families in 1963.

2. This series uses the Census data, which began in 1959.

3. U.S. Census, Money Income and Poverty Status in the United States 1989, Series P-60, No. 168. Poverty. U.S. Bureau of the Census, Washington, DC.

4. Ibid.

5. U.S. Committee on Ways and Means, *Green Book: 1990,* pp. 1390 and 1391.

6. Shiffman and Motley (1990) argue that a holistic plan that includes social, physical, and economic aspects of neighborhoods is needed to develop opportunities for personal, group, and community growth. This integrative approach does not fit the funding agencies' categorical needs and forces the CDOs to operate and dance to the tune of projects rather than comprehensive plans.

7. Avis C. Vidal is the principal investigator of *Community Economic Development Assessment: A National Study of Urban Community Development Corporations* by the Community Development Research Center, Graduate School of Management and Urban Professionals, New School for Social Research.

8. Neal R. Peirce and Carol F. Steinbach, *Enterprising Communities: Community-Based Development in America, 1990.* The Council for Community-Based Development, 1990, p. 15.

9. Renee Berger, The National Congress for Community Economic Development and by the Community Information Exchange, *Against All Odds: The Achievements of Community-Based Organizations,* 1989.

10. There is some evidence that the costs of using the private sector to provide capital necessary for low-income housing are very expensive. Case (1990); Stegman (1990).

11. General Accounting Office, September 1989.

12. Mayer, p. 9.

13. On the average, 59% of all board members of CDOs have these strong community ties and are responsible for the direction of the group (Vidal, Table III-7).

14. Vidal, 1989, Tables III-1 and III-5.

15. Executive Order 12612, October 26, 1987.

16. Local Initiative Support Corporation, *Annual Report: 1989*

17. Skelly, 1987, p. 267).

18. U.S. Committee on Ways and Means, *Green Book.* OMB, CBO, CRS, Low-Income Housing Information Service and the Center on Budget and Policy Priorities.

19. Chapters 3 & 4, HUD evaluation of neighborhood Development Demonstrations.

20. Vidal, p. II-6.

REFERENCES

Apgar, Jr., William C., DiPasquale, Denise, Cummings, Jean, and McArdle, Nancy. *The State of the Nation's Housing, 1990*. Joint Center for Housing Studies of Harvard University, 1990.

Case, Karl E. "Investors, Developers, and Supply-Side Subsidies: How Much Is Enough?" in *Preserving Low-Income Housing Opportunities: Principles for a 1990s Housing Preservation Strategy*. Fannie Mae Annual Housing Conference, 1990.

Cook, Dick. *Study of the United Way Donor Programs*. Washington, DC: National Committee for Responsive Philanthropy, 1986.

Exploratory Project on Financing the Nonprofit Sector. *Part of the Solution: Innovative Approaches to Nonprofit Funding*. Washington, DC: Institute for Public Policy and Administration, Union for Experimenting Colleges and Universities, October 1988.

Henry, Jennifer, and Paprocki, Steven. *United Way's Donor Option Program*. National Committee for Responsive Philanthropy, February 3, 1989.

Jaynes, Gerald, and Williams Jr., Robin. *A Common Destiny: Blacks and American Society*. Washington, DC: National Academy Press, 1989.

Johnson, Robert M. *The First Charity: How Philanthropy Can Contribute to Democracy in America*. Cabin John, MD: Seven Locks Press, 1988.

Leigh, Wilhelmina A. "Black Americans and Federally Subsidized Housing." One-Third of a Nation: African American Perspectives Conference, November 1989.

Leonard, Paul A., Dolbear, Cushing, N., and Lazere, Edward B. *A Place To Call Home: The Crisis in Housing for the Poor*. Washington, DC: Center on Budget and Policy Priorities and Low Income Housing Information Services, April 1989.

Massey, Douglas S. *American Apartheid: Segregation and the Making of the Underclass*. Chicago, IL: University of Chicago and Social Demography Group, Population Research Center, June 1989.

Mayer, Neil S., and Marshall, Sue A. *Neighborhood Organizations and Community Development*. HUD Contract H-5255, January 1983.

Mayer, Neil S. *Neighborhood Organizations and Community Development: Making Revitalization Work*. Washington, DC: The Urban Institute Press, 1984.

Mayer, Neil S. "Preserving the Low-Income Housing Stock: What Nonprofits Can Do Today and Tomorrow." Papers of Fannie Mae Annual Housing Conference, 1990.

National Committee for Responsble Philanthropy. *Community Foundations: At the Margin of Change Unrealized Potential for the Disadvantaged*. Washington, DC, September 1989.

National Congress for Community Economic Development. *Against All Odds: The Achievements of Community-Based Development Organizations*. Washington, DC, March 1989.

Newman, Sandra J., and Schnare, Anne B. *Subsidizing Shelter: The Relationship Between Welfare and Housing Assistance*. Washington, DC: Urban Institute, 1989.

Newman, Sandra J. "Housing Assistance As A Route to Independence: A Case That Has Yet To Be Made." The John Hopkins University for Policy Studies, Occasional Paper No. 3, January 1990.

Odendahl, Teresa. *Charity Begins At Home: Generosity and Self-Interest Among the Philanthropic Elite*. New York: Basic Books, 1990.

Peirce, Neal R., and Steinbach, Carol F. *Enterprising Communities: Community-Based Development in America, 1990*. Washington, DC: Council for Community-Based Development.

Pratt Institute Center for Community and Environmental Development (The). *An Evaluation of the Neighborhood Development Demonstration*. Washington, DC: Office of Policy Development and Research, U.S. Department of Housing and Urban Development, July 1988.

Riesenberg, Charles E., and Line, Carolyn P. *Principles and Practices of Community Development Lending: A Five-Step Investment Model to Strengthen Bank Community Development Lending Programs*. Minneapolis, MN: Federal Reserve Bank of Minneapolis and First Bank System, 1989.

Shiffman, Ronald, and Motley, Susan. *Comprehensive and Integrative Planning for Community Development*. New York: Community Development Research Center, Graduate School of Management and Urban Policy, New School for Social Research, March 1990.

Skelly, Daniel F. "Focus on Nonprofit Charitable Organizations, 1982." Paper given at Annual Meeting of the American Statistical Association 1986–1987 in *Statistics of Income and Related Administrative Record Research: 1986–1987*. Washington, DC: Internal Revenue Service, Department of the Treasury, November, 1987.

Stegman, Michael A. "The Excessive Costs of Creative Finance: Growing Inefficiencies in the Production of Low-Income Housing," in *Preserving Low-Income Housing Opportunities: Principles for a 1990s Housing Preservation Strategy*. Fannie Mae Annual Housing Conference, 1990.

Sternlieb, George, and Hughes, James. "Private Market Provision of Low-Income Housing: Historical Perspective and Future Prospects," in *Preserving Low-Income Housing Opportunities: Principles for a 1990s Housing Preservation Strategy*. Fannie Mae Annual Housing Conference, 1990.

Struyk, Raymond. "Preservation Policies in Perspective." in *Preserving Low-Income Housing Opportunities: Principles for a 1990s Housing Preservation Strategy*. Fannie Mae Annual Housing Conference, 1990.

Underhill, Jack. *A Summary of the Literature on the Extent and Causes of Poverty and the Effectiveness of Efforts to Overcome Poverty*. George Mason University, School of Public Affairs, May 7, 1990.

U.S. Committee on Ways and Means, U.S. House of Representatives. *Overview of Entitlement Programs: 1990 Green Book*. June 5, 1990.

U.S. General Accounting Office. *Partnership Projects: Federal Support for Public-Private Housing and Development Efforts*. September 1989.

U.S. General Accounting Office. *Rental Housing: Observations on the Low-Income Housing Tax Credit Program*. August 1990.

U.S. General Accounting Office. *Partnership Projects: A Framework for Evaluating Public-Private Housing and Development Efforts*. May 1990.

U.S. House of Representatives. *Cranston-Gonzalez National Affordable Housing Act: Conference Report to Accompany S. 566*. Report 101-943, October 25, 1990.

Vidal, Avis C. *Community Economic Development Assessment: A National Study of Urban Community Development Corporations—Preliminary Findings*. New York: Community Development Research Center, Graduate School of Management and Urban Professions, New School for Social Research, July 5, 1989.

Vidal, Avis C., Howitt, Arnold M., and Foster, Kathleen P. *Stimulating Community Development: An Assesment of the Local Initiatives Support Corporation*. Cambridge, MA: The State, Local, and Intergovernmental Center, John F. Kennedy School of Government, Harvard University, June 1986, p. IV-10.

Weinbaum, Eve S., and Ray, Talton F. *Expanding Horizons: Foundation Grant Support of Community-Based Development*. Council for Community-Based Development, April 1989.

10 Lessons from LISC for Corporate Philanthropy

Avis C. Vidal and Arnold M. Howitt

INTRODUCTION

Corporate philanthropic contributions and related investments have become an increasingly important source of support for community revitalization efforts since 1980. During that period, the community development movement expanded rapidly; the number of locally rooted community development organizations (CDOs) increased to approximately 2,000, and their ability to make a difference in their communities has been increasingly acknowledged.[1] This growth has been supported by the private sector and has, in turn, provided corporate philanthropy with an array of opportunities to invest in communities.

Recent growth in corporate grants to support the work of CDOs illustrate this trend. In 1987, 53 corporations provided $8 million for community-based development. In 1991, only four years later, 282 corporations provided $23 million—a 187 percent increase in the amount granted and a more than four-fold increase in the number of donors. Ten of the top

50 funders of community-based development in the country were corporations (33 were independent foundations and seven were community foundations).[2]

Corporate philanthropic support for community development follows two channels. Some funds flow directly from corporations to individual organizations and projects. Others flow through financial intermediaries that identify and support community development activities. The number of corporate grants made directly to community-based organizations outnumbered grants to intermediaries 1906 to 1199, but local and national intermediaries received about 70 percent of the funds awarded.[3]

Although increased corporate support for community development has not been limited to the intermediaries, their role has been central. The best known of these intermediaries, Local Initiatives Support Corporation (LISC), the Enterprise Foundation, and Neighborhood Investment Corporation, are national in scope. Their activities are complemented by the work of local public–private partnerships, most notably the more than 60 local housing partnerships active in cities across the country.

Active since 1980, LISC is the largest of the nonprofit intermediaries supporting community-based development. Begun with $9.35 million provided by 6 corporations and the Ford Foundation, total commitments to LISC from 1100 corporations, foundations, government agencies, and individuals had reached approximately $880 million by 1992.[4] Its experience provides important insight into the elements of successful corporate sponsorship of community development. This essay, based on an in-depth evaluation of LISC's activities through the mid-1980s, underscores these key lessons.

THE EVALUATION OF LISC

From 1983 to 1986, a research team from Harvard University's John F. Kennedy School of Government evaluated LISC on behalf of its board of directors. The evaluation's purpose was to describe LISC's methods, evaluate their effectiveness, and draw lessons for LISC and others.[5]

The heart of the evaluation was extensive field investigation in seven LISC Areas of Concentration: Boston, California, Chicago, Cleveland, Indianapolis, Philadelphia, and the South Bronx. The study focused on 34 individual community organizations, 72 of their LISC assisted projects, and 113 separate LISC program actions. The research team interviewed more than 325 individuals, including:

- staff and board members of the community-based organizations
- members of each Area's Local Advisory Committee

- people active in each Area's "community development community"
- LISC program officers, national staff, and members of its board of directors.

THE LISC MODEL

LISC is a national nonprofit lending and grantmaking institution. It was founded in 1980 to marshal private financial and technical resources to help revitalize deteriorated communities.

LISC invests these resources in various projects—including housing rehabilitation and new construction, and commercial and industrial revitalization—undertaken by nonprofit community development organizations. Through such investments, LISC seeks to help CDOs improve local physical and economic conditions, while also increasing their own financial strength and strengthening their management and financial capabilities. LISC packages its support so that local banks and other private and public sector funding sources invest in each project, ensuring that its own funds amount to a small portion of total project costs.

LISC operates through a national office in New York City and a nationwide network of 31 local Areas of Concentration (each covering a metropolitan area or larger territory). In each Area of Concentration, a local LISC raises its money from local corporations and foundations. These resources are matched by funds from LISC's national capital fund.

LISC is neither a traditional bank nor a traditional philanthropy. Three alternative "images" of LISC illustrate different aspects of LISC's approach.

As a *social banker,* LISC worries about the social returns on its investments, not only the economic returns. It is eager for the assisted organization and the public to receive these returns, not just itself. And it cares about the social risks of a project, as well as about the financial risk.

Viewed alternatively as a *hard-nosed philanthropist,* LISC insists that projects be financially sound and produce economic returns, not just produce social effects. LISC hopes to get some of this return for itself, not to have it all accrue to the CDO, so that LISC can recycle funds to other groups.

LISC can also be viewed as a *social experiment,* both testing a "technology" to promote economic and social change by using CDOs as its instruments and encouraging a partnership between business and philanthropies on one hand, and community organizations on the other.

LISC's community revitalization work is guided by an underlying theory which consists of four major hypotheses:

1. LISC can identify sizable numbers of community organizations with the capacity to do neighborhood development projects and can help them complete these projects successfully.

2. The assisted projects and their sponsoring organizations will generate improvements in the quality of neighborhood life.

3. These projects will strengthen the community development organizations that implement them by giving them new skills, improving their financial circumstances, and increasing their access to sources of capital.

4. Demonstration of the success of this development approach will increase the supply of social capital available (including capital from corporations and corporate philanthropies) to support the neighborhood revitalization efforts of CDOs.

Evaluating LISC's activities around these four hypotheses, this essay organizes the effects of LISC's work, and its lessons for corporate philanthropy, into four corresponding categories:

1. project effects;
2. neighborhood effects;
3. organization effects; and
4. community development community effects.

PROJECT EFFECTS

When LISC began, the most visible and controversial part of its social experiment was demonstrating the effectiveness of a new "technology" for neighborhood development. This hinged on enhancing the ability of CDOs to:

- devise and carry out activities that promote the development of their neighborhoods
- arrange appropriate financial support for their activities
- meet project related financial obligations in a timely and businesslike fashion

LISC has been highly successful in developing this new technology. At the conclusion of the evaluation field work, LISC had committed $7,198,194 to the 34 CDOs included in the study. Returns on these investments included extensive physical improvements in low-income neighborhoods, including:

- construction of 379 new housing units
- rehabilitation of an additional 808 dwellings
- construction or rehabilitation of 350,000 square feet of commercial and industrial space

LISC had also supported 18 ventures (both for-profit and nonprofit), most of which were newly established; 11 of these had become self-supporting. Remaining project activities varied widely, including support for management development, real estate projects being planned or constructed (including 238 units of new housing), and neighborhood improvement projects such as arson and crime prevention programs.

LISC assisted projects are typically small—only 3 of the 19 housing developments cost more than $3 million, for example—but are not simple. They often involve technically complicated activities, and the financial arrangements are often complex.

The evaluation looked at 66 projects. It assessed:

- whether the project was completed as planned
- whether the CDO received its expected financial benefits
- whether LISC received its expected financial return

In 79 percent of these cases, funded CDOs produced the outcome expected (a "success") or something reasonably close (a "qualified success"). Seventy percent of the projects produced at least some financial return for the CDO, and 50 percent produced about the return expected. LISC, moreover, was regaining its funds as anticipated from 81 percent of projects on which it expected a return.

Likelihood of success varied according to two major factors:

1. the nature of the market for each project; and
2. the sponsoring group's previous experience with similar projects.

Markets for LISC assisted projects are of three types: those created to meet an assured demand, those created to meet a speculative demand, and those that are not marketed.

A significant portion of LISC aid goes to activities designed to meet an *assured demand*. They include:

- development of low-income housing, which is always in demand because it is subsidized
- pre-leased commercial developments
- new ventures with a captive market, such as a housing management company established by a CDO which owns enough housing to keep the management company operating in the black

These projects accounted for slightly less than half of the financial commitment LISC made to CDOs in the evaluation.

Other projects involve a *speculative demand*—that is, they entail production of a good or service for which demand is uncertain and must be cultivated. Among these projects are new ventures, both for-profit and nonprofit, and speculative real estate. These projects accounted for slightly less than half of the financial commitment LISC made to projects included in the evaluation.

Some LISC projects produce a socially valued product that is *not marketed*. Examples include:

- a service like arson or crime prevention for which the sponsoring group is not compensated
- a direct effort to strengthen management capacity of the assisted group, such as an improved financial management system

These projects accounted for about 5 percent of LISC dollar commitments in the evaluation.

Likelihood of project success varies substantially across these market types. Of projects in the evaluation, 86 percent of the assured demand projects were successful and 14 percent were qualified successes.

In contrast, only 45 percent of speculative demand projects were successes, while 23 percent were qualified successes. All projects in which the expected outcome failed to be achieved involved speculative demand.

Assessment of financial returns to sponsoring CDOs also revealed substantial differences by project type. Three–quarters of assured demand projects, but only one–quarter of speculative demand projects, produced financial returns roughly as expected. Half of the speculative demand projects failed to meet their financial objectives at all.

The sponsoring CDO's prior experience with similar projects also affected the probability of project success. For assured demand projects, where the group had worked on relatively similar projects before, 93 percent were successful, and the remainder were qualified successes.

For projects that moved groups into new activities, the success rate was only 67 percent. Financial success followed a similar pattern. Four-fifths of the assured demand projects, where a group had experience, produced the expected financial returns. But only 60 percent of the projects that required new activities produced expected returns.

Prior experience had an even more dramatic effect on speculative demand projects. Groups working on speculative demand projects, that were relatively similar to their previous ones, were successful 78 percent of the time. In contrast, only one-third of those involving new activities were successfully completed. Financial returns were also disappointing. Only 20 percent of speculative new activity projects produced expected returns, and almost 60 percent were not financially successful at all.

The inherent riskiness of speculative projects and new kinds of work does not imply that LISC and other supporters of community development should avoid assisting projects of this kind. Moving CDOs into new and more ambitious community development activities is an integral part of LISC's mission and essential to the task of revitalizing communities. But understanding the sources of project risk can help LISC identify projects that may need special financial or technical support. It can also help LISC structure a portfolio of investments that carries the level of risk it desires.

In addition to assessing project outcomes, the evaluation sought to identify how critical LISC's role was in achieving these results. To do this, the evaluation specified on a project-by-project basis both the outcome and the most likely outcome if LISC had not been involved. The difference between this "alternative future" and the actual outcome was regarded as LISC's net impact on a project (characterized as large, medium, or small).

Measured this way, LISC's impact on projects varied noticeably by project type (but did not vary by project size). One-third of LISC's funds went to assured demand projects in which LISC had a large role in making the project happen. Projects in which LISC's role was small or medium each received comparable levels of financial support.

In contrast, LISC's financial resources were more likely to support speculative projects in which LISC's impact was large. LISC had a large impact on about half of the speculative demand projects in which it participated, and these projects received 45 percent of the dollars committed to projects of this type.

These findings indicate that LISC, like other investors in community development, faces a tradeoff. Assured demand projects are much more likely than speculative demand projects to be completed successfully and to produce the financial returns anticipated by their sponsors. But the share of the result in assured demand projects that can be attributed to LISC is lower than in speculative demand projects. That is because the lower level of risk in the former projects helps to attract funding from other sources.

In contrast, speculative demand projects are riskier. Therefore, CDOs have a harder time pulling together necessary resources. Consequently, LISC's ability to make a big difference is comparatively higher.

These riskier projects present both opportunities and challenges for corporate philanthropic managers, especially those who seek to promote economic development (which is commonly more difficult for CDOs than housing since it is more likely to involve speculative markets and to move them outside their previous range of experience). Working with a skilled intermediary, in collaboration with others, allows philanthropies to invest in projects that carry different levels of risk and thus to make a difference in riskier circumstances.

It is important to note that LISC's support for projects is not purely financial. LISC program officers provide CDOs with a variety of less tangible forms of assistance. Alternative sources of this kind of support and technical assistance are increasing in number but are still in short supply in many locations. The technical expertise of LISC and other intermediaries contributes to their attractiveness as vehicles for corporate philanthropic support in this field. At the same time, the clear need for a stronger network of locally available technical support for CDOs provides a potentially attractive funding opportunity for corporate philanthropy.

NEIGHBORHOOD EFFECTS

LISC hopes to affect the neighborhoods in which it works beyond the impact of any one project; broad neighborhood improvement is a central objective of community development. But such "neighborhood effects" are one of the most difficult of LISC's contributions (or the contributions of individual CDOs) to observe.

First, neighborhood effects take time to develop, but LISC is still relatively young, and the evaluation spanned a short time period. Second, neighborhood change is difficult to measure, at best. Capturing changes in intangibles, such as residents' energy and hopefulness and willingness to invest in themselves and their neighborhoods, was beyond the scope of the evaluation.

Finally, revitalization in distressed neighborhoods will necessarily be the product of many forces, not LISC alone. So improvement in these neighborhoods cannot be clearly attributed to any single actor.

For these reasons, the evaluation did not include a systematic analysis of neighborhood change in the target areas of the 34 CDOs studied. The evaluation did, however, develop an analytic framework for evaluating neighborhood effects and carried out prototypical analyses in two areas of the South Bronx served by LISC assisted CDOs.

Because neighborhood impacts are hard to observe, the two examples were selected precisely because the evaluators believed real improvement had occurred. These analyses illustrate that LISC assisted activities clearly have the potential to improve distressed neighborhoods.

They also suggest that advantages may be derived from geographically concentrated redevelopment. Although these analyses cannot be taken as evidence that improvements of this scale result from the typical LISC investment, they do indicate the kinds of change that might reasonably result from LISC's activity at its best.

Overall, the search for LISC's effects on the quality of neighborhood life should be undertaken with realistic expectations. The neighborhoods in which LISC works face an imposing array of social and economic problems. LISC can make a solid contribution to the process of change, but the work of many others—public, private, and nonprofit—will also be necessary.

ORGANIZATION EFFECTS

LISC has made a commitment to build strong, viable community development organizations in low-income neighborhoods, as well as to help improve physical and economic conditions. LISC therefore promotes the organizational development of the CDOs it assists both indirectly (helping a CDO "stretch" by undertaking and completing ambitious projects) and directly (with financial assistance and strategic advice, technical assistance, networking, and credibility enhancement).

The 34 CDOs in the evaluation sample varied in organizational capacity prior to their involvement with LISC. None would be regarded as substantial in size even in the world of small business. Only two had 30 or more paid staff members, and 40 percent had three or fewer.

The typical group had $200,000–$300,000 of revenue annually. Only four had assets over $1 million. Most had moderately strong relationships in their local communities, and some ties with government, but far fewer had relationships with the private sector.

Participation in LISC assisted projects enabled many CDOs to make solid improvements in their internal organizational capacity. Almost 70 percent were able to undertake activities that departed significantly from their previous operations.

Most of the rest were able to increase the scale or complexity of an existing line of activity. About 80 percent of the groups gained new or enhanced staff skills while working on LISC assisted projects. More than half of the CDOs, notably the smaller ones, increased staff size as a consequence of LISC aided projects.

Information about group finances is spotty and sometimes qualitative. However, it appears that about 70 percent of the 27 groups for which data was available increased their financial scale, generally by a modest amount; about 15 percent declined in scale.

Information on assets was particularly unsatisfactory, but it appears that about half the groups secured an equity interest in real property or other assets as a result of participation in LISC-aided projects. In some cases these assets are valuable, but in many others the asset is illiquid and of uncertain market value. Significantly, in only three cases did the evaluation find evidence that a CDO had suffered financial harm from participation in a LISC aided project.

LISC supported projects helped CDOs improve their ties with potential collaborators. Most groups established broader or closer relationships with their neighborhoods. The fundamental character of government relationships remained unchanged, but many groups created and maintained good working relationships with government agencies in carrying out projects. Two-thirds of the groups established relationships with at least one new funding source: private, philanthropic, or public.

More than half the sample established new financial relationships with a private sector source, although these were generally of modest character.

LISC's assistance has generally benefited the organizational development of the groups. In a minority of cases, groups are substantially stronger as a result. In the vast majority of the remaining cases, the groups are noticeably stronger but not dramatically so.

Taken as a whole, the impact of LISC's organizational development efforts seems modest. Assisted CDOs typically remain relatively small and fragile, vulnerable to the departure of key staff or leadership transitions. Reliable financial support for overhead remains a pressing problem for most. Corporate philanthropy could be extremely helpful in this regard.

EFFECTS ON THE COMMUNITY DEVELOPMENT COMMUNITY

LISC attaches great importance to the goal of increasing overall support for CDOs from the "community development community." This includes the network of public and private institutions in each Area of Concentration that are or could be involved in neighborhood revitalization.

LISC has sought to influence this network by:

1. altering the pattern of corporate and philanthropic giving so that the pool of resources available to community development organizations is increased;
2. improving the lines of communication between the corporations and foundations;
3. drawing the public sector formally or informally into the partnership;
4. increasing contacts between community groups and private sector funding sources; and
5. promoting institutional change in the community development community.

In each Area of Concentration, LISC's effectiveness has been shaped by the pre-existing local setting. It varies particularly by:

- the prior degree of private sector concern with neighborhood revitalization
- the number and sophistication of existing community development organizations
- the extent to which government provides both technical and financial support for CDOs

In 6 of the 7 evaluation sites, LISC raised more than $1 million—much of it money that would not have otherwise gone to support the work of CDOs or neighborhood development. LISC proved to be an attractive vehicle for corporate social investment.

In the seven sites, 98 corporations contributed to LISC. Forty-four percent gave again in second round fundraising. For many foundations, which generally had more experience than the corporations in supporting community organizations, LISC proved a cost-effective way to enter a complex new field, housing and economic development, in which they had little in-house expertise. Working through an experienced intermediary provides the same potential benefit for corporate philanthropies, particularly those of modest size.

Despite concern by a number of CDOs, the evaluation found no evidence that money previously committed to community organizations was being shifted to LISC. It did not appear that LISC's fundraising made it more difficult for CDOs to raise money from traditional sources. However, some of these sources seemed to be moving independently toward providing support for projects rather than general operating funds.

LISC expanded substantially the amount of corporate and philanthropic money available in these seven Areas of Concentration to support CDOs and neighborhood development. But the evaluation found no evidence that the overall supply of funds committed to social purposes was expanded equally.

LISC's local operations appear effectively to promote better linkages among members of the community development community. At most sites, participation in LISC's Local Advisory Committee had brought the corporate sector and foundations together to work on projects—often for the first time. Many LISC projects also involved government agencies, though LISC was not always responsible for bringing these participants into projects.

LISC has also had an important effect on community development by supporting innovative institutional changes such as:

- legal reforms in Boston and Cleveland to facilitate community developers' access to abandoned property
- new vehicles for the provision of technical assistance to CDOs in Boston, Philadelphia, and Chicago
- financing for a new pooling arrangement for neighborhood housing rehabilitation in Cleveland

LISC worked to create citywide institutional initiatives to support the ongoing work of CDOs: the Chicago Housing Partnership and the Boston Housing Partnership.

The Chicago Housing Partnership is a citywide development and financing organization that works through CDOs. It includes the Chicago Equity Fund, which pools corporate funds to give CDOs equity in projects that they sponsor.[6] LISC also took the lead in founding the closely related Community Equity Assistance Corporation, which provided technical assistance to CDOs engaged in housing development.

The Boston Housing Partnership was established in 1983, with LISC's support, as a citywide development and financing organization to rehabilitate housing through CDOs. It has an active board of top corporate executives, public officials, and CDO directors.

CONCLUSIONS AND STRATEGIC IMPLICATIONS

LISC's community revitalization work is guided by an underlying theory. This theory is the structure of LISC's "social experiment" and has four major elements.

1. LISC can identify sizeable numbers of community based groups with the capacity to do neighborhood development projects and can help them successfully complete such projects.
2. These projects and their sponsoring organizations will generate improvements in the quality of neighborhood life.
3. The assisted projects will strengthen the community development organizations that execute them by giving them new skills, improving their financial circumstances, and increasing their ties to sources of capital.
4. Demonstration of the success of this development approach will increase the supply of social capital available to support the neighborhood revitalization activities of community development organizations.

LISC's experience provides considerable evidence that these propositions form the basis for successful social investment to strengthen poor communities. It also demonstrates practical strategies that corporate philanthropy can use—working either directly with CDOs or in concert with LISC or other intermediaries—to provide effective support for community-based neighborhood revitalization.

NOTES

1. National Congress for Community Economic Development, *Changing the Odds: The Achievements of Community-Based Development Corporations* (Washington, D.C.: December 1991).

2. Council for Community-Based Development, *Expanding Horizons III: A Research Report on Corporate and Foundation Grant Support of Community-Based Development* (Washington, D.C.: Spring 1993).

3. Ibid.

4. Local Initiatives Support Corporation, *From Within Our Cities: 1992 LISC Annual Report*.

5. Complete results of the evaluation are contained in Avis C. Vidal, Arnold M. Howitt, and Kathleen P. Foster, *Stimulating Community Development: An*

Assessment of the Local Initiatives Support Corporation (Cambridge, MA: Taubman Center for State and Local Government, John F. Kennedy School of Government, Harvard University, 1986).

6. The concept piloted in the Chicago Equity Fund was subsequently expanded through the formation of the National Equity Fund, the vehicle through which LISC raises equity for CDO sponsored housing developments using the Low Income Housing Tax Credit. Tax credit investments are now a major source of nonphilanthropic corporate support for community development.

Part III
Philanthropy and African-American Development Innovations

11 National Neighborhood and Housing Development Models

Lance C. Buhl

According to the Census Bureau, in 1991, 35.7 million Americans, more than 40 percent children (14.3 million), lived below the poverty line, trying to support a family of four on $13,500 per year. Safety net supports, food stamps and the like, added $1,000.

Most folks trapped in poverty, against great odds, have turned to peculiarly American devices for social renewal—self-help and the nonprofit option. Through nonprofit CDCs (community development corporations), low- and moderate-income people work to rebuild the physical, economic, and social health of their neighborhoods.

Extensive and accurate research on this has been reported by the National Congress for Community Economic Development. NCCED's study, *Changing the Odds,* catalogues impressive productivity. Conservatively, NCCED estimates 2,000 (some say 4,000) community-based organizations. Seventy-five percent of them produce housing, 320,000 total units. The rate of production has accelerated, and 87,000 of these were completed in 1988–1991. Nonprofits, since 1982, produced more low-income housing units than for profits or government. They also offer credit counseling, weatherizing, and other home improvements.

CDCs are also players in other forms of economic development. One-quarter of the 1,160 organizations responding to NCCED's 1991 survey report that they develop commercial and industrial real estate—producing 17 million square feet of space. Other CDCs fill capital gaps, brokering with mainstream financial institutions or making small to medium sized loans and equity investments (most less than $100,000) directly for small business development.

NCCED estimates that CDCs created or retained 90,000 permanent jobs since 1986. Economically, CDCs fill the role previously played by forprofits—developers, builders, housing and commercial real estate managers, banks.

Each CDC is different, fashioned by trial and error to respond to unique landscapes of disinvestment and civic culture. There is no one model. Every neighborhood must invent its own. But there are five necessary core activities—requisite skills—that CDCs must employ to stabilize and restore neighborhood health. Not every organization must demonstrate maturity in all five to deserve support. But, each must demonstrate interest and ability to develop across all five over some reasonable time to merit continuing support. The five operate as a reinforcing set of activities, not necessarily different stages of growth. "Model" CDCs exhibit working maturity in all five areas. The assessment questions are:

1. Is the CDC adept at organizing? Each CDC must create a covenant with people in its neighborhood and must periodically affirm, even modify it. This is problem identification, agenda setting, leadership development, community celebrating, connecting people, place, institutions, and values. It is analogous to organizational development in corporate life, with an equally important link to effectiveness, but usually with a more democratic flavor. Who's out there? What do they think? Are they with the program, neutral, or against it? What are their problems? What assets can they add? Who has leadership potential? How to get them involved?

Foundations tend to neglect this aspect of CDC life, and consciously underfunded it, more out of fear than out of enlightened self-interest. But where organizing neighbors, around block clubs, churches or settlement houses, is neglected, developmental investments tend to do poorly. They were not bad investments to begin with, but they were not managed by alert, organized neighbors.

2. Is the CDC skilled at advocacy? Once the neighborhood's developmental agenda is set, a CDC must be able to articulate and translate the neighborhood's voice. Sometimes this involves confrontation, more often with public officials than with private leaders, sometimes with both. Usually that struggle is to get a place at the resource table. Once there, the premium is on negotiating on behalf of neighborhood needs. At bottom, advocacy relates to values, and clearly stating and articulating needs for justice.

Interestingly, advocacy, the ability to become part of the political decision making system, is increasingly recognized by CDCs as essential to effectiveness. Often, CDCs band together to establish a political presence. In Ohio, for example, CDCs formed the Ohio CDC Association, to lobby the government. Other states have similar organizations. NCCED, the Center for Community Change, LISC, and Enterprise Foundation on Capital Hill—all reflect and carry forward the need for political presence. Maturing CDCs figure out how to get connected.

3. Is the CDC adroit at deal making? Effective CDCs not only organize and advocate, but they figure out how to get the houses rehabbed or built, make retail services available, develop land, build bridges to mainline sources of capital, and make sure a range of needs get met.

It's not necessary that the CDC be the developer, general contractor, lender or investor, human service provider, or new business and job creator, though many do all these. CDCs can be effective as the broker, translating the agenda for development into reality by finding and qualifying, for example, a for-profit builder. It is important, however, that the CDC develop a broad view of the community's needs.

4. Does the CDC have a real goal of creating wealth? This is the "vision thing." Successful deal making is not sufficient. Deals must not be the end but the means to real, persisting differences in economic circumstances and capacities of people. That requires a strategic sense of economic intervention, financial and network leveraging to generate wealth, and return the neighborhood to the economic mainstream through comprehensive neighborhood renewal. Any CDC that hopes to be effective must think in these larger terms of development to find elevating aspirations. And grantmakers or investors in poor communities must hold to that vision, realizing that achievement is years off.

5. Finally, does the CDC demonstrate a track record for capacity building? Growth in capacity is, of course, subsumed in each of the first four activities in the cycle. It's emphasized for the same reasons corporations focus on human resource and organizational development. Like activity four, CDCs must undertake systematic "inreach," or there's a tendency for organizing, advocacy, deal making, and even visioning to become discrete developmental tasks.

Each may be done well, but do they cohere organizationally? Is the neighborhood's (and the organization's) need for leadership renewal being met? Are the organization and its people flexible and creative? Is the organization—its staff and its board effective—working harmoniously? Is the organization a good place for professionals to work? Can it recruit the talent it requires? Are its resources adequate and properly deployed? To be effective over time, a CDC, like a for-profit business, needs to attend to its human resource needs. So foundations should also support programs to strengthen the human infrastructure of the industry through training, compensation, leadership development, and provision of adequate core support.

So, rather than pointing to a "model" CDC, here are five ways, a model of interconnecting and mutually reinforcing CDC activities, to help decision makers determine whether to invest. Common sense applies. If the organization is young, some of the activities will not be occurring. But, whatever the age, each CDC over time ought to demonstrate its commitment to developing each of the five.

But why do so few companies, relative to other categories of grant making and social investment underwrite community-based development? Is it because they don't understand? Are they put off or frightened by the noise, grit, and politics of poverty?

CDCs use a businesslike orientation to production, job creation, and a bottom line concern for the marketplace. Given that fit, there are opportunities for synergy between for-profit institutions and CDCs. The Community Reinvestment Act and the Low-Income Housing Tax Credit provide bases for action. Many bankers continue to see CRA as an unwarranted intrusion. But, alliances between banks and CDCs, forced by CRA pressures, mean good, often new business for the former and solid gains for distressed neighborhoods, whose renewal depends on the ability to access and circulate capital from conventional sources.

Successful partnerships depend on flexibility by both sides—around qualifying credit seekers, for instance. The Federal Low-Income Housing Tax Credit is a worthy avenue for involvement. Purchasing tax credits, as a means of investing in low-income housing, works. It's safe. Companies realize, typically, an IRR of 18 percent (after tax, net present value). Ninety percent of low-income housing, 1986–1991, was financed (usually up to 40 percent per deal) through tax credits purchased by corporations. CDCs involved learn the discipline of the market and its investment mechanisms. It's win/win/win. Yet, sales are hard to make. Corporations should get involved.

12 Black Self-Help and Philanthropy

Emmett D. Carson

INTRODUCTION

One of the most intriguing debates in black America today involves the extent to which blacks are engaged in activities to help themselves. This debate was initiated in earnest when a small group of black conservatives began to question whether blacks, more specifically well off blacks, were sufficiently engaged in activities to help poor blacks. Although a consensus has begun to grow among both liberals and conservatives that blacks should take a more active role in helping their own poor,[1] there is little understanding of the long standing philanthropic traditions of blacks or their contemporary giving patterns.[2]

Black conservatives have made considerable headway in shaping the discussion on black self-help and in creating a public consensus that blacks can and should do more to help themselves than they are currently doing. Implicit in this argument is the belief that blacks are more lax in this regard than other racial or ethnic groups due, in part, to an overreliance on government. While acknowledging the importance of government action in addressing problems in the black community, Glenn Loury, a prominent black spokesperson for black self-help states:

Self-reliance is essential to black dignity and a key ingredient for black progress. . . . But meeting the challenge facing black America today—the challenge of taking control of our future by exerting the leadership, making the sacrifices, and building the institutions necessary for black social and economic development—does ultimately depend upon black action. It is unwise and dangerous to rely on the government to remain sufficiently committed to such a program of black revitalization over the long haul.[3]

Unfortunately, statements such as the one above fail to recognize the critical role that black philanthropy has played in advancing black interests. Over the years, black philanthropy has taken on new forms as both the black community and the larger society have changed, socially, economically, and politically. Before the Civil War, black philanthropy centered on helping slaves escape from the South, primarily through the Underground Railroad, and on helping them cope with the hostile society they met elsewhere. Early black philanthropic efforts were carried out in secrecy, particularly in the South, and most were limited to helping individuals survive day to day. When one compares this with the work carried out by black churches and a host of social protest organizations during the civil rights movement—through which national protest was openly encouraged—one begins to grasp how closely tied black philanthropy has been to the nation's social and political climate.

The racial climate throughout our nation's history has driven black philanthropy in a different direction from that of white dominated efforts. Unlike the missionary approach that characterizes much of white charitable activity, with the well off giving their excess to the poor, the approach of black philanthropists has more often seen self-reliance as the gift the poor most need. Today especially, the black community can draw on a strong tradition of people helping others to help themselves.

This chapter draws on the Joint Center for Political and Economic Studies' 1986 and 1987 surveys to examine the attitudes that blacks and whites expressed concerning four basic issues:[4] first, whether the middle class is doing what it should to aid the poor and whether the poor are doing enough to help themselves; second, which governmental and private organizations should bear the primary responsibility for helping the poor; third, which problems most urgently need to be addressed by charitable groups; and fourth, how much trust is placed in charitable organizations to help the poor.

If blacks and whites have decidedly different views on how far the poor should be expected to help themselves—or if they have different views on how far charitable organizations can be trusted—such differences might be key to explaining why their charitable giving differs, in those areas where it does differ. Moreover, to the extent that one is interested in using the charitable giving of blacks to develop new and/or expand existing social service delivery programs or to spur community economic development, understanding the philanthropic attitudes of blacks is essential.

DO MIDDLE CLASS BLACKS DO ENOUGH FOR POOR BLACKS?

A central premise underlying black self-help arguments is that the black middle class should do more to help poor blacks. Tables 12.1 and 12.2 show how whites and blacks rate efforts to help the poor by the middle class of both races. Table 12.1 concerns the efforts of the white middle class, and Table 12.2 concerns the efforts of the black middle class.[5] For

Table 12.1
"Do Middle Class Whites Help Poor Whites as Much as They Should?"
—Responses by Race, 1986 and 1987

	1986		1987	
	Blacks	Whites	Blacks	Whites
Do as much	12.0%	16.0%	17.5%	18.3%
Do not do as much	77.4	61.6	64.8	72.7
Nothing they can do	5.4	1.9	NA	NA
No opinion	5.1	20.5	18.2	8.9
No. of observations	868	916	918	916

NA indicates this response was not offered by the questionnaire.

Table 12.2
"Do Middle Class Blacks Help Poor Blacks as Much as They Should?"
—Responses by Race, 1986 and 1987

	1986		1987	
	Blacks	Whites	Blacks	Whites
Do as much	19.9%	21.0%	13.5%	15.8%
Do not do as much	65.1	66.0	74.5	66.4
Nothing they can do	3.3	2.4	NA	NA
No opinion	11.6	10.5	12.0	17.8
No. of observations	868	916	918	916

NA indicates this response was not offered by the questionnaire.

both years surveyed, a solid majority (more than 60 percent) of both
blacks and whites responded that middle class whites do *not* do as much
as they should, while less than 20 percent of both racial groups responded that whites in fact do as much as they should do.[6]

Likewise, a similar majority of blacks and whites (more than 65 percent of each) responded that middle class blacks do not do as much as
they should, as Table 12.2 shows. (The figure rose among black respondents by 10 percentage points between 1986 and 1987, suggesting a vola-
tility between the two years for which there is no ready explanation.)

These data suggest that the belief that the middle class makes an insufficient effort to help the poor is as widely held concerning the white
middle class as concerning their black counterparts. The conviction, in
short, seems to be color blind.

DO THE POOR HELP THEMSELVES ENOUGH?

The next two tables show the extent to which blacks and whites believe
the poor do as much as they should to help themselves (a question asked
in the 1987 survey only). Table 12.3 shows that a solid majority of both
blacks (65 percent) and whites (78 percent) believe poor whites do not
do as much as they should, and Table 12.4 shows that, likewise, a majority of both groups (72 percent of blacks and 80 percent of whites) believe
the black poor are not doing enough. Interestingly, more than twice as
many blacks as whites feel that poor blacks are indeed doing as much
as they should to help themselves (1 percent versus 8 percent).

Table 12.3
**"Do Poor Whites Do as Much as They Should to Help Themselves?"—Responses
by Race, 1987**

	Blacks	Whites
Do as much	17.1%	11.5%
Do not do as much	65.1	78.2
Don't know	17.9	10.3
No. of observations	918	916

Table 12.4
**"Do Poor Blacks Do as Much as They Should to Help Themselves?"—Responses
by Race, 1987**

	Blacks	Whites
Do as much	16.9%	7.7%
Do not do as much	72.2	80.0
Don't know	10.8	12.3
No. of observations	918	916

Overall, these findings suggest that both blacks and whites believe that while the middle class of both races should do more to help the poor, the poor nevertheless should do more to help themselves. The prevalence of this second belief would seem to confirm the view that Americans in recent years have become less sympathetic toward the poor. At the same time, responses concerning the middle class' efforts seem inconsistent with this generalization, suggesting that most Americans believe that those who are relatively better off should be more charitable.

WHO SHOULD BEAR RESPONSIBILITY FOR THE POOR?

Although Americans seem to want the middle class to do more for the poor, it is obvious that a single segment of our society can only be expected to do so much. Who, then, should bear the primary responsibility? At one end of the spectrum of responsibility is the government— and at the other end the poor themselves. By examining public attitudes on this question, we may be able to determine who or which institutions would be most likely to generate the necessary financial and volunteer support.

If it turns out, for example, that the public believes the federal government bears primary responsibility, then the public may be receptive to increasing the level of federal funds and strengthening policies aimed directly at helping the poor. Alternatively, if the poor themselves are believed to bear the primary responsibility, the public may be less receptive to government efforts or even to private charitable activity.

Responses to the question of who has the greatest responsibility are shown in Table 12.5. Blacks are more likely than whites to hold that the federal government has the greatest responsibility, with reponses in 1987 showing them nearly twice as likely to hold this view (43 percent versus 24 percent). Moreover, the percentage of blacks who felt the federal government has the largest responsibility for the poor rose by more than 10 points between 1986 and 1987, from 31 percent to 43 percent. (White attitudes on this question remained relatively constant over the same period, with close to 25 percent citing the federal government in both years.) One explanation for the notable shift among blacks may be their perception that changes in the weakening economy has been hurting them disproportionately and the sense that overt racism might again be on the rise.

Attitudes toward the primacy of state and local government's role, by contrast, revealed little difference between the two racial groups, hovering between 11 and 15 percent between the two survey years.

Concerning this question of who holds greatest responsibility, only minor differences are evident between black men and black women and among blacks with different levels of education or household income.

Table 12.5
"Which Group Has the Greatest Responsibility for Helping the Poor?"—1986 and 1987 Responses, by Race

	1986		1987	
	Blacks	Whites	Blacks	Whites
Federal government	31.4%	24.6%	42.9%	23.7%
Churches	26.3	24.7	17.3	20.5
State & local governments	13.3	14.7	10.6	14.1
Poor themselves	3.8	12.7	5.2	17.3
Relatives of poor people	3.4	7.6	3.4	4.8
Other private charities	3.9	6.0	3.0	5.0
Someone else	0.9	0.4	1.7	0.5
Don't know	17.1	9.3	15.9	14.2
No. of observations	868	916	918	916

Significant differences do emerge, however, among blacks of different ages and from different regions of the country (Table 12.6). A significantly smaller percentage of younger blacks (ages 18 to 29) than older blacks (age 50 and over) cite the federal government as holding primary responsibility for the poor; 40 percent versus 48 percent. Conversely, a higher percentage of younger blacks (7 percent) than older blacks (2 percent) responded that the poor themselves have the greatest responsibility.

This generation gap is perhaps most easily explained by the fact that blacks under the age of 30 belong to the post-civil rights era. They have little firsthand knowledge of the social and legal barriers blacks faced before the civil rights legislation of the 1960s, and they are less likely than others to know what a forceful hand the federal government had to use to knock down those barriers. Older blacks, with their firsthand

Table 12.6
Groups That Blacks Believe Have the Greatest Responsibility for Helping the Poor, by Age and Region, 1987

	Federal Gov't.	Churches	State or Local Gov't.	The Poor Themselves	Relatives of the Poor	Other Private Charities	Someone Else	Don't Know
Age								
18-29	39.6%	12.0%	13.3%	6.5%	6.2%	3.2%	2.2%	17.1%
30-49	42.4	17.9	8.6	6.5	3.3	4.1	1.9	15.3
50 and over	48.0	22.7	10.1	2.3	0.6	1.4	1.1	13.8
Region								
East	44.8	12.7	12.5	7.8	3.9	4.8	1.6	11.8
Midwest	37.3	19.1	14.6	6.5	3.1	1.0	0.3	18.1
South	46.4	19.3	6.8	4.2	3.7	3.2	1.5	14.9
West	30.2	15.8	16.8	0.0	1.7	0.9	6.6	27.8

knowledge of the civil rights era, are more apt to realize that barriers of discrimination were responsible for much of the poverty that then prevailed in the black community.

More important perhaps, older blacks remember that it was the federal government that protected their rights as American citizens when many state and local governments, especially in the South, were attempting to abridge those rights in nearly every area of life. Thus, it is not surprising that the survey findings show a much smaller percentage of Southern blacks than those from any other region believe that state or local governments have the greatest responsibility. Likewise, a slightly greater percentage of blacks in the East and South believe the federal government has the greatest responsibility for the poor.

WHY HAVE POOR BLACKS BEEN UNABLE TO ESCAPE POVERTY?

Black poverty has been on the national agenda in some form or another since the 1960s. Nevertheless, there is increasing concern that the socioeconomic status of *poor* blacks has changed little over the last two decades.[7] In fact, this is one reason many people are now calling for more and stronger black self-help efforts. Clearly, an individual's opinion as to why so many poor blacks have failed to rise out of poverty may help explain that person's preference for government, private institutions, or others as the most effective agents in aiding the poor.

Table 12.7 suggests that blacks and whites differ dramatically on this issue. Blacks are far more likely than whites (28 percent versus 7 per-

Table 12.7
"What Is the Main Reason Poor Blacks Have Not Been Able to Rise Out of Poverty?"—Responses by Race, 1987

	Blacks	Whites
Job discrimination	28.3%	7.1%
Not enough education	24.3	37.5
Not enough motivation	16.0	31.7
Not enough available jobs	11.8	7.4
Discrimination in education	10.6	7.3
Individual blacks' fault	1.1	0.4
Society's fault	0.7	0.1
Less in-born ability	0.5	3.0
Other	0.2	0.5
Don't know	6.6	5.0
No. of observations	918	916

cent) to believe that job discrimination is the primary barrier to the advancement of poor blacks. By contrast, the poor's own lack of motivation is cited far more often by whites than by blacks (32 percent versus 16 percent) as a primary reason. Clearly, large proportions of blacks and whites hold widely differing views on why black poverty remains largely unresolved.

WHICH PROBLEMS SHOULD CHARITIES TARGET?

In general, both liberal and conservative proponents of black self-help, especially in recent years, have failed to address the matter of deciding on which issues the black community must focus its attention. This decision is critically needed because, regardless of how much self-help any single ethnic or racial group practices, only a limited number of causes can be adequately supported at a given time.

Traditional economic theory, extended to explain the nonprofit charitable sector, would suggest that any community's priority problems could be identified by observing which charitable organizations receive the greater number and amount of contributions. However, this reasoning may not always adequately explain the behavior of giving. It is reasonable to assume that people may prefer to contribute to charitable organizations whose history they are most familiar with or whose philosophy or outlook they support, rather than preferring only those that support specific services. Indeed, many organizations operate a variety of services, and few organizations receive contributions targeted by the donor for specific uses.

To shed some light on the community problems donors and others believe most deserve to be solved by charitable effort, the survey asked respondents to select from a list of widely recognized problems the one they considered most important for charitable organizations to address. Table 12.8 summarizes the responses.

Overall, there are few meaningful differences between the responses of blacks and whites. Two exceptions to this are the issues of unemployment and health problems. Twice as many blacks (15 percent) as whites (8 percent) believe unemployment is the most important problem for charitable organizations to try and solve. In contrast, many more whites (17 percent) than blacks (10 percent) feel that health problems, such as AIDS and cancer, should be charities' priority. Despite these differences, the problem of drug abuse received the largest responses from both blacks and whites (19 percent and 22 percent, respectively).

Tables 12.9 and 12.10 show the responses of blacks to the same question, broken down according to the respondents' socioeconomic characteristics. While the responses vary noticeably according to educational levels, they vary little between the different levels of household income.

Table 12.8
Problems Respondents Believe Are Most Important for Charitable Organizations to Address, by Race, 1987

	Blacks	Whites
Drug abuse	19.2%	21.5%
Unemployment	15.2	8.1
Health problems	9.5	16.5
Housing	9.5	13.7
Poverty	8.8	10.8
Teen pregnancy	7.5	4.2
Crime	6.9	4.8
Problems of the elderly	4.7	8.9
High school drop-outs	4.1	3.7
Environment	0.5	2.3
Other	0.5	0.7
Unreported	13.5	4.8
No. of observations	918	916

Very significant differences show up among different educational levels concerning the problem of teenage pregnancy (Table 12.9). College graduates showed considerably more concern over this issue; the percentage among them who chose this as the most pressing problem for charitable organizations to address was at least double the percentages of those from every other educational level. The opposite pattern emerges concerning the issue of drug abuse. Slightly more than 20 percent of blacks with less than a high school education and those who have only a high school diploma checked off drug abuse as the priority problem for charities, whereas 17 percent of those with some college and only 7 percent of college graduates chose drug abuse.

The income levels of respondents (Table 12.10) reveal interesting differences concerning the issues of poverty and unemployment. Among low-income blacks, far more felt that charities should tackle unemployment (18 percent) than poverty (8 percent). Wealthier blacks, on the other hand, expressed precisely the opposite priorities: 16 percent cited poverty and only 9 percent cited unemployment. These divergent patterns may be evidence of division between socioeconomic classes: poor blacks would rather obtain jobs to end their poverty, while upper income blacks are more likely to recognize only the poverty itself—a symptom brought on by unemployment—and not its underlying cause. These findings may be particularly important in assessing the degree to which eco-

Table 12.9
Six Most Frequently Cited Problems Blacks Think Should Be Addressed by Chari-table Organizations, by Educational Level, 1987

	Drug Abuse	Unemployment	Health Problems	Teen Pregnancy	Poverty	Crime
Less Than High School	21.9%	13.8%	8.8%	7.9	7.6%	7.9%
High School Graduate	20.9	18.8	10.7	6.5	7.2	6.6
Some College	16.9	14.1	8.5	5.4	11.4	7.8
College Graduate	7.2	8.9	9.5	14.5	15.8	3.4

nomic development efforts should focus on employment and income generation.

LEVEL OF TRUST IN CHARITABLE ORGANIZATIONS

To understand why blacks and whites exhibit particular patterns of char-itable giving, it is useful to have some measure of the trust they put in charitable organizations' ability to effectively help the poor. This is important because, historically, black charitable organizations have tended to be informal groups, operating within neighborhoods and often through local churches. Thus, until recently in the black community, donors and recipients would have been very likely to know each other, either directly or indirectly. By contrast, if blacks today have strong misgivings, however mistaken, about the ability of larger charitable or-ganizations to serve the poor, they may be more inclined to reject efforts by these larger groups to solicit from them at higher levels.

The responses of blacks and whites to the question of how much trust they have in charitable organizations' ability to help the poor are shown in Table 12.11. Whereas only 19 percent of blacks and 16 percent of whites reported having "a lot" of trust, about half of both groups (47 percent of blacks and 55 percent of whites) reported having "some trust." Only one-fifth of either group reported having "very little" trust

Table 12.10
Six Most Frequently Cited Problems Blacks Think Should be Addressed by Chari-table Organizations, by Household Income of Respondents

	Drug Abuse	Unemployment	Health Problems	Teen Pregnancy	Poverty	Crime
Less Than $12,000	16.7	18.0	8.0	9.3	8.2	7.1
$12,000–$24,999	19.0	10.6	12.8	6.8	10.2	11.0
$25,000–$39,999	17.7	14.5	12.8	9.0	6.7	7.3
Greater Than $40,000	19.0	9.2	8.7	10.6	16.1	0.0

Table 12.11
Degree of Trust Placed in Charitable Organizations' Ability to Help the Poor, by Race, 1986

	Blacks	Whites
A Lot	18.7%	16.4%
Some	47.2	54.7
Very little	22.0	20.1
None	6.0	3.5
It depends	3.9	3.2
Don't know	2.3	2.1
No. of respondents	868	916

in charitable organizations, and less than 6 percent reported having no trust at all. This suggests that, as with whites, the majority of blacks are not overly concerned that charitable organizations will fail to deliver promised services to the poor. This view, however, may have changed significantly, given widespread media coverage of the 1992 United Way of America scandal.

BLACK PHILANTHROPIC ACTIVITY

While some aspects of the data presented thus far, particularly in the section on who should bear responsibility for the poor, would appear to support the hypothesis offered by some black conservatives that blacks are more likely to look toward the government to address the problems of the poor, a strong argument can be made that these data present an incomplete picture of black efforts to help themselves. There is a sharp difference between whether one believes that a specific entity should have primary responsibility to provide certain services to the poor and whether one waits for that entity to take responsibility. In other words, while the data provide statistical support for the belief that blacks look toward government as having primary responsibility for aiding the poor, they do not provide the required evidence to suggest that blacks are idle while waiting for government to meet its responsibilities as perceived by a large percentage of blacks.

One measure of whether blacks are engaged in helping the poor is to examine their actual giving to charitable organizations. Charitable giving is the traditional method whereby individuals who are relatively better off attempt to provide some assistance to those who are worse off. Table 12.12 shows the total contributions of blacks and whites to charitable organizations in 1986, controlling for differences in income. (This is because, one would imagine, that the more household income that one has available, the greater the amount that is available for charitable giving).

Table 12.12
Total Contributions of Blacks and Whites to Charitable Organizations in 1986 by Household Income

	Less Than $12,000		$12,000 – $25,000		$25,000 – $40,000		More Than $40,000	
	BLACK	WHITE	BLACK	WHITE	BLACK	WHITE	BLACK	WHITE
Less than $50	13.1%	17.3%	10.0%	9.9%	3.1%	6.1%	3.3%	0.9%
$50–$99	9.3	10.7	13.5	8.2	9.9	11.5	6.7	4.2
$100–$499	20.0	24.0	35.9	38.8	27.8	36.2	24.7	27.3
$500 or More	7.9	11.5	14.2	26.5	33.2	35.9	55.8	58.4
NO CONTRIBUTIONS	44.1	34.9	24.6	13.9	19.9	7.4	6.4	8.2
UNKNOWN	5.6	1.7	1.8	2.7	6.2	2.9	3.2	1.0
Observations	325	168	221	241	122	221	78	186

Notwithstanding some exceptions, the data indicate that, controlling for differences in household income, similar percentages of blacks and whites report making the same level of total contributions to charitable organizations.[8] However, regardless of household income level, larger percentages of blacks than whites report having made no contribution at all. The differences were largest between blacks and whites with household incomes between $12,000–$25,000 and $25,000–$40,000, the middle-income groups that are often the focus of discussions on black self-help. While these data provide some support to the notion that the black middle class might be able to do more, the overall conclusion is that blacks as a community are, in large measure, as active as whites in charitable giving. This is remarkable when one considers that the median white wealth is 12 times greater than median black wealth ($39,1350 and $3,397, respectively).[9] Moreover, there is mounting evidence that black giving is more resilient to downturns in the economy than any other group.[10]

CONCLUSION

The data presented here strongly suggest that black conservatives are largely wrong when they suggest that the black community is somehow unique or different in its views toward self-help and the poor. A majority of blacks and whites hold the view that neither poor blacks nor whites do enough to help themselves, nor does the black or white middle class of either race do enough to help its respective poor. Further, contrary to the implicit argument of the black conservatives that blacks are content with their current efforts of self-help, again, few blacks thought that the black middle class or poor blacks were doing enough.

The data, however, strongly support the contention of the black conservatives that blacks look toward government as having the primary responsibility to aid the poor. These views among blacks are not wholly unexpected given the federal government's role in securing fundamental rights of equality for blacks. Moreover, when one examines the actual charitable giving of both blacks and whites, there is little evidence to suggest that even though blacks believe that the government should have the primary responsibility to aid the poor that blacks are significantly less likely than whites to make donations to charitable organizations. Other findings, not presented here, also suggest that a large percentage of total black charitable dollars are donated to black organizations, refuting suggestions that blacks do not support their own charitable institutions.[11] This raises important questions as to how much calls for self-help that rely exclusively on blacks helping blacks will be successful. On the other hand, multiracial charitable efforts may ultimately hinge on the degree of control and influence blacks are able to exert within multiracial organizations to solve community problems that affect blacks.

Finally, successful fundraising efforts will depend, in part, on the extent to which organizations focus on causes that are of interest to different segments of the population. The findings suggest that blacks and whites, while sharing similar attitudes that philanthropy should be used to address some community problems, diverge on others. To the extent to which these areas of divergence between the two groups can be resolved, the more encouraging the prospects will be for either exclusively black or multiracial charitable organizations and, ultimately, for efforts to use black philanthropy to encourage community economic development.

NOTES

1. See: American Council on Education and the Education Commission of the States, *One-Third of A Nation,* a report of the Commission on Minority Participation In Education and American Life, May 1988; and Committee on Policy for Racial Justice, *Black Initiative and Governmental Responsibility* (Washington, D.C.: Joint Center for Political Studies, 1987).

2. Emmett D. Carson, "The Evolution of Black Philanthropy: Patterns of Giving and Voluntarism," in *Philanthropic Giving: Studies In Venture and Variety,* ed., Richard Magat (New York: Oxford University Press, 1989); and "Patterns of Giving in Black Churches," in *Religion and Giving: Changing Patterns of Faith and the Future of America's Voluntary Spirit,* ed., Robert Wuthnow and Virginia A. Hodgkinson (San Francisco: Jossey-Bass, Inc., 1990).

3. Glenn Loury, "Misguided Public Policy Is Harming Minorities," *American Visions* (May/June, 1986), p. 11.

4. Both the 1986 and 1987 surveys, conducted by the Gallup Organization, sampled a nationally representative cross-section of adults in the continental United States.

5. Here and in all the tables in this chapter, the margin of error between black and white responses is plus or minus five percentage points.

6. Unlike the survey questions on charitable activity, which ask respondents to recall their behavior during the calendar year preceeding the survey, the attitudinal questions asked respondents about their feelings at the *time of the interview*.

7. National Research Council, *A Common Destiny: Blacks and American Society* (Washington, D.C.: National Academy Press, 1989).

8. These findings are largely consistent with those of other studies of charitable giving at the time. For example, "Independent Sector," *Giving and Volunteering in the United States,* (Washington, DC: Independent Sector, 1988).

9. U.S. Department of Commerce and Bureau of the Census, *Household Health and Asset Ownership: 1984* (Household Economic Studies, Series P-70, No. 7, July 1985), p. 5.

10. See: Virginia A. Hodgkinson, *Giving and Volunteering in the United States. 1992.*

11. Emmett O. Carson, "Contemporary Trends in Black Philanthropy: Challenging the Myths," in Dwight F. Burlingame and Lamont J. Hulse, *Taking Fund Raising Seriously* (San Francisco: Jossey-Bass Publishers, 1991), pp. 219–238.

13 How Corporations Can Support Fundraising and Other Strategic Development Innovations

Richard F. America

How can corporate philanthropy support economic development innovatively in Afro-America, rural and urban? This chapter suggests a package that could accelerate income and wealth growth and that could help solve many chronic problems that plague the black under classes.

FUND REFORMS OF THE NAACP AND NATIONAL URBAN LEAGUE

First, there are two major organizations traditionally looked to for leadership in civil rights and in advocating the interests of Afro-America. These are the NAACP and the National Urban League. They are also catalysts and sometimes managers in economic and small business development, employment training, and placement. In some cases, they also participate in housing development and rehabilitation.

Corporate foundations should look for ways to strengthen these two key economic development/civil rights organizations. Over the next 30 years, their primary concerns likely will be more in economic development than in the past. And the skills they will need in national and local leaders will accordingly change. No longer will civil rights advocacy be the background most required. Instead, hard management skills and a track record of successful administration will be preferable. Other internal organizational reforms should also be forthcoming, to remove the decades of dysfunctional tradition that has handicapped both organizations and kept them from functioning optimally.

Philanthropic supporters can use their leverage to help produce these overdue structural and cultural changes by insisting on management and organizational overhauls before granting funds. This, of course, has to be done in a way that is not seen as undue interference with internal matters. But the fact is, these organizations are too important to the future of economic development in distressed urban areas to be allowed to go along with outdated, inefficient methods and structures. Philanthropy can assist greatly by funding high quality organizational development and consulting reviews and evaluations and followup implementation of recommendations for reform.

Once that fundamental work is completed, foundations will be able to work with the new professional managers in the streamlined, state of the art NAACP and NUL, to accomplish important developmental goals.

HELP THE NAACP AND NUL BECOME
FINANCIALLY INDEPENDENT

After funding organizational development reforms and acquisition of quality professional management, the second priority for philanthropy should be to help the organizations become financially independent of philanthropy. So paradoxically, philanthropy should be interested in helping the NAACP and NUL arrive at a stage of self-sufficiency so they will never again have to turn to philanthropy for operational or program support.

The way this should be accomplished is for foundations to supply sufficient funds for fundraising and membership development so that both organizations can finally, at long last, create a stable large membership and donor base. Five years of large scale grant support, earmarked for use in hiring top flight professional fundraisers and for direct mail, can make it possible for the long term financial needs of both to be met internally.

So foundations that truly seek to contribute to the long term healthy development of Afro-America will adopt this strategy of putting the key developmental organizations on an independent footing, after they have cleaned up their operations and management. Something on the order of $5 million a year to each for five years should be sufficient to allow this work to be accomplished. It will afford the acquisition of mailing lists, the hiring of the best fund raising counsel and staff, and the use of the most attractive and effective direct mail materials, so that the grassroots potential membership and contributors, that have always been there, can finally be energized.

CREATE AN AFRICAN-AMERICAN FUND

Third, foundations should work with Afro-America to create another source of permanent independent funding for development. There needs to be a powerful annual fundraising program like the Catholic Charities, United Jewish Appeal, or United Way. There needs to be an African-American Fund. This would tap the eight million households in Afro-America, and any other contributors, individual and institutional. It would generate funds for supplemental programs in health, recreation, education, neighborhood development, crime prevention, housing, and small business development. It would operate through local units and would create a growing permanent National Fund, perhaps in the form of an endowment.

The potential exists for the AAFund to receive upwards of $1 billion a year from internal individual contributions averaging $100 to $200. If an effective organization and apparatus is created that is professionally run, scrupulously audited, and uses state of the art fund raising techniques (including payroll checkoff), then African-Americans will be able to rapidly become self-sufficient and, through their internal charity, take care of much of the community's needs.

There have, of course, been efforts along these lines, such as the Black United Funds, the United Black Funds and the NAACP Special Contributions Fund. But none has ever been managed properly or had sufficient startup funding to realize the full potential that exists. It takes money to raise money. Philanthropy, on the order of $10 million a year for five years, is needed to create the kind of organization needed to buy the mailing lists, talent, and materials needed to do the job right. Once these sources of initial support are in place, the AAFund will take off and be self-sustaining at a very high level. In this way, corporate strategic philanthropy can complete the development of economic self sufficiency.

FUND VENTURE CAPITAL

Fourth, philanthropy can work with the venture capital community to create pools of resources that can accomplish serious business development at a significant scale. For the past 20 years, foundations have funded some Minority Enterprise Small Business Investment Companies licensed and regulated by the federal government. The same has been done with other private nonregulated funds like The Cooperative Assistance Fund, Opportunity Capital Corporation, and the UNC Corporation. The trouble is, none of these funds has had the resources to participate in the kind of acquisition and leveraged buyout programs needed to accelerate the growth of competitive firms at a larger scale.

Foundations should, for the next ten years, supply to a handful of the best MESBICs and investment organizations, funds for investment on the order of $10 to $20 million for each selected firm. This will make it possible for African-American investor/managers to acquire major manufacturing and sophisticated service firms in sectors of the economy heretofore not even remotely penetrated at that scale, if at all.

CREATE AN ENDOWMENT TO ENABLE BLACK UNIVERSITIES TO COMPETE FOR STAR QUALITY FACULTY

Fifth, the Historically Black Colleges and Universities (HBCUs) need resources to make them strategically competitive. They need funds to help with student assistance in loans and grants, bricks and mortar and equipment, and research funds. Every budget line item could benefit from added outside support for these 120 schools. But resources are limited and their market and the needs they can serve are changing.

Philanthropy already continues its long standing support. But there are innovations and targeted priorities that could make major differences in how some of the strongest schools function.

An informal survey of deans, senior faculty, and presidents in these turned up an interesting proposition. Asked what assistance they would find most useful, the consensus was for help in competing for and retaining star quality young faculty. Obviously, they also needed everything else on the list, but if there is one overriding ingredient with which they could go on to build strong institutions, it is help in claiming their share of the brightest young fresh Ph.D.s coming out each year and an occasional established, specialized, tenured professor. These people will then form a critical mass in departments and universities and will solve the other problems, in time.

Out of this insight came the idea for the BASE Endowment. Certain programs and departments especially relate to long term community small business and economic development. These include, Business Administration, Agriculture, the Sciences, Engineering, and Economics (BASE). Obviously, the arts and letters and humanities also deserve support and also have a lot to do with community development. But given limited resources and the desire to focus in ways that will make the schools engines of overall development and problem solving, these programs stand out as the ones to receive special attention. So philanthropy should create a huge permanent endowment, $100 to $200 million.

This would be through a public–private partnership with government grants, with individual and alumni contributions also adding to the accumulation. But foundations could take the lead and be the catalyst. The BASE Endowment would be administered by either an existing organization with a good track record, like the UNCF, or by the NAFEO, or perhaps by one of the other educational entities serving land grant colleges or higher education in some other way. Or a new organization could be created specifically and solely to accomplish this mission.

The procedure would call for an annual competition in which selected schools, whose departments meet certain criteria in advance, would submit proposals for funds. They would then receive grants on the merits that would allow them to pay competitive salaries and offer other perks, research support, and total packages, so they would take a back seat to no other universities in material inducements.

Initial foundation grants of a few million dollars a year for the first three years could entice matching government and corporate support, so the endowment could achieve full size within ten years, and would then operate in perpetuity. Again, the idea is to create an institution that has ongoing life and is independent of outside interference and second guessing once its management and oversight mechanisms have proven themselves.

FUND INNOVATIONS IN BEHAVIOR MODIFICATION AND CRIME PREVENTION

Sixth, a primary impediment to community and economic development is dysfunctional behavior. This self-destructive, antisocial activity undermines all other attempts to improve life, raise incomes, and build institutions.

Crime, teenage pregnancy, school dropouts, and other expressions of lack of discipline discourage academic performance and residential and business investment. They are a principle barrier to employment generation.

It might be preferred that public policy intervene with programs budgeted at levels sufficient to turn the situation around, but for complex reasons, that is improbable. Therefore, it becomes the responsibility of the community and its leaders to find ways to persuade large numbers of people to change their attitudes and behavior. This is strategically crucial and no significant investment and development is likely to occur until the communities come to be viewed as safe, clean, hospitable environments in which to do business, work, and shop.

The remedy for behavior breakdown is complex. It involves upgrading the formal criminal justice/penal system to accommodate the hard core criminal who cannot be persuaded to change. But the vast majority of people, behaving suboptimally, can probably be reached through one-on-one counseling, neighborhood group activities, and through modern persuasive mass communications, print and electronic. This is a kind of social marketing.

The NAACP and the NUL could sponsor a program of intense communication. And there is reason to believe it could effectively change the circumstances dramatically. Corporate foundations should be in the vanguard developing this approach. It should be a priority, and a public–private partnership, with some government funds, would be the instrument for launching and sustaining a five- to ten-year campaign.

The program would use commercial techniques and commercial firms. It would not rely on Public Service Announcements or donated services. Those would be welcome and would be part of the package. But this is important enough to approach the way corporations sell products and services with budgeted funds.

The idea is, we can "sell" the idea of right living, of compliance with law and expected norms of responsible behavior. A multimillion dollar budget should be committed for this essential element in an overall strategy of development.

FUND THINK TANKS AND INTELLECTUAL INSTRUMENTS

Seventh, community revitalization and development in Afro-America requires that its advocates effectively participate in the battle for public opinion. They have to develop and use the instruments of intellectual and analytical struggle that shape the political and legislative atmosphere. That means they must create and edit first rate influential magazines, journals, newsletters, and radio and television public affairs shows.

One of the principle reasons why those who wish to see progressive policy have been consistently disappointed is that they have been negligent or derelict in this regard. The NAACP publishes "The Crisis," and the NUL publishes the "Urban League Review" and the annual "State of Black America." None have much impact, or influence. And that fact helps explain why progressive policy viewpoints have been consistently losing in the struggle for influence.

Foundations should proactively work with organizations like the NAACP and NUL, and with others, to create a handful of first rate policy journals that can advance the point of view of those seeking economic justice and community revitalization. These organs typically require continuing subsidies, and foundations should recognize that this form of philanthropy is critical to a comprehensive strategy of community development in distressed areas.

FUND ANTITRUST REFORM

Eighth, another major impediment to African-American business and economic development exists in the form of a kind of **social monopoly.** For several generations, and until fairly recently, it has been impossible for black investor/manager/entrepreneurs to enter most kinds of business. Access was blocked by regulation and formal law in some cases, and by widespread policy and practice in banking, insurance, and in business relationships generally.

These high barriers to entry benefited established businesses as a class and provided them an unjust enrichment. But this monopoly by race and exclusion by race also had the same shortcomings as monopoly in the usual sense; it restricted output, distorted prices, and discouraged innovation.

Now it is time to establish the concept of social monopoly, support a full research agenda to quantify the consequences of the behavior, and find remedies both legislative and judicial.

Foundations should support a full program of research and writing, with seminars, conferences and full discussion of the concept. This is a key element in an overall approach to business development for the previously excluded African-American business community.

FUND RESEARCH ON RESTITUTION THEORY

Ninth and finally, there is the issue of the social debt, of reparations and restitution. In the late 1960s, the concept was made public, but had little impact, in part because it was presented in an emotional, threatening way, and in part because it had not been well thought through. But the idea is sound and deserves a thorough and consistent place in the total discussion of how to create sound development policy.

The processes of slavery and discrimination, beginning in 1619, diverted income and wealth interracially. Exclusion, discrimination, and exploitation produced immense class benefits. These benefits were then bequeathed, carried over, and transferred intergenerationally.

They accumulated and are enjoyed currently by the upper income groups, those in the Top 30 percent of the income distribution. In general, the haves benefit from historic injustices committed by their collective ancestors against the ancestors of the have nots. This unjust enrichment can be studied, analyzed, quantified, and monitored.

There needs to be a continuing review of labor and capital market discrimination and discrimination in educational investments to determine the magnitude of the social debt annually. The NAACP and NUL, or some other institution, could carry out this continuing research program, announcing the findings the way we announce price index, employment, interest rate, exchange rate, and other economic indicators.

Philanthropy should proactively support the development of theory and technique for measuring the debt and should provide institutional subsidies to insure that the work is accomplished in a quality manner.

The public policy implications of these annual reports would be important. The redistributive implications of the research findings would buttress progressive policy proposals for increased investment in community revitalization and education and training. In effect, the monies required for these programs are owed by the haves to the have nots. Without this concept, it is unlikely there can be sufficient analytical and intellectual muscle ever generated in favor of redistributive policy on the correct scale.

Part IV
Philanthropy and Small Enterprise

14 Job Training Partnerships for Economic and Employee Development

Sandra A. Waddock

EXECUTIVE SUMMARY

The Job Training Partnership Act, passed in 1982, has provided the opportunity for many companies worried about the availability and quality of future human resources, a central issue in economic development, to become involved in intensive partnerships with public sector agencies. Called Private Industry Councils, these partnerships have sometimes come under attack but frequently are beginning to make inroads into the serious problems associated with training the disadvantaged for positions in the private sector. In this chapter, the experiences of a number of successful PICs are analyzed so that those factors that are associated with success are drawn out.

Shared vision, de-emphasis on politics, shared power, local networks and initiatives, building mutual trust and support among partners, and skilled implementation are among the factors associated with success in these social partnerships. In turn, these factors present a series of paradoxes for the partnerships attempting to manage them. Conclusions are drawn about the processes associated with building successful partnerships.

In the 1980s, for both the private and public sectors, the partnership concept became almost ubiquitous. American companies engaged in joint ventures with Japanese companies to produce cars and computers. Collaborative research projects, exemplified by the alliance of Hoechst Chemical with Massachusetts General Hospital, became more common. Wendy's agreed to sell Baskin Robbins ice cream in an effort to increase sales of both products. Members of the American Association of Advertising Agencies joined with numerous talent and trade groups to form the Partnership for a Drug-Free America, an effort to "denormalize" the use of illicit drugs through advertising. These partnerships are aimed at numerous competitive, economic, and social problems. Yet another type of partnership—that between government and business—has taken on a great deal of currency in the economic development and human resources arenas.

Throughout the 1980s, government agencies and businesses joined in increased numbers of social partnerships, often under the mandate of the Job Training Partnership Act's (JTPA) Private Industry Councils (PICs). PICs are specifically designed to tackle the difficult problem of job training for the disadvantaged. As the labor pool shrinks over the next decade, many companies have begun to realize the potential that training the disadvantaged has for filling entry level positions, enhancing skills, and improving company performance. Many of JTPA's PICs programs have ranged far beyond their initially mandated goals of job training for the disadvantaged to deal with other work force issues such as economic development, literacy, improving basic education, community development, and skill enhancement. The successes of some of these partnerships, as well as the publicity they have received, combined with increasingly scarce governmental resources and more recognition of the interdependence of the private and public sectors, ensures that such "social partnerships" will continue to proliferate in the 1990s. While these partnerships are strictly speaking not corporate "philanthropy," in some cases, corporations enter into them out of philanthropic motives. When these partnerships work, however, the philanthopy becomes a part of the enlightened self-interest of the firm. Almost by default, the firm may find itself "doing well by doing good."

In a very real sense the PICs established by JTPA are the "granddaddies" of the partnership concept that has taken on so much accuracy, despite the existence of social partnerships (a.k.a. public–private partnerships) for many years (e.g., Brooks, Liebman & Schelling, 1984; Fosler & Berger, 1982). JTPA replaced the much criticized CETA (Comprehensive Employment and Training Administration) program of the

1970s. Passed under the banner of the "new federalism," JTPA provides for a federal job training initiative aimed at helping the disadvantaged become employable in the private sector. These goals are accomplished through the direct participation in and control over local job training initiatives by a partnership of private and public sector sector representatives on the PICs. The representatives, familiar with both local employment and social conditions, as well as industry needs, are able to make decisions that are appropriate for the needs of their region.

Specifically designed to overcome some of the well publicized failures of the CETA programs (e.g., training the disadvantaged for dead-end public sector jobs), JTPA mandates partnership in the form of Private Industry Councils (PICs). In doing so, it often taps into pre-existing networks established under CETA. PICs, for example, existed under Title VII of CETA, although they did not have the power of JTPA's PICs to actually make resource allocation decisions within the job training spheres. They did, however, provide a foundation of relationships among private and public sector actors, many of which have continued under the JTPA legislation. While most observers agree that PICs alone cannot substitute for the loss of federal spending in the area of job training for the disadvantaged or provide a full foundation for economic development, there is evidence that sometimes they work extremely well to bring the needs of the private sector for a literate and job ready work force quite directly into line with the goals of the public sector to improve the lot of the disadvantaged.

JTPA AND THE PICs: BACKGROUND

A Private Industry Council is a group of individuals representing the top decision making levels of major private and public sector organizations in a region. Appointed by the governors of each state, following a nomination process in which numerous general business and community organizations participate (e.g., local Chambers of Commerce), PICs have direct responsibility for developing and overseeing implementation of local job training programs within a region, called a Service Delivery Area (SDA). They are authorized to spend the federal monies allocated to job training for the disadvantaged within their SDA. By the terms of JTPA, each PIC must have at least 51 percent private sector representation among its members. As a result, a majority of the interests represented on the PIC are those of the private sector. PIC representatives are from the top management ranks of important local organizations. In theory (and sometimes in practice), they have enough decision making clout to "speak" for their organizations regarding PIC decisions without constantly having to "check in" with higher authorities. The law provides what are essentially "block grants" to the SDAs for which the PICs are responsible. PIC programs are administered through a Service Delivery Agency, also chosen by the governor (and which frequently is the same as the agency that had administered CETA programs in the past). PICs are directly responsible to a local elected official (LEO), often the mayor of the largest city within the SDA.

What is different about JTPA's PICs from past efforts to incorporate private sector actors into decisions about job training for the disadvantaged is the amount of authority vested in them by the Act. Rather than serving as simple advisory boards to local training agencies, the PICs are actually responsible for the allocation of funds, for strategic planning for the SDA, and for overseeing the implementation of local programs. By virtue of their majority private sector representation and the authority vested in them, the PICs are presumed to be able to speak directly to the interests of the local business community, thereby enabling job training efforts to meet the needs of industry better than many of CETA's efforts. Federal level "control" of PIC/SDA activities is related to output oriented standards, such as placement and program retention rates, rather then more process oriented aspects of training programs. Thus, the overall thrust of JTPA is to provide a federal "umbrella" of standards and overall resource allocation to a diverse group of local efforts. The principle behind the legislation is that local groups will be better able to design programs that meet local needs than will a more centrally run effort.

JTPA and its PICs have been criticized for "creaming" or taking only those individuals who are most "job ready" into their programs (Lee, 1986), for not addressing the right problems (e.g., literacy and poverty or economic development), and for lack of real partnership and programmatic impact (Bernick, 1984). Others have noted the limitations of using market forces to initiate public policy changes. The National Commission for Employment Policy points out the need for balance among local needs and JTPA standards, for reduced emphasis on cost standards, for assisting states in developing appropriate policies with regard to JTPA, and for possibly reorienting the JTPA youth programs. The 1987 National Alliance of Business assessment of JTPA presents a mixed picture of effectiveness. Still others have suggested that JTPA has not been funded at consistent or high enough levels to achieve its purposes.

Despite the criticisms and problems inherent in any major effort at social change such as JTPA, however, there is evidence that some PICs have begun the long term process of making major changes in the development and administration of programs to reduce unemployment among the disadvantaged and thereby improve local conditions. Some of these changes are slowly beginning to affect the way in which employment and training for the disadvantaged—as well as a wealth of other related concerns—are dealt with by companies. For example, the National Alliance of Business has noted that 90 percent of PIC chairs and SDA administrators rated their relationships as "good" to "excellent," an evaluation by Westat concluded that most state/SDA relations could be characterized as "positive and reasonably cooperative . . . though certainly not all," and an MDC/Grinker-Walker report pointed out that positive gains have been made in power sharing between PICs and local governments. Liebschutz reported improved relations among partners in JTPA over those under CETA. Lee indicates that JTPA's results are "better than nothing and better than CETA" but suggests that real partnerships still need to be developed. By 1987, some declines in satisfaction with JTPA were in evidence in the National Alliance of Business survey over previous years; however, the overall assessment was that relationships were generally very positive. The 1987 NAB study concluded that JTPA is maturing into a network of significant relationships among public and private sector actors that can potentially have a major impact on employment training.

Thus, despite the numerous criticisms of JTPA and the limited successes some of its PICs appear to have had, there are numerous examples of PICs that *have* had recognized successes in developing working partnerships between the private sector business and public sector agencies engaged in PIC activities. It is within these partnerships that the potential for long term change rests, yet exactly what makes one partnership work, while others falter, is still unclear. In the rest of this chapter, some of the factors that appear to be at work in making those successful partnerships work will be explored. Based on analysis of telephone interviews with key participants in partnerships drawn from successful PICs across the country, the results of the research presented below illustrates that a number of themes emerge consistently in successful PICs.

MANY MODELS WORK

The first thing that becomes apparent, when analyzing PICs that have been successful in meeting federal and their own goals, is that there is not a single "PIC model" that works under all conditions. For example, the combination of urban, suburban, and rural regions under the control of effective PICs varies widely. Successful PICs range from a huge consortium of 27 rural counties in Oregon to a combination of metropolitan and farming areas in the Ozarks to a single city model in Boston. Some successful PICs require that only chief executive officers (and no alternates) attend meetings and make decisions; others permit lower level organizational representatives. Nor does structure seem to make the difference; successful PICs sometimes set up their own staff to help with administration of the program and sometimes work with only the SDA agency as staff. Neither does it seem to matter whether the SDA area is experiencing rapid growth in employment, as are some high technology (and largely suburban) areas of Massachusetts, or has declining employment opportunities with large industry closing down or leaving, as in St. Louis.

Whether large or small businesses participate in the PICs does not seem to be a determining factor for success either. This is especially true in many rural areas where there are few large businesses able to participate, yet many rural PICs are successful in spite of that gap. Program focus also does not seem to make or break a PIC. Some successful PICs have focused exclusively on job training; others have branched out into literacy and school support programs; still others work in areas of economic or community development, as well as job training for the disadvantaged. Further, different leadership styles appear equally effective in different circumstances. Leaders of some effective PICs and SDAs become deeply involved in hands-on program details in some areas but maintain an arms' length distance from programmatic efforts and stick to policy making in others. Sometimes there has been a single "visionary" leader who initially pulled together the PIC and created sense of direction as happened in Boston; other times there are multiple civic entrepreneurs scattered throughout the system, as in the Oregon Consortium, which encompasses 27 rural counties and an enormous geographic spread.

Given the diversity of the models exemplified in successful PICs, the question that arises is what are the elements in common across this diversity? What factors are attributable to successful PICs, from which lessons can be drawn and applied to other less successful PICs, so that companies wishing to improve the quality of entry level employees by actively participating in their training can be successful at doing so?

COMMON SUCCESS FACTORS IN PICs

Shared Vision

One critical element is the presence of a set of overarching goals or purposes on which participants agree and around which they develop a shared set of values. In essence, this set of overarching goals represents a shared vision of or perspective on the area contained within the SDA. In many successful PICS, shared values culminate in an almost missionary zeal among PIC, SDA, and LEO (local elected official) members about the purpose(s) of the PIC. It does not seem to matter if this shared vision is the relatively negative one of "we could only get better," experienced by the PIC on the Navaho reservation in Fort Defiance, AZ, or the similar "it couldn't go down; it had to go up" sense, shared by members of St. Louis PIC when it started because of the city's deteriorating economic condition. Often, however, a more positive sense of what the region is all about develops, for instance, the strong "sense of knowing what we are about: jobs and education" developed by the Gulf Coast Business Services Corporation (Gulfport, MS).

What does matter is that out of the presence of this common sense of what a region is all about arises a sense of community among all of the participants on the PIC. This gives rise to a common perspective on what the issues facing the area are and a general set of expectations about what can be done about those issues. Shared vision is related to the development of purpose for a PIC in that it draws people together, creating the bonds of a community among participants. This shared vision can be expressed as the "we care attitude" experienced by the PIC working at the Navaho reservation in Arizona or by the fact that "people get hooked" into working within the Oregon Consortium. Shared vision is related to other factors that are critical to PIC success, including a de-emphasis of "politics," power sharing among subgroups within the PIC and SDA, and development of mutual trust and support, which will be discussed in the next sections.

De-emphasizing Politics

Members of successful PICs also seem to develop an ability to de-emphasize the political overtones of their activities, reducing tensions among the interests represented by the local elected official(s), the PIC members, who are predominantly from private sector organizations, and the SDA, which is predominantly oriented toward public sector interests. In de-emphasizing politics, PIC members pay particular attention to reducing potential "turf battles" among the various constituents involved within an SDA. For example, tensions can arise from the mingling of interests of different regions contained within an SDA, particularly around turf issues fostered by different elected officials' perspectives on their constituencies' desires, from historical competition or conflict among districts now combined into a single SDA, or simply from combinations of very different types of communities (e.g., rural, farming communities combined with larger cities). De-emphasizing politics means subordinating political gains for one constituency (e.g., the SDA director or a local mayor) to the good of the overall effort.

The PIC of Southern Connecticut, for example, was able to bridge wide differences in the communities united in the SDA, which spanned a wealthy city with numerous corporations, an urban rust belt city, and an isolated rural area. Issues of territorialism, parochialism, and mistrust among the newly integrated regions had to be submerged to a common interest, rather than the political agendas of any one area. By de-emphasizing the political agendas of each locality, while emphasizing the shared concerns over high levels of unemployment in one area combined with the need to recruit qualified individuals in other areas, PIC members were able to bridge the gaps between the communities and provide a balance of shared interests to which all could agree. As the SDA director puts it, the downplaying of political agendas enabled the PIC to "stop talking about money and who was going to get it and start talking about training slots;" i.e., they focused on appropriate issues on which few could disagree.

In another instance, eight PICs enabled their SDAs to cooperate on programs, market information, and clients so that the needs of the entire region could be met. By crossing SDA and county boundaries in this manner, these groups were better able to meet long term objectives of enabling the harder to serve population to achieve permanent employment, since clients trained in one SDA could be hired by employers in a nearby SDA. This was appropriate because of the transportation-dependent nature of the region. It would not have been possible, however, if each PIC had chosen to maintain its political and geographic autonomy.

Power Sharing

A characteristic of successful PICs related to their ability to de-emphasize the politics of the situation is that they tend to be willing to share power among decision making groups within their purview. Frequently, this power sharing is discussed in terms of having a "democratic" organization, one in which decision making occurs from the "bottom up" or at the local level, under the broader umbrella provided by guidelines developed within the PIC. The Oregon Consortium, for example, stresses that its success is due in large part to the empowerment by the Consortium of numerous local entities operating within the nine districts (comprising the 27 rural counties) that make up the Consortium. The Consortium works by recognizing that there are "many right points of view," depending on the local perspective and by delegating the responsibility to those in the communities to design and develop programs particularly suited to that area.

In other instances, power sharing takes place among potentially competing groups that might otherwise engage in battles for control; for instance, between local elected officials, PICs, and SDA agencies. In Alameda County, CA, for example, the PIC and the board of local elected officials share decision making power equally, along with a staff support organization that helps them minimize turf battles as well as duplication of efforts. Power sharing helps them to recognize the different contributions that each sector can make to resolve local issues and has also enabled them to develop a tight, consistent focus on job training and development, leaving educational and economic development programs to other agencies.

Still other PICs de-emphasize political actions by any one group and spread power among relevant parties by carefully delineating the boundaries and responsibilities of each decision making entity so that power and authority are explicit. In the Job Council of the Ozarks, for example, the LEO works in the political sphere and the PIC develops policy, planning, and program design, while the SDA is responsible for implementation. Obviously, in each of these instances, the ability to share power depends on the willingness to de-emphasize one's own political gain for the good of the whole, noted above, and the presence of mutual trust and support among actors involved in designing and implementing PIC initiatives, to be discussed below.

Mutual Trust and Support

Public officials do not always trust those in the private sector to understand or be interested in public policy issues, such as job training for the disadvantaged. Similarly, business people may have little confidence that the public sector has the ability to carry out directives, especially when the "bottom line" is at stake, since public and private sector goals tend to be quite distinct. Developing trust and mutual support among actors from different economic sectors, as well as actors from different regions in large or newly combined SDAs, can be a problem for a PIC. The de-emphasis of politics noted above, along with the willingness to delegate authority and share real power by central authorities, which results in the development of necessary trust and support, is a common element among effective PICs.

In Gulfport, MS, for example, there was initially much skepticism on the part of public sector representatives about whether private sector people would really want to be involved in JTPA or the PIC. Over time, however, representatives from both sectors were able to develop a shared sense of the ways in which the PIC could work to implement JTPA that would benefit all. Combined with a democratically run PIC, in which all opinions are welcome—and actually listened to—this shared vision enabled PIC members to begin to trust the motivations, commitment, and abilities of each other.

Often, developing trust and support systems takes a great deal of time and a good deal of working together. Starting small also helps. In Boston's PIC, for instance, participants indicate that breaking down the barriers between the public and private sector took years of working on issues and "a lot of drinking together." Without this trust, however, the potential for "politics" or power grabbing (rather than sharing) is high. Successful PICs work hard to assure that PIC members, LEOs, SDA agency members, and other participants in the process of providing job training for the disadvantaged understand each other and learn the ropes of how to work together.

Local Knowledge and Networks

Two other factors consistently crop up in successful PICs, the SDAs they work with, and the LEOs. One is that they are comprised of individuals with both broad and deep knowledge of local conditions. The second factor is that key PIC members or key SDA implementers have, and themselves constitute, an extensive network of local contacts; these networks provide a vital source of ideas, resources, clients, talents, and placements for highly developed PICs.

Knowledge of local conditions is essential, especially when decisions are delegated to states and locally to successful PICs as JTPA mandates. That those with knowledge of local conditions could better develop programs than those at a distance, in fact, is an underlying premise of the JTPA legislation. Successful PICs bear out the accuracy of this assumption.

In-depth local knowledge enables PIC or SDA members to diagnose where the potential for shared vision lies more accurately than they could with less direct knowledge. Even more important, it provides them with an ability to accurately target key local trends, problems, and issues that might be overlooked by individuals less familiar with the area. One PIC credits its success in part to the fact that PIC members were instrumental in alerting the SDA to the fact that economic conditions were changing "180 degrees," from a labor surplus economy to a labor shortage economy, thereby shifting the program focus from seeking jobs for clients to seeking clients for jobs.

Local networks are important, too, for they provide much more immediate access to employers, to extra sources of funding, to government officials who can reduce bureaucratic snaggles, and to sources of trainees for the programs generated by the PICs. In St. Louis, there is an extensive network of community based organizations, neighborhood groups, city agencies, training subcontractors, and small businesses linked through the Agency on Training and Employment (the local SDA agency) to work on economic development issues. Though sometimes difficult to maintain, such networks assure that necessary skills, abilities, and contacts are available when they are needed.

Local Initiatives

Whatever they do and however they are arranged, successful PICs understand the need to generate initiatives locally. Connected to the power sharing and delegation of responsibility noted above, the development of local initiatives is an important aspect of JTPA at the federal level as well as within the more successful PICs. Delegation to the local level is particularly apparent in a PIC like the Oregon Consortium, which contracts with program operators in the nine districts that make up the Consortium. Each district is supported by a Local Advisory Group that helps program operators design programs specifically for local needs, rather than more generically across a rather diverse group of counties.

Although the structure is very different from the Oregon Consortium, the Alameda (CA) County PIC provides another instance of the importance of designing initiatives for the specific locale, rather than generically. This PIC combines its intimate knowledge of the labor market, and the training needed to meet the needs of that labor market, with a "bottom line" orientation and an ability to make "independent, local decisions" with a minimum of state or federal intervention.

SKILLED IMPLEMENTATION

All of the factors mentioned above lead to the final success factor identified in this research: skilled implementation. Implementation for PICs occurs on two levels, both of which are important. First is the level of relations among PIC members and between the PIC and the SDA agency that is authorized to carry out the PIC's agenda. Continuing attention to PIC relations, as well as feedback about programmatic happenings, is necessary if the PIC is to work successfully. The second level on which skilled implementation is important is in the area of program development and implementation, often delegated directly to the SDA agency's staff or contracted out by the SDA to other organizations.

Skills in implementation are required for each of the other success factors to exist. To understand the importance of de-emphasizing politics, for example, and to actually carry out policies that reduce potential political tensions among vastly different actors, requires attention to individual personalities, organization stakes in the issues at hand, and broader societal interests as well. Further, it is obvious that most PICs would not be considered successful if their programmatic efforts failed to achieve the objectives they set forth. Hence, skilled implementation forms the final success factor for PICS.

THE PARADOXES OF SUCCESSFUL PICs

Each of the characteristics discussed above is associated with PICs that are considered highly successful. Yet it may be obvious by now that integrating these success factors means that PICs are forced to deal with inherently paradoxical realities. As scholars of organizational effectiveness have recently pointed out, effective organizations deal successfully with the inherent paradoxes and complexities they face. Maintaining a shared vision, while permitting local initiatives with distinctive goals, poses one of these paradoxes. Centrally controlling PIC/SDA activities, while permitting local decision making autonomy, is another. Clearly understanding the political realities embedded within a PIC/SDA relationship, while at the same time de-emphasizing politics to avoid turf battles, is still another. These paradoxes will be discussed in greater detail below.

Shared Vision/Local Initiatives

Among the paradoxes successful PICs face are those of generating a vision shared by all participants in the PIC and SDA and shared sense of overarching purpose, while simultaneously not only permitting but encouraging local entrepreneurial initiatives. Here, it is the nature of the shared vision that is critical. Successful PICs develop shared visions that involve in-depth understanding of the nature of the SDA region, its problems and opportunities, the trends it faces and its people. The visions that develop out of this understanding do involve development of a common purpose or set of ends, but those ends are general rather than specific. These general purposes or overarching goals permit the development of local initiatives, with goals that are specific to the program and which can be established at the local level, where program planners are intimately familiar with needs and conditions. The shared vision thus provides an umbrella under which numerous diverse local initiatives can develop, as long as they are working toward the same general ends. It is the character of the umbrella that is important: it must be broad enough to cover a variety of options and local initiatives; at the same time, it must constrain local entrepreneurs to a set of shared values and ends, while permitting them the freedom to do what is right for their own locality. And, as with any set of overarching goals, implementation by a strong staff is critical, as is feedback to those who have developed the plans.

As with the Los Angeles County PIC, successful PICs tend to develop overarching objectives, e.g., serving the harder to serve population to achieve long lasting employment, meeting standards that go well beyond the federal guidelines and are dictated largely by local conditions. The PIC, with its support staff, works to formulate long range goals and strategies without specifying to local communities how their program goals should be established. By working with larger issues, such as "what direction should we be going?" the PIC frees up the eight cooperating SDAs it oversees to establish individualized local programs with their own goals and objectives.

Similarly, the "many right points of view" permitted under the vast Oregon Consortium umbrella represent another example. In the Consortium, the larger staff umbrella organization supporting the PIC is responsible for generating policies that affect all nine districts, while at the same time permitting local initiatives to grow. The Executive Director of the Oregon Consortium notes that the type of thinking needed in this circumstance is distinctly "nonlinear," by which she means that local initiatives are permitted to grow on their own, spreading out in waves as others see their value, rather than being programmed for the entire consortium. The central Consortium authority is responsible for general policies and oversight of local activities; at the same time, it permits numerous local "dots" or specific programs to sprout and to grow constantly larger, spreading to other regions if they are successful, but with no intention of going in a straight line from point A to point B.

Central Authority/Local Decisions

Successful PICs also seem to understand the nature of delegation, while still maintaining control over products or outputs, a tension that has been termed centralizing to decentralize. JTPA federal guidelines provide some help here, as they designate certain output measures that PICs can use to determine the productivity and success of any given local effort. The output measures provide indicators of success, without dictating how a program is to be designed, developed, or implemented. They provide means for the central authority to control local efforts and know when they are working, but they enable that same central authority, the PIC, to delegate to the local level appropriate decisions. Successful PICs use the federal model to guide their local operations.

The strong neighborhood or community-based network that comprises the St. Louis PIC represents an example of this tension. The SDA agency makes policy recommendations and develops a general action plan, which is reviewed by the LEO and PIC, who are responsible for overseeing it and for developing the broad policy guidelines within which the SDA operates. Then local programs are subcontracted to numerous community based organizations. But the PIC has made a clear decision to reduce the emphasis on "playing the numbers game," and attempting to ensure that basic skills are provided so that people are truly motivated and ready for work when they finish programs. This means that local programs must take into their own hands key decisions that affect the outcome measures, such as job placement rates or trainee retention rates, but such decisions clearly fit within the broader policy umbrella established by the PIC to "serve the hard to serve population and return St. Louis to a good community for its citizens."

Astutely Political/De-Emphasis of Politics

Perhaps a greater tension, particularly for PICs working closely with their local elected officials or in SDAs where past tensions or conflicts have been high, is to manage the political realities of the situation while simultaneously de-emphasizing politics. Only with an acute sense of what the political realities are can PIC effectively work around the inter-county, intercity, interorganizational, interpersonal, and intertown conflicts that might otherwise occur. Balancing the understanding of the political realities with the downplaying of political agendas is a delicate but necessary business. It is also critical so that the shared vision that is so important to success can be developed and because internecine conflict can paralyze a PIC if not subordinated to the greater good. The shared vision is a particularly important component of the ability to downplay political agendas because it provides a common basis for interaction. Smart PICs thus look for the common ground and avoid what is not in common.

A particularly striking instance of the ability to avoid such potential conflicts is provided by the PIC of Southern Connecticut. Here a local mayor was instrumental in minimizing the distrust that had previously existed between very different localities combined into a new SDA. Despite being the "lead mayor" or key decision maker for the PIC, he spoke of "equal sharing" among the cities combined into the PIC rather than automatically assuming authority and the leadership position. The mayor clearly understood that the past history of territorialism and mistrust among the four areas now combined could get in the way of a productive partnership, especially if he stepped into the lead and assumed the power position. Only by understanding this political reality—and by de-emphasizing his own political agenda in favor of pulling together the four areas—was he able to begin the process of bringing together PIC members from all four areas into a united effort.

CONCLUSIONS—AND WHEN IT WORKS?

By reviewing the characteristics and paradoxes embedded within successful PICs, one can gain a sense of the processes through which PICs become successful. The processes are not easy ones, nor do they necessarily happen quickly. The processes revolve primarily around resolving the paradoxes noted above; that is, being able to develop a sufficiently broad umbrella of shared vision and values, while encouraging local initiatives, maintaining centralized control together with local autonomy, and remaining astutely political, while de-emphasizing the politics of the local SDA situation. Resolving these paradoxes involves hard work, much discussion, some constructive conflict, and a willingness to work together to balance multiple interests and needs. Resolving them relies on having skilled individuals available who are willing to take risks when necessary, who understand the situation, and who are able to accomplish the goals they set forth.

These efforts must come from both private and public sector representatives to the PIC, from the local elected officials, and from the SDA agency directors and their staffs, as well as those who implement programs when they are subcontracted. In short, the process of developing a successful PIC is one of real partnership, which means giving as well as getting, which means balancing the good of the whole with one's own good. This balancing act, when done well, enables the PIC and those who work with it to recognize and develop the broader themes that can engage the community, the businesses, and the social service agencies encompassed within an SDA. Doing this successfully requires focusing on elements of community and cooperation rather than discord, finding the common threads among the many disparate views that might otherwise fragment an area into separate units, and, quite frequently, subordinating at least temporarily personal or group benefits to the greater benefit of the whole.

Successful PICs start by working together to develop a common understanding of local conditions, problems, opportunities and trends; that is, an accurate diagnosis of local conditions that is intimately dependent on the local expertise of PIC members and their networks. This understanding, which is articulated through the shared vision and happens as a result of much hard work, helps PIC members come to a realistic perspective on what the critical needs of the region are, whether they involve a narrow focus on job training for the disadvantaged, attention to the school system as well as job training, literacy programs to support job training, or broader forms of economic development to attract industry. The diverse needs of different regions are in large measure responsible for the many successful PIC focuses; accurate diagnosis of local conditions means that the PIC has targeted appropriately and has a much better chance of actually meeting the region's needs. Obviously, coming to the initial diagnosis is part of the process of developing the vision appropriate for a region, but it is also a continuing process of revising that vision as local conditions change and communicating those changes throughout the PIC.

Very likely, the process of developing common understanding comes only with a simultaneous process involving the development of mutual trust and respect among PIC members, both public and private. This educational process happens in part as PIC members diagnose the situation and become more knowledgeable about local conditions and as they begin to know each other and how they work as a group. Often, the process is aided by educational efforts, by dialogues, and by information distribution among PIC members and, equally importantly, between PIC members and the SDA and LEO contacts.

Does it take a visionary leader to develop this vision? It would seem that the answer is maybe: sometimes yes, sometimes no. Some successful PICs were initiated by visionary leaders who articulated a perspective in which all could believe, but in others the vision emerged from the PIC itself only after a long and difficult struggle. What is obvious from the need for local initiatives is that civic entrepreneurship must be encouraged within the shared vision at multiple levels within the scope of the PIC's domain, as well as in multiple localities. Some form of leadership is critical; it may, however, be from an individual willing to take a back seat to the group, focusing more on ensuring that the PIC "owns" its own vision than on his or her personal leadership agenda.

What does matter is that the shared vision exists and that as the PIC moves from vision to implementation, the other processes associated with successful PICs take place. That is, once the vision is in place and understood (although not in such linear fashion as this statement makes it seem), then the PIC must set in place processes involving power distribution among relevant constituent groups so that local programmatic efforts will reflect local needs and conditions, so that local efforts will be "owned" by locals, and so that local networks can be tapped as necessary. The shared vision provides an umbrella set of goals and values that gives a sense of "belonging" to those who participate and that is in part responsible for the almost missionary zeal with which some PIC and SDA participants seem to approach their work.

In sum, while not all of the PICs that JTPA established are working successfully, it is clear from the brief review presented above that there are many that are working. It is also notable that these successful PICs have in common characteristics, such as shared values and shared vision, a de-emphasis of politics, power sharing within the ranks, development of mutual trust and support, and local knowledge, networks, and initiatives, that are not easily tabulated. It is not the program focus, the structure, the level of representatives, or local conditions that determine success, but rather more qualitative elements, especially managing the paradoxes inherent in this type of enterprise, that seem to be most likely to have successful outcomes.

REFERENCES

Bailey, T. R. "Market forces and private sector processes in government policy: the Job Training Partnership Act." *Journal of Policy Analysis and Management,* 1988, 7 (2): 300–315.

Bailis, L. N. "The more things change . . ." A study of the status of PY 85 JTPA coordination and PY84 JTPA activities. Washington, D.C.: National Commission for Employment Policy, 1987.

Bernick, M. "The truth about job-training programs." *Journal of Contemporary Studies* (Winter 1984): 37–43.

Brooks, H., L. Liebman, and C. Schelling. (eds). *Public–Private Partnership: New Opportunities for Meeting Social Needs.* Cambridge, MA: Ballinger, 1984.

Cameron, K. S. and D. A. Whetten. (eds). *Organizational Effectiveness: A Comparison of Multiple Models.* Chapters 1 and 12. New York: Academic Press, 1983.

Cameron, K. S. "Effectiveness as paradox: consensus and conflict in conceptions of organizational effectiveness." *Management Science,* 32 (5), May 1986, 539–553.

Fosler, R. S. and R. A. Berger. *Public–Private Partnership in American Cities.* Lexington, MA: D. C. Heath, 1982.

Johnston, J. W. "The Job Training Partnership Act: A Report by the National Commission for Employment Policy." Washington, D.C.: National Commission for Employment Policy, 1987.

Lee, C. "What's the Word on JTPA?" *Training* (May 1986): 54–61.

National Alliance of Business. "What's Happening with JTPA? A Complete Analysis of NAB's 1984 Survey Data." Washington, D.C.: National Alliance of Business, 1985.

National Alliance of Business. "Is the Job Training Partnership Working? The 1985 NAB Survey of PIC Chairs and SDA Administrators." Washington, D.C.: National Alliance of Business, 1986.

National Alliance of Business. "JTPA Operations at the Local Level: Coordination or Discord?" Washington, D.C.: National Alliance of Business, 1987.

National Commission for Employment Policy. "The Job Training Partnership Act." In *The Job Training Partnership Act: A Report by the National Commission for Employment Policy.* Washington, D.C., 1987.

National Commission for Employment Policy. "Evaluation of the effects of JTPA performance standards on clients, services, and costs." Washington, D.C.: National Commission for Employment Policy, 1988.

Perrow, C. "The bureaucratic paradox: the efficient organization centralizes in order to decentralize." *Organizational Dynamics,* 1977, 5: 3–14.

15 Corporate Philanthropy and Affordable Housing

Steven D. Lydenberg

This chapter looks at trends and developments in corporate philanthropic support for affordable housing initiatives, documenting several of the important and innovative programs. Three factors in particular prompted a substantial growth in these programs:

1. The emergence of national and local "intermediaries" on housing issues (e.g., the national Enterprise Foundation or the local Cleveland Housing Network). These channeled corporate contributions—large and small—to neighborhood organizations and provided technical assistance on housing projects.
2. The Tax Reform Act of 1986. This grants tax benefits to corporate investments in low income housing.
3. The crisis in affordable housing.

This chapter examines three types of initiatives that are particularly successful:

1. Cash charitable giving—where, working through an intermediary, large scale giving by a corporation, singly or as part of a coalition of philanthropies, was directed toward a broad systematic solution of fundamental affordable housing problems.

2. In-kind contributions—where major commitments of corporate resources or personnel in a highly visible and public manner lent substantial political support to community-based urban revitalization initiatives.

3. Low-income loans or tax advantaged investments—where syndicated partnerships raised multimillion dollar pools of funds to be invested with non-profit community groups.

A fourth issue is also examined briefly: affordable housing as ordinary business.

INTRODUCTION

Housing as an initiative for U.S. corporations goes back to the time when New England mill factories provided minimal shelter for workers. In the context of urban revitalization, however, corporations were most recently confronted with housing issues in the 1960s. With urban centers deteriorating and President Johnson's War on Poverty the slogan of the day, a few major U.S. companies with social concerns took direct part in urban revitalization projects.

Two of the most major efforts were those of Ralston Purina in St. Louis, Missouri, and General Mills in Minneapolis, Minnesota. In both cases, the corporations became the lead developers in targeted neighborhoods, committing substantial resources and personnel. Both projects cost the companies money.

While these programs were successful in revitalizing the neighborhoods, they raised questions about the direct intervention of large corporations in specific neighborhoods, "gentrification," and the retention of control of revitalization programs at the local level. These models were not replicated.

In the late 1970s, a new alternative for corporate involvement in affordable housing initiatives emerged. Neighborhood groups wishing to tackle economic development grew phenomenally. Fledgling organizations, they slowly gained experience and expertise. In their wake followed the creation of intermediaries to channel funds from corporations and foundations to community-based groups.

These intermediaries became keys in creation of increasingly popular "public–private partnerships" for affordable housing. Most of the corporate initiatives involve such partnerships.

Charitable Cash Contributions: Corporate giving of cash is most often thought of as corporate "philanthropy." It has been opposed on occasion by those on the conservative right. Milton Friedman, for example, has argued that profits are not the corporation's to give away, but belong to shareholders and employees. On the left, John Steinbeck, for example, argued that philanthropy only perpetuates the problems it professes to alleviate. Within the corporate community, however, cash grantmaking has broad acceptance.

In contributing to affordable housing initiatives, several differing corporate approaches can be distinguished. The most usual is the giving of small (under $50,000) operational support grants to local affordable housing organizations. This lends general support but entails no large scale commitment by the corporation nor any systematic attempt to deal with affordable housing problems.

Two other primary approaches to grantmaking take a broader view. First, large grants ($50,000 to $1 million) are given to intermediary organizations (usually national in focus) devoted to working with local housing groups. The concept is that corporate grantmakers, wishing to make substantial contributions in a meaningful manner, often do not feel competent to distinguish among local groups. Experienced intermediaries offer advantages as a vehicle for large-scale corporate giving. They have proven their ability to choose local groups capable of completing projects. They have the capability to aid these groups should they run into problems. And they have the capacity to coordinate multiple grants for a single project.

Second is local giving in collaboration with other large donors to address a single issue. This approach recognizes both the fact that a well funded project is more likely to succeed than an underfunded one and that multiple sponsorship can broaden political support for a project and lessen the risk of controversy.

NOTABLE INITIATIVES

Affiliated Publications, parent company of the *Boston Globe*, has been a generous philanthropist through traditional giving by its *Boston Globe* Foundation. The company's goal is to give 4 percent of pre-tax profits to local charities each year. Community-based housing initiatives consistently receive substantial support.

Until 1987, the Globe Foundation's general practice in housing had been to give small grants to a dozen or so community-based development groups. In 1987, however, the Globe Foundation decided to take part in an unusual collaborative effort among Boston grantmaking organizations. The result was the Neighborhood Development Support Collaborative (NDSC), a $4.5 million pool of funds to provide annual grants of $50,000 to $60,000 over five years to ten local community development groups.

Crucial in the formation of NDSC were Boston's United Way, LISC and the Ford Foundation. In 1986, for the first time in its history, Boston's United Way was seriously considering support for community development groups in housing, but was unsure of the best approach. The Ford Foundation, encouraged by this, offered to match United Way contributions. And LISC's Carol Glazer, an executive on loan from Boston Edison, assessed the needs of local housing groups. She found small staffs hampered, in effect, by their own success. Having undertaken one project, these groups' resources were strained, and they were unable to take advantage of further opportunities. NDSC was created to strengthen and expand the administrative infrastructures of these community organizations.

The United Way ultimately contributed $1.8 million and the Ford Foundation, $1.5 million. The Globe Foundation pledged $150,000 over three years.

Another illustration of how to use an intermediary is Upjohn's 1987 decision to support local initiatives in Kalamazoo, Michigan. Historically, Upjohn's charitable giving focused on education. In 1986, 65 percent of its $4.3 million in cash contributions was to education, primarily for research at colleges and universities. Starting in 1985, the company received increasing requests from community housing groups. The company, however, felt it had no expertise in evaluating the proposals. So Upjohn commissioned LISC to do a citywide study of housing needs and resources. LISC found a particular need for housing rehabilitation and proposed a comprehensive program (under LISC's coordination). Upjohn pledged $850,000, and LISC contributed $250,000 over two years.

A second example is BP America (formerly Standard Oil of Ohio) and the Enterprise Foundation in Cleveland. BP America's contributions to housing programs are large, with $10 million since 1980.

With the support of BP America, the Enterprise Foundation was instrumental in creating the Cleveland Housing Partnership (CHP). CHP brought together the Cleveland Housing Network—a coalition of nine local neighborhood organizations—and Cleveland Tomorrow—a coalition of 40 corporations. Through tax syndication agreements, the corporate community invested $2.3 million over five years in housing projects by the community groups.

BP America's contributions are large: $976,000 out of $13 million (7.5 percent) in 1986. Cash contributions were allocated to education, primarily research grants at colleges and universities.

IN-KIND CONTRIBUTIONS

Another traditional form of corporate philanthropy is contribution of goods or services at no charge, referred to as "in-kind" contributions.

Three broad types of in-kind contributions can be distinguished, with differing advantages and drawbacks.

1. Gift of goods or property is what the phrase "in-kind" contributions usually calls to mind. Such gifts often involve goods or property of little material value to the corporation (i.e., damaged products, outmoded product lines, real estate with no useful function). In addition, these gifts are at least partially tax deductible. No long term (and perhaps unpredictable) commitments to the donees are implied. Furthermore, what is being given, and its value, can be easily stated.

These gifts do not usually involve attempts to grapple with underlying structural issues, either within the donee's nonprofit organization or within the social context of the problem ultimately addressed.

2. The gift of professional expertise is also often a part of in-kind giving. Usually this involves lending (on company time) or volunteering (on employees' time) of knowledgeable staff to assist nonprofit organizations. Occasionally, the services involve larger scale studies of underlying structural causes of social problems and/or comprehensive assessments of solutions and place corporate actions in the context of these solutions.

In general, donation of services involves the corporate donor more directly and on a longer term basis than does a gift of goods. It has the potential to affect positively structural problems within community organizations or more broadly at the societal level.

3. The gift of political commitment is more nebulous but is in certain ways more substantial. Included are a range from the decision to keep— or locate—corporate headquarters or major production facilities in economically deteriorating neighborhoods, to the public commitment by top officers to head or support coalitions to tackle problems. These commitments involve the full weight of the corporate name in a community. They risk involving the corporation in complicated political battles with unpredictable outcomes. But they also promise the reward of bringing change to fundamental structural issues underlying social problems.

OTHER IMPORTANT INITIATIVES

During the 1970s, Pitney Bowes was involved in revitalization projects in its headquarters, Stamford, Connecticut. One was the New Hope apartments, to which the company lent $10,000, and later, when the project ran into financial difficulties, another $85,000 as part of a syndicated limited partnership that completed the development.

In the early 1980s, the company faced a decision on where to build new headquarters. Its headquarters was in the South End of the city. A peninsula cut off from the rest of Stamford by a railroad line and the Connecticut Turnpike, this ethnically mixed community had not shared in the revitalization of downtown. The company commissioned an $85,000 study of problems facing this neighborhood and possible solutions. The study was conducted through the Stamford Economic Assistance Corporation and "donated" to the city for future planning purposes.

The company viewed its ultimate decision, to stay in the South End, as a positive force toward revitalization of the neighborhood. As it happened, a cemetery wanted to sell six acres, and Pitney thus avoided problems acquiring and destroying neighborhood properties. At the same time, the company sold for a dollar a parcel of land valued at $250,000 in the South End to New Neighborhoods, a local affordable housing organization, for construction of 12 moderate-income condominiums. The company also loaned $150,000 to Neighborhood Housing Services for low-income housing.

Corporate decisions to build in deteriorating areas have generally been viewed as important in revitalization (e.g., Johnson & Johnson in New Brunswick, New Jersey; Campbell Soup in Camden, New Jersey; or Clorox in Oakland, California). In Pitney Bowes' case, its decision involved a political commitment, as well as gifts of property, cash, and expertise. The Chairman described the decision as without "misplaced altruism" and involving "no federal intervention, no Urban Renewal, no neighborhood destruction, no gentrification," but instead fostered preservation of affordable housing.

In-kind commitments of personnel by State Street Bank to affordable housing in Boston is another example of contributions beyond the ordinary. For many years, State Street's chief executive was prominent on behalf of the corporate community, promoting public–private partnerships. As with similar partnerships in Chicago and Cleveland, the basic principle is to bring together a wide variety of public and private resources to support local nonprofit revitalization.

The corporate financial role in the Boston Housing Partnership's first effort—renovation of 700 apartments—was confined to securing a $4.5 million low interest loan from the city by letter of credit from Boston banks. In addition, the corporate community donated to the administrative expenses of the BHP $240,000 in one year. The second stage—renovation of 950 more units—involved tax syndications through which $17 million was raised in corporate investments.

LOW INTEREST LOANS AND TAX ADVANTAGED INVESTMENTS

In financing construction or rehabilitation of affordable housing, there are multiple opportunities for corporate support through investments or

loans. Advocates of this approach, as opposed to outright gifts, argue
that loans or investments:

- Allow funds to go farther since they can be reinvested or loaned out again
  after completion of a project
- Promote self-sufficiency rather than dependency
- Can, in the case of tax advantaged investments, provide substantial returns
- Allow for the influx of large amounts of capital to the community level with-
  out taking control of projects away

Loans and investments differ. Below market rate loans are particularly appropriate for banks or insurance companies. For banks, the
Home Mortgage Disclosure Act and the Community Reinvestment Act
provide extra impetus for participation. For insurance companies, an informal prompting to greater social involvement—including investment in
social projects—comes from the Center for Corporate Public Involvement, a trade association of the insurance industry that promotes and
publicizes corporate social responsibility among members. Among insurance companies, Aetna, Prudential, and Equitable stand out for strong
efforts in housing, with Travelers, Metropolitan Life, and Cigna also being active. Tax advantaged investments by corporations was spurred by
the Tax Reform Act of 1986, which emphasized low-income housing as
a corporate tax shelter.

FURTHER NOTABLE INITIATIVES

Amoco has been a leader in Chicago, supporting community-based housing revitalization through loans or investments. In the 1980s, it provided
a $230,000 below market mortgage to the Organization for the Northeast
to rehabilitate an apartment house and restaurant. It pledged $2.5 million
in risk capital as part of a $20 million renovation of 304 low-income
housing units in the deteriorating Rogers Park neighborhood.

It became a chief supporter of the Chicago Equity Fund, purchasing a
$1.5 million share of CEF's $6 million pool in its first year. CEF grew
out of the Chicago Housing Partnership, which involves the city, numerous nonprofit community organizations, and the private sector. CEF was
the pioneer in what has now become a model for raising capital for community-based, affordable housing. The basic principle is tax advantaged
syndication. In practice, community groups take the role of general partner in a syndicated housing rehabilitation or construction project. The
CEF (with funds from the corporate community) is the limited partner.
The general partner is responsible for designing and managing the project, but the tax advantages pass to the limited partner and ultimately to
its corporate investors.

The National Equity Fund (NEF) was created on this model. Fourteen companies invested $1 million in the first pool. A fair number of banks and insurance companies have programs for placing below market rate loans with community-based or minority owned projects.

Three Chicago banks (First Chicago, Harris, and Northern Trust) have lending programs for low-income neighborhoods. Among factors prompting these agreements was the review—due to impending mergers or acquisitions—under the Community Reinvestment Act.

The Harris Trust and Savings program totals $35 million. These funds were earmarked for a variety of below market rate loans: single and multifamily residential mortgages; home improvement loans; mixed use real estate rehabilitation; and commercial property loans. All projects are carried out by nonprofit, community-based development organizations. A review board, made up of representatives of community organizations and representatives of the bank, oversees the program.

At the time that it announced the program, Harris Trust also pledged $600,000 in charitable grants, over 5 years, to community development groups to which it would be lending. Increasingly, companies making below market loans (or foundations making program related investments) also set aside grants for these organizations. Often this is to assure that nonprofit and often small groups have an adequate infrastructure to successfully manage the projects for which they are receiving the loans.

AFFORDABLE HOUSING AS ORDINARY BUSINESS

While not strictly within the realm of this chapter, it is appropriate to mention those exceptional corporations that incorporate affordable housing into daily business. One model is the small, though remarkable, South Shore Bank of Chicago. It began in 1974 with the acquisition of the only bank in a deteriorating neighborhood by a racially mixed coalition of investors. Beginning with single family mortgages and extending gradually to multifamily rehabilitation projects, South Shore has neighborhood revitalization as its central goal. The company received substantial support from the corporate community. Insurance companies, notably Equitable and Travelers, purchased packages of their loans on the secondary market.

South Shore Bank expanded into another low-income neighborhood and then purchased a small bank in Arkansas, to apply lessons learned in urban settings to problems facing the rural poor.

Mention should also be made of the Federal National Mortgage Association (Fannie Mae) which operates primarily through the secondary market for mortgages. It has tackled various low-income housing questions through charitable giving and investments in syndicated housing partnerships.

CONCLUSIONS

The change in attitude during the 1980s on affordable housing, within the corporate community, was in many ways remarkable. Those handful of companies supporting the first innovative partnerships and local efforts were pioneers in corporate philanthropy. Now opportunities abound.

Several factors were important in making support for affordable housing initiatives attractive to the corporate community.

1. The risks that affordable housing projects will not be successfully completed diminished as local groups and larger intermediary organizations strengthen and as sophistication increased for packaging of finances for these projects.
2. Systematic, large scale attacks on affordable housing problems were made possible through the partnership approach.
3. The risks of community relations problems diminished as control of revitalization increasingly rested at local levels.

16 Philanthropy and Venture Capital

C. Robert Kemp

Venture capital is key in financing medium to high technology businesses. The resulting job generation is an important source of new jobs.

The role of philanthropy in social and in business development has been highlighted in the popular press and in foundation journals. Institutional investors also have claimed credit for corporate social responsibility initiatives implemented via corporate foundations. But venture capitalists are, thus far, reluctant to invest in small businesses in distressed areas or in businesses owned and operated by African-Americans. Conversely, foundations and socially responsible corporations principally make grants, loans, and program related investments in only those kinds of businesses.

Venture capitalists, thus, use different criteria than do foundations. And this reality exacerbates the problem of capital formation in distressed areas.

Foundations can invest in certain venture capital firms, and insure that market discipline is applied even though the objective is to create jobs and businesses that are nontraditional. Venture capital firms can, with additional foundation capital, assure capital adequacy for selected firms, and make available management and technical assistance.

HOW CORPORATE FOUNDATIONS CAN HELP GENERATE VENTURE CAPITAL FOR AFRICAN-AMERICAN BUSINESSES

The *Wall Street Journal,* on April 20, 1987, headlined: "Enterprise Lost," "Newark, New Jersey, Cable-TV Firm Sadly Cashes In Its Chips When Financing Tightens," and "Between a Rock and a Hard Place, Black Cable-TV Franchise Gives Up On Newark."

A careful reading told a different story. The sale of the cable TV franchise made the entrepreneur a multimillionaire and earned a 40 percent compounded annual return for the company investors. The company began in 1982 with $9.5 million of debt. It sold in 1986 for $33 million. That is capital formation at its best. Yet, this story points up a number of concerns.

The report highlights the problem facing blacks in securing capital. The company didn't give up on Newark, rather, the capital source gave up on the entrepreneur and on Newark. Let's examine the main capital sources for minority business enterprise (MBE).

Banks

Capital, of any description, is scarce for minority business. Historically, bank debt was the primary source, but banks are becoming less important for minority business. Investment banks and "nonfinancial" firms have moved into areas like interest bearing money market accounts and home equity loans. And this competition has hurt commercial banking.

Corporations decreased reliance on banks by issuing short term securities and commercial paper, in place of short term bank borrowing. Commercial paper now amounts to $190 billion. Securitization of mortgage portfolios followed, taking another $600 billion.

Now auto loans have been securitized, taking another $8.6 billion. As a result, bank profitability has been deteriorating. It is estimated that 25 percent of the 14,000 U.S. banks are losing money, and the losses will continue. Loans that remain with banks are of decreasing quality, in oil related activity, farming, real estate, and Third World debt. Bad debt writeoffs were $15 billion in 1984, $16 billion for 1985, $21 billion for 1986, and then rose dramatically in the late 1980s.

By the early 1990s, banks had curtailed much traditional lending. It's likely that the banking and related savings and loan crises will continue to adversely affect minority business. Since banks already perceive minority loans as risky, it is unlikely they will lend to MBE startups and expansions unless there is underlying collateral, or verified repayment sources, equal to or greater than the requested debt, or both.

SSBICs

Minority Enterprise Small Business Investment Companies, MESBICs, are intended as a source of near equity. (MESBICs are now referred to as Specialized SBICs or SSBICs.) And since the early 1970s, SSBICs have been the only investors willing to finance minority ventures. But they were often unable to meet the full demand. Many start-ups, expansions, and acquisitions by minorities have been financed by SSBICs and SSBIC syndicates. The Newark cable TV company is an example.

To take one illustrative year, in 1984, SSBIC investments helped to create or maintain 14,000 jobs. These gains were achieved in the face of tough barriers. Theoretically, for every dollar of paid in capital, SSBICs have available four dollars of leverage from the Small Business Administration (SBA) in the form of preferred stock and debentures. But actual leverage to SSBICs is only 1 to 1. That's because SSBICs are required to invest at least 65 percent of paid in capital before they can be *ELIGIBLE* to apply for leverage. Then, after application, they typically wait months for the leverage funds.

Another hurdle is that most SSBICs are thinly capitalized. They therefore cannot cover operating expense from the income they receive from debt investments they have made with their remaining capital, while awaiting the Federal matching leverage funds. Added to this dilemma is the requirement that SSBICs lend and invest at specified rate ceilings and terms. This can mean that their cost of capital exceeds what they can earn from loans and investments.

The fiscal year 1986 budget appropriation for SSBIC leverage, for example, was $39 million. But the potential leverage request was $260 million. For fiscal year 1987, the budget request reduced the $39 million to $20 million. Since then there have been no major increases.

Regulatory constraints are also onerous. SSBICs can only hold 49 percent SSBIC ownership in any portfolio business, and they may invest no more than 30 percent of their capital in any one venture. These constraints, combined, can contribute to difficulties, especially the inability to control portfolio firms.

Assuming SSBICs had improving access to private capital and increasing liquidity and stability, SSBICs could foster small business development, job creation, and innovation. Additional benefits would include: replacement of public funds with private investment, helping reduce the Federal deficit, and generating new tax revenues.

INSTITUTIONAL SOURCES

Institutional investors include primarily mutual funds, pension funds, and insurance companies. In the 1980s, many insurance companies modified their investment strategies. All had a consistent policy that lending to, and investment with, minorities is classified as Corporate Social Responsibility, not regular investment. But their insistence on the corporate social responsibility classification stigmatizes minority ventures and, in many instances, penalizes the venture.

In the Newark cable TV case, for example, the insurance company lender would lend only through its special "social investment" program because of "a policy against financing cable operations, and . . . . the founding entrepreneurs' lack of management experience and funds of their own violated the usual 'risk-reward criteria.' "

But "a credit-worth-minority entrepreneur doing business in our home city" fits our social investment criteria. For their $3 million in senior debt, the insurance company received a market rate interest plus a kicker, presumably a risk adjusted premium, of 5 percent of the gross sales price whenever the company was sold.

But when the company later needed $2 million more from its senior lenders, the insurance company first agreed to provide an additional $1 million, but then balked and asked for an appraisal. After market value was estimated at $25 million, the insurance company still refused to lend more money.

The minority group investors offered to find a replacement for the insurance company, and the insurance company agreed to be replaced, but refused to give up the 5 percent equity kicker.

Because of the recalcitrance of the insurance company, the SSBIC syndicate was required to put up an additional $1.3 million on top of the original $2.5 million in near equity and find a substitute lender for the insurance lender. So the insurance lender was repaid, earned interest during the loan term, and received 5 percent of the sales price net of debt, for its "social investment."

Yet the insurance company says the return doesn't justify what it put into the deal. Had the capital been available when needed, the company might still be owned by blacks. However, the point is that the sale was forced because the company was viewed as a social investment, but the return to the insurance company exceeded traditional market return. This resulted in an exorbitant cost of capital for the minority business.

It would appear from this illustration that any rate of return is justified on social investments despite the dual requirement that the return meet standard criteria and corporate social responsibility criteria. The question is, where does that leave us on the subject of capital formation for MBEs? And what can corporate philanthropy do to help accelerate this process?

The desired goal of equitable redistribution of income and wealth will not be realized through equal opportunity and affirmative action. The courts are ruling that many more people are in groups entitled to set asides. So the net effect is that set asides become less effective as a tool for correcting social injustice.

Banks have serious problems. Government is drying up as a primary source of risk capital, and institutional investors view MBEs as difficult customers. Therefore, foundations can step in with more creative financing approaches. It also appears that the other remaining potential source of risk capital is the African-American community itself.

The question is: How do we gain access to our risk capital? The institutions to whom we have entrusted our funds are not doing well for themselves or for us. Why not afford minority business the opportunity to realize its upside potential?

RESTRUCTURING AMERICAN BUSINESS AND INDUSTRY

American industry is experiencing a transformation. Deregulation, increasingly interconnected global markets, and pressure for short term results fueled a period of merger mania. In 1986, 4,000 large companies spent $200 billion to transform themselves. That was four times the amount spent in 1983. Stock buybacks by companies targeted for takeovers handed $75 billion to shareowners in 1984 and 1985. Managers, who previously had worried about growth, ROI, and earnings per share tried to manage the gap between share price and the breakup estimate of the would be raider.

The market in new "junk" bond debt grew from $1.5 billion in 1978 to $40 billion in 1986. Junk bonds came to account for 21 percent of the corporate bond market. Mergers, acquisitions, LBOs, and stock repurchases reduced corporate equity by $200 billion just during one stretch from 1984 to 1987.

In 1953, institutions controlled 15 percent of equities on the New York Stock Exchange. Their trades were 25 percent of market transactions, measured by volume or value. Today's institutional trades are 80 percent of transactions. With more than $2 trillion in assets, pension funds own one-third of the equity of all publicly traded companies and 50 percent of the equity of large corporations.

Most of the 20 largest corporations are not doing well. Look at GM's apparent inability to deal with quality problems, AT&T's incapacity in marketing anything but long distance telephone calls, IBM's failure to understand the importance of creating compatible systems in a world of distributed processing, Exxon's disasters with office equipment and electrical machinery, and Sears' financial services mistakes.

These illustrate the dangers to large corporations when the environments in which they have flourished turn unstable and unpredictable.

And it suggests that, despite their troubles, their contributions and foundations strategies should seek to work with other public and private partners to help firm up the weakest portions of the general social environment.

GENERATING MBE VENTURE CAPITAL

Of the $8 billion invested in venture capital in 1985, only $15 million was available to MBEs. Severe limitation on access to credit and capital for MBEs is the reason for the creation of Opportunity Funding Corporation (OFC) and its affiliated venture capital firms. Let's look at this approach and at how corporate philanthropy could participate through it to generate economic development in distressed areas.

The SSBIC syndicate that financed the Newark cable TV company was led by Syndicated Communications Company (SYNCOM) and its wholly owned SSBIC, Syncom Capital Corporation (SCC). One of the other SSBIC Investors was Fulcrum Venture Capital Corporation (Fulcrum).

Both of these venture fund sources were created by OFC. The notion was to utilize leverage to create capital pools. OFC would use its limited assets to establish financing intermediaries, such as SYNCOM and Fulcrum, and attract investors.

In the 1970s, OFC concluded that attractive investment opportunities for minority ownership were available in broadcast communications and in manufacturing. Our reasoning was that minorities owned less than 0.5 percent of all broadcast properties. This could be quickly changed through acquisitions, and leveraged buyouts of manufacturing concerns by minority managers would make factory jobs available to blacks and other minorities.

With the help of the Federal Communications Commission, the first part of the strategy worked. In addition to OFC, other investors in these financing intermediaries included the Presbyterian Economic Development Corporation (PEDCO), The Cooperative Assistance Fund (CAF), The Ford Foundation, and subsequently, two institutional investors.

In the 15 years following the establishment of the two venture firms, SYNCOM has made more than 50 communications investments in AM/FM radio, VHF/UHF TV, cable TV, cellular radio companies, and print media. Fulcrum has invested in eight LBOs of manufacturing concerns and has another ten investments in medium/high technology, mainly in computer related companies.

In the aggregate, the OFC Group had gains of $1.4 million in 1985 and $4.8 million in 1986. These accomplishments are from an initial capital base of $7 million in 1970. By 1994, they constituted a consolidated asset base of $162 million.

Although the OFC Group has achieved a measure of "success," we are just beginning to address the capital needs of minority business. There could be an OFC Group in every city, and they still could not meet the MBE capital demand.

However, the OFC Group does not have access to traditional private capital, increasingly it does not have access to public capital, and its limited assets cannot command debt capital at adequate levels. Most importantly, it has not organized its own capital. But corporate philanthropy could help jump start African-American internal capital formation as discussed in several other articles in this volume.

Here's one more proposed remedy. As an example, if millions of African-Americans knew that a substantial portion of their savings accounts, money market funds, IRAs, insurance cash values, mutual funds, and pension funds were invested in the equities of troubled corporations, and in the less credible junk bond market, they undoubtedly would be worried about their funds at risk. But they probably wouldn't withdraw their funds because their alternatives are limited.

But if they were given the chance to authorize allocation of just 10 percent of their invested funds for minority businesses, it's a good guess that many would do that. They are already at risk in an unstable, unpredictable environment. And even if they lost the 10 percent minority allocation, they would still retain 90 percent of their funds.

That's not too bad a deal, especially with the promise of value appreciation on the 10 percent. The black population is 12 percent of total population—34 million persons. They have annual income of $200 billion and spend $180 billion. But only 7 percent, or $12.6 billion, is spent with black businesses.

Additionally, the seven major black denominations have combined membership of 19 million, with annual receipts over $3 billion. Their total deposits in black banks and savings associations is $2.5 billion. In partnership with foundations, some of these resources could flow into black business.

Insurance companies' investment and social investment programs include minority business. Other industries, including nonconsumer producers in natural resources, heavy equipment, construction, electronics, defense, and transportation, could channel their foundation funds likewise.

Pension funds total more than $2 trillion. African- and Hispanic-Americans comprise roughly 25 percent of the population. Twenty-five percent of $2 trillion is $500 billion. Ten percent of $500 billion, or $50, in an investment pool would make a substantial impact on business development. Creative foundations could reach out to initiate the partnerships that would attract that kind of funding.

To illustrate, the Congress of National Black Churches, CNBC, has established an insurance agency to handle property/casualty insurance needs of the seven denominations. A direct and immediate benefit is a substantial reduction in premiums, plus earnings from ownership of the agency.

Collective banking and collective purchasing also help stimulate development and job creation, increase yields on investment, and generate discretionary funds, which can help capitalize black businesses, especially at larger scale. All of these innovations can be catalyzed with the help of creative corporate philanthropy.

17 Corporate Philanthropy and Small Business Opportunities

John Nelson

This chapter reviews a project that helped create mechanisms to help public housing residents plan, start, and manage businesses. From 1986 to 1989, the United States Department of Housing and Urban Development (HUD) worked with Opportunity Resource Institute (ORI), a New York-based nonprofit community development corporation, to fund, plan, and implement the project.

The project was to stimulate local private–public partnerships to support resident entrepreneurs. Their enterprises are seen as part of a broad self-employment strategy. The project featured outreach to tenants, a 16-week business planning workshop, individual technical assistance and "mentoring," and a high risk revolving loan fund. It served Dade and Broward Counties in Florida, New Haven, Connecticut, and Cleveland, Ohio.

In each, an advisory board was formed to support and manage the program, along with the lead public agency that received the HUD grant. By 1989, 35 "graduates" of the first planning workshops had begun ten businesses.

These businesses illustrate the results possible:

Word Processing	Sewing—Tailoring
Preschool Child Care	Snack Bar
Clothing Import—Retail	Cosmetology
Answering Service	Car Wash
Appliance Repair	T-Shirt Printing
Convenience Store	Secretarial Service
Laundromat—Dry Cleaning	Mobile Oil Service
Wedding Services	Fruit and Vegetable Stand
Bookstore	Convenience Shop
Hair Styling	

There were several spinoff benefits from the project. They include private foundation grants attracted, stimulation of Job Training Partnership Act activities in the form of funded Private Industry Councils, state support, and application for a Comprehensive Improvement Assistance Program (CIAP) called "Economic Initiatives."

But the most exciting and tangible parts of the project were the high hopes of the workshop graduates and the transformed lives of those who launched their businesses. One graduate, in Broward County, spoke before a nationwide audience of the National Association of Neighborhoods. She credited the program with giving her a shot in the arm as a person—changing her appearance, clothing, social and work attitudes, and personal sense of self-worth. She started an air conditioning appliance sales and repair business.

The SBO program is a component of comprehensive community economic development. Public housing authorities can join with private partners, including corporate foundations and contributions programs, and work with public agencies to promote the SBO.

CONCEPT AND STRUCTURE

The project stimulated enterprise development in four sites. Each project varied depending on resources—private and public—which were locally available and on the needs being addressed.

Here is a summary description of one project. In Miami, a 501C corporation was established to manage the project. The Metro–Dade Office of Community and Economic Development provided financial and staff support. Metro–Dade Community College coordinated workshops and offered oncampus technical assistance and an entrepreneurship education center. The public housing authority supported the project as a partner and helped reach the tenants.

In New Haven, the coalition advisory group included the housing authority, Science Park, and the minority Chamber of Commerce, and was part of the city's "Enterprise Corporation." In Cleveland, the focus was on one housing project's convenience store. The project expanded to include other residents via the resident management groups.

Then, in a twist on the original model, something called the Bay Consortium Private Industry Council (Bay PIG) started a project called "Opportunities Unlimited." It was to serve public housing in mostly rural eastern Virginia. The Levi–Strauss Foundation approached ORI to explore the feasibility of doing the project in communities where Levi had a presence. ORI, in turn, assessed Warsaw, Virginia, Albuquerque, and El Paso for Levi.

Levi eventually funded the Bay PIG for a 2-year project starting in 1988. The project completed two rounds of workshops. Nine promising businesses were created in the first phase. The project had one staff person and a "coalition" of private–public sector representatives that oversaw and provided policy direction—all under the legal accountability of the nonprofit PIG. The Bay PIG and ORI then agreed to promote and implement the project as a joint venture to other Private Industry Councils throughout the United States and launched this in 1989 in Phoenix to a national gathering of PIGs.

This program illustrates the possibility of using Job Training Partnership Act funds for workshop training and local PIGs to manage the projects. Various private organizations have expressed an interest in sponsoring SBO type efforts. An ecumenical church in Florida, for example, is interested in promoting entrepreneurship training, not only in its own community, but in various cities. Public interest groups with a neighborhood focus have approached ORI about national expansion of the SBO concept in cooperation with their existing community-based organizational structure.

The "Congress of National Black Churches," the "National Association of Neighborhoods," and New York's "Project Strive," among others, are also potential partners. These and others could work with proactive corporate philanthropists to generate businesses in public housing and other chronically distressed areas. Such innovations, using volunteers, show how foundations can work with public housing and community groups to generate jobs.

CONCLUSIONS AND RECOMMENDATIONS

Volunteerism and private–public sector partnerships, including imaginative philanthropy, can generate jobs in areas of chronic high unemployment. Public housing residents can succeed in starting their own businesses to serve their communities.

SBO type projects can go beyond public housing residents to serve the needs of other low-income, minority, and women entrepreneurs, and rural communities.

Selected Bibliography

Bratt, Rachel, et al. *The Private Sector and Neighborhood Preservation*. Medford, MA: Tufts University Press, 1983.

Brooks, H., L. Liebman and C. Schelling, eds. *Public–Private Partnership: New Opportunities for Meeting Social Needs*. Cambridge: Ballinger, 1984.

Bruyn, Severyn. *The Field of Social Investment*. Cambridge: University Press, 1987.

Burlingame, Dwight F. and Lamont J. Hulse. *Taking Fund Raising Seriously*. San Francisco: Jossey-Bass, Inc., 1991.

Fosler, R. S., and R. A. Berger. *Public–Private Partnership in American Cities*. Lexington, MA: D.C. Heath, 1982.

Levitan, Sar A. *Progress to Aid the Poor*. Baltimore: Johns Hopkins University Press, 1985.

Magat, Richard, ed. *Philanthropic Giving: Studies in Venture and Variety*. New York: Oxford University Press, 1989.

Powell, Walter W., ed. *The Nonprofit Sector: A Research Handbook*. New Haven: Yale University Press, 1986.

Sclar, Elliott, et al. *Shaky Places: Homeownership and Social Mobility in Boston's Suburbanization*. New York: Columbia University Press, 1984.

Warren, Donald. *Helping Networks: How People Cope With Problems in Their Community*. South Bend, Indiana: Notre Dame University Press, 1981.

Weisbrod, Burton. *The Nonprofit Economy*. Cambridge, MA: Harvard University Press, 1988.

Wuthnow, Robert and Virginia A. Hodgkinson. *Religion and Giving: Changing Patterns of Faith and the Future of America's Voluntary Spirit*. San Francisco: Jossey-Bass, Inc., 1990.

Index

About the Editor and Contributors

RICHARD F. AMERICA is a Senior Program Manager in the U.S. Small Business Administration. He is an Adjunct Lecturer in Business Administration at Georgetown University. He has been a Lecturer at the University of California, Berkeley, and a Visiting Lecturer at Stanford Business School.

KENNETH A. BERTSCH is a consultant on corporate philanthropy based in Washington, D.C.

LANCE C. BUHL was formerly Director of Corporate Contributions for British Petroleum America and is now a consultant as Principal of Lance Buhl and Associates in Cleveland, Ohio.

EMMETT D. CARSON is President of the Minneapolis Community Foundation.

PHILLIP L. CLAY is Associate Professor in the Department of Urban Studies and Planning at the Massachusetts Institute of Technology.

ROBERT DESMAN is Associate Professor of Management and Entrepreneurship at Kennesaw State College in Marietta, Georgia.

VIRGINIA HODGKINSON is Director of Research at Independent Sector in Washington, D.C.

ARNOLD M. HOWITT is Executive Director of the A. Alfred Taubman Center for State and Local Government at the John F. Kennedy School of Government at Harvard University.

C. ROBERT KEMP is President of Family Savings Bank in Los Angeles. He has also been a venture capitalist, and was Director of the Interagency Council on Minority Business in the Department of Commerce during the Carter Administration.

RITCHIE P. LOWRY is Professor of Sociology at Boston College and Founder and President of Vermont-based *Good Money* Publications, Inc., publishers of newsletters, reports, guides and other materials for socially concerned investors.

STEVEN D. LYDENBERG is a partner in the consulting and social investment management firm of Kinder, Lydenberg and Domini of Boston.

TIMOTHY S. MESCON is Dean of the School of Business Administration at Kennesaw State College in Marietta, Georgia.

JOHN NELSON is a Principal with Enterprise Strategy Group and a Managing Director of the Pearlman Group in Washington, D.C.

JAMES E. POST is Professor of Management at the School of Business Management at Boston University.

JEROME SMITH is a Program Manager at the United States Department of Housing and Urban Development.

RICHARD STEINBERG is Associate Professor of Economics and Philanthropy in the Department of Economics at Indiana University/Purdue University at Indianapolis.

RAPHAEL THELWELL is Professor of Business Administration at Howard University.

DONN J. TILSON is Adjunct Professor of Business Administration at Kennesaw State College in Marietta, Georgia.

AVIS C. VIDAL is Director of The Community Development Research Center and Associate Professor in the Graduate School at The New School for Social Research in New York City.

SANDRA A. WADDOCK is Associate Professor of Management in the School of Management at Boston College.

JENNIFER R. WOLCH is Professor and Chair of the Department of Geography at the University of Southern California.

ISBN 0-313-28809-7

90000>

EAN

9 780313 288098

HARDCOVER BAR CODE

DATE DUE

DE 2 5 '03			